PITCH BLACK

PITCH BLACK

THE STORY OF BLACK BRITISH FOOTBALLERS

EMY ONUORA

Biteback Publishing

First published in Great Britain in 2015 by
Biteback Publishing Ltd
Westminster Tower
3 Albert Embankment
London SE1 7SP
Copyright © Emy Onuora 2015

ISBN 978-1-84954-814-4

10 9 8 7 6 5 4 3 2 1

A CI   tish Library.

To Niki Eltringham, Lloyd, Sean, Amaka, Anayo and Lota,
without whom I'd never have got to this place

CONTENTS

CONTENTS

PREFACE

IT'S A FREEZING cold January afternoon and it's a third-round FA Cup tie. The atmosphere is that combination of euphoria and cockiness you get when your team's comfortably ahead and the opposition are just going through the motions. Mixed in with that cheery, swaggering arrogance is anticipation. Anticipation that at any time you might get another goal to really drive home your dominance. Familiar songs are sung in homage to our heroes. It's like New Year's Eve.

The opposition make a change. It's not made with any conviction that things can be turned around, but just to give the substitute a run-out. As the sub does the familiar handshake with his departing teammate and runs onto the pitch, passing on instructions and tactical changes, the party atmosphere suddenly changes, as if he's said something loud and offensive to the host. For the final ten minutes or so, the focus of the crowd is on this one player. All the singing has stopped and the cheery atmosphere dissipates into a sea of bitterness and hatred. They can't wait for him to get possession so they can have their few seconds of vitriol. Every touch, every pass, there's no let-up. The player himself seems not exactly oblivious – how could he be, such is the noise? – but seems determined to concentrate on the job in hand. He plays gamely, but doesn't really have any effect on the rest of his teammates, who just want the match to end. The final whistle goes and he retreats to the dressing room with his teammates, pausing to shake hands with home team players. The player in question is an eighteen-year-old striker called Garth Crooks. I was in the crowd that day and was just eleven years old. It was the first time I'd ever really thought about an opposition player. I kept wondering, what must he really be thinking? Did he want to jump into the crowd and take them all on, Bruce Lee-style? What would I have done if he had? Would I have joined in with him? Could the two of us have taken on every one of the 40,000-odd people in the crowd together? The significance of that event for me as an eleven-year-old football fan has led – in a roundabout way, and several years later – to the writing of this book. I'd seen black players before, on *Match of the Day* and the regional football programmes that ITV showed on Sunday afternoons. I was interested in them, of course – their relative scarcity gave them a kind of novelty value – but something had changed after I thought about Garth Crooks, and I began to develop an enduring empathy with all black players. I wanted to know what they really thought.

Throughout the 1970s, when Crooks was making his name as a slippery, predatory striker, the nature and level of racism that existed within the professional game was at a level that exceeded anything seen today in southern or eastern Europe. Black players were routinely subjected to the most vile racist abuse imaginable. From the terraces, black players were routinely subjected to monkey noises and racist chanting.

Bananas were thrown at them; they were spat at and received death threats. Far-right groups openly sold racist literature both inside and outside football grounds without opposition or condemnation from clubs. Terrace abuse wasn't solely confined to away fans, either. Home fans abused their own black players mercilessly and sent letters to clubs and the local press, vehemently condemning decisions to include black players in teams.

On the pitch there was often no hiding place from the abuse that black players suffered. Routine racist abuse from opponents was commonplace, as was abuse from teammates in dressing rooms and training grounds.

Racist myths steeped in historical justifications for slavery, colonialism and racial discrimination were widespread. Black players were admired for their strength, speed and flair, but also denigrated for their lack of intelligence, application and courage and their inability to play in cold weather. Coaches and managers ascribed these popular myths to players under their charge and stereotyped their ability and performances.

The FA, as the governing body of the English game, and its Scottish and Welsh counterparts were complicit in all this by their refusal to take action or provide even the most cursory of condemnation – that is, until they were forced by pressure from grassroots anti-racist campaigns to take a stand and provide some semblance of leadership.

The media blindly peddled the same racist myths without either disapproval or qualification and often ignored some of the nastiest examples of racism, so they were tacitly and overtly complicit in the racism that was raging around the game. Black players were routinely described as 'black pearls' or 'black gold' and their achievements described as 'black magic'.

That image of the game seems like something from a bygone age. Certainly it is a generation away from today's multi-camera, 24/7, wall-to-wall football coverage. Racist chanting of the massed, four-sides-of-the-ground variety is almost unheard of, at least in English football stadiums, and is curbed by legal statutes and powers against such behaviour. The media is willing to condemn such behaviour in outraged tones, and coaches and fellow professionals are quick to jump to the defence of fellow teammates subjected to these displays of racism. But while overt racism is condemned, racism in more subtle forms remains. There are still few players of Asian origin playing in the professional game, in spite of the widespread popularity of the game within their communities, and there remains a chronic shortage of black coaches and managers.

There are an increasing number of books on issues of race both in sport and in football in general. Phil Vasili's excellent *Colouring Over the White Line* (Mainstream Publishing, 2000) provided a well-researched encyclopaedia of black footballers who have played in the British professional game. However, the critical difference between Vasili's book and this one is that this book serves as a history of black British footballers from the perspective of those footballers themselves, and an analysis of the key events that have shaped the experience of black footballers today. The sometimes angry, moving and humorous testimonies from current and former players demonstrate the strategies they adopted to deal with and respond to the racism they suffered.

However, although *Pitch Black* differs in approach from *Colouring Over the White Line* in many other respects, its starting point is the place at which Vasili's book ends. *Colouring Over the White Line* provided an overview of the start of an era in which black footballers were beginning to come of age, or 'exploding into maturity', as Vasili put it. Vasili's book supplied evidence of a black presence since the birth of the professional game in England and ended in the 1980s

just as a crop of talented young black footballers were starting to make their mark. *Pitch Black* concentrates specifically
on UK-born or -raised players. Therefore, there's no Thierry
Henry or Patrick Vieira. No Shaka Hislop, Lucas Radebe or
Jimmy Floyd Hasselbaink. Also, because it's about British-
born black players, Republic of Ireland internationals Paul
McGrath, Chris Hughton and Terry Phelan don't feature,
even though they were born in west London, east London
and Manchester respectively, though Chris Hughton does
count as a manager. However, players such as Cyrille Regis,
Brendon Batson, Eric Young and John Barnes, all of whom
were born outside the UK but were raised in Britain and
played at international level for one of the home nations, are
featured in these pages.

This book takes an historical approach, beginning in the
1970s and charting the black British presence in the national
game, and ending with an assessment of contemporary issues
and an analysis of future developments.

The issue of racism in football just doesn't seem to go
away. Every incident brings about a familiar pattern. De-
nouncement, outrage, soul-searching, finger pointing. The
event is analysed from all angles and eventually things
move on once the incident has been milked for all its worth,
until the next incident and the old familiar circular pattern
emerges again. The purpose of this book is two-fold. Firstly,
to provide greater understanding of the issues involved
and to allow the debate around racism in football to move
away from its familiar arguments. Secondly, it's intended to
provide a voice to those at the sharp end of racism in the
game, but a voice that goes beyond the familiar knee-jerk
responses, articulating a considered, thoughtful analysis of
players' own experiences and their role within the game.

INTRODUCTION

IT IS 12 April 1982. Paul Canoville is warming up on the sidelines getting ready to come on as substitute for Chelsea against Crystal Palace. He is met with a torrent of racist abuse, mainly from his own fans. Monkey chants and cries of 'Sieg Heil' rain down from all four sides of the ground. When Canoville replaces his teammate, the abuse becomes louder as he enters the field of play. He is visibly shaken as he runs on to make his debut for Chelsea. He is just twenty years old.

17 June 2007. Nedum Onuoha is playing for England in the UEFA under-21 European Championship against Serbia. He is met with a volley of racist abuse from a large section of Serbian supporters. Onuoha stares and observes the Serbian fans. His head is held high. He appears cocky, arrogant, but above all dignified. He is twenty years old.

At first glance, the different reactions of Canoville and Onuoha may simply be explained by differences in the personalities of the two young men. In reality, enormous changes took place in the intervening twenty-five years that shaped the two players' responses. Huge strides have been made in British football to eliminate the type of racist abuse suffered by Canoville. These changes reflect growing opposition to overt forms of racism in wider society, which provides a broader context for Onuoha's reaction to the racism he suffered.

Onuoha would not have been allowed to react that way had he played in Canoville's era. Almost certainly, he would have received some form of condemnation from within the media and other commentators on the game for making a stand. He may even have received a fine or a ban. Canoville and his contemporaries were expected to take the abuse, say nothing and concentrate on playing football. In Canoville's time there was no question of support or sympathy; instead, it was expected that these incidents would build a player's 'character'. In 2007, the reaction Onuoha received from the media, fellow professionals, football coaches and the FA was overwhelmingly supportive. If only it were always this way.

The story of black British footballers is linked inevitably with post-war immigration to the UK from the West Indies and, to a lesser extent, from west Africa. There has been a consistent black presence within the game in Britain right throughout the professional era. Many notable players were born outside the UK, in British colonies, like the South African Albert Johanneson. Others were from Britain's black communities, which, prior to the Second World War, were largely atomised and dispersed, with the exception of black communities within British seaports. The post-Second World War migration from the Caribbean and other Commonwealth countries saw black communities settle not in seaports for the most part, but in manufacturing and industrial centres. It was the sons of this generation of migrants who formed the cohort of black players who, by their numbers and endeavours, collectively began to have an impact on the beautiful game throughout the UK.

Of course, there were black professional footballers plying their trade from the beginning of this era. There was the Bermudan Clyde Best at West Ham, who had made his debut for the Hammers at the start of the 1969/70 season. Local boy and pacy winger Johnny Miller played for Ipswich and Norwich from 1968 until 1976 and was in some, albeit limited, circles touted as a possible first black player to play for England. The East End-born Charles brothers, John and Clive, played for West Ham in the early 1970s. But it was a younger group of players, those who first came to prominence in the mid- to late 1970s onwards, whose impact was so significant. This wave of black footballing pioneers, whose presence paved the way for the normalising of a black footballing presence within the British game, differed in two important respects from those who had gone before.

Firstly, those players such as Laurie Cunningham, Cyrille Regis, Viv Anderson, Brendon Batson and others were born or at least raised in the UK and grew up within emerging black communities. The places they grew up in and the schools they attended were mainly based in working-class areas where football was ingrained within the fabric of the community. Football was, and is, extremely popular in the Caribbean and in Africa, where the pioneers of the black professional game in the UK drew their heritage from. A generation of young black boys played football and flourished, building on the game's appeal within black communities and in working-class sporting culture, which became particularly potent following the success of the 1970 Brazil World Cup side. This multiracial team, with its style and skill and brand of flowing, graceful and above all exciting football, personified by its stars, Pelé and Jairzinho, provided the role models that this generation could follow and emulate.

Secondly, sport was one of the few areas black communities in Britain were actively encouraged to excel in. Black British footballers remain vastly over-represented in the professional game compared to their overall proportion within the general population. Some 20 per cent of professional footballers are black, compared to around 3 per cent of the general population. In the 1970s, the experience of black pupils in schools was characterised by widespread and systematic underachievement and discrimination. Black pupils typically received an educational experience that was distinctly below par, to use a sporting metaphor. In London, where the vast majority of migrants from the West Indies lived, some 70 per cent of pupils in schools for the educationally sub-normal (as students with learning difficulties were then termed) were of West Indian origin, in spite of this group making up only 20 per cent of the overall school population. In addition, school expulsion figures were dominated by children of West Indian origin. Parents of these children consistently complained about the low expectations that teachers had for their sons and daughters, and about the unfair application of discipline and sanctions. Sport often remained the only part of school life where teachers had high expectations and actively nurtured and supported any aspirations these children had.

Therefore, a combination of football's widespread appeal within black and working-class communities, the encouragement and support for black sporting achievement (largely at the expense of academic study), and the inspiration provided by the all-conquering Brazil side would provide the British game with a pool of footballing talent from within its black communities in excess of the handful of black footballers who had participated in the professional game up to that point.

Black footballers have always reflected the changing styles and fashions of Britain's black community. George Berry and

Vince Hilaire's afros, Ricky Hill's 'wet look', Les Ferdinand's 'flat top' and Rio and Anton Ferdinand's cornrows, as well as the young Paul Ince's quite frankly woeful hairstyle, have provided sources of admiration, amusement and downright disgust amongst black football fans and the wider black community. Black players' goal celebrations – the high five, the touch, the grip, the bogle, body popping and backslides – all reflected shifts in black popular culture. These symbols were extremely important to black players throughout the 1970s and beyond. In the face of widespread racism within the game, they reflected the solidarity that existed between black players, and their role in helping footballers deal with the racism they suffered on and off the pitch cannot be underestimated.

These ordinary black men from ordinary black communities instantly became role models, pioneers, ambassadors and the focal point for debates around national identity, just at the point at which they got their first foothold in the professional game. Most if not all of the players who feature in this book were ill prepared for the responsibility associated with their new-found status as professional footballers, let alone as role models and pioneers. Many of them managed to live up to the responsibility, but often at a price, both to their dignity and pride, and to their families and close friends. For black communities, an empathy and understanding of their plight, based on often bitter experiences in school, on the streets and in the workplace, is the reason pioneers such as Regis, Barnes and Wright remain extremely popular amongst black football fans regardless of which team they support.

Beyond black communities, the impact of black footballers has played another important role. It provided a glimpse, albeit a narrow one, into the culture of young black Britain. Fashions, hairstyles, musical preferences all provided a lens through which many whites viewed black communities. More importantly, in supporting their heroes who play week in, week out for the teams they support, many white fans took their first steps towards a stand against racism. Football became the arena in which the stupidity and folly of racism was cruelly exposed, and led to a sea change in football grounds around the country. It is the one place that many if not most football fans receive any kind of anti-racist education or challenge to their racist behaviour and it helped to challenge the most overt expressions of racism not only in football but in society as a whole.

Of course, the level of racism suffered by black players in the 1970s and '80s differs radically from that suffered by black players today. Today, cases are more isolated and less socially acceptable. Official responses to racism within the game are more likely to condemn the racists as a matter of course. Players have been sent off and clubs have been fined where allegations of racial abuse have been confirmed, but there remain deep-rooted problems within the British game. The lack of black coaches at managerial level is an ongoing issue which those responsible for running the game continue to be slow to address. Sympathy is offered and highly qualified black coaches are told to be patient and that their time will come, yet it seems that the number of black managers never rises past three or four, while younger and less-qualified white coaches are given high-profile managerial and coaching positions. In addition, football clubs and the respective Football Associations have done little to bring their considerable influence to bear to protect black footballers in their care and employ from racist abuse and discrimination, particularly when those players are representing their clubs and countries in European competitions.

It would, however, be wrong to define the participation of black footballers solely in terms of racism. The life of a professional footballer is a good one, even a great one. It remains the envy of many small and not-so-small boys and has caused untold heartache to those whose chances to join its ranks have been cruelly denied through bad luck, injury or lack of talent. Even before the Premier League era, when the financial rewards for players, including those of modest ability, became downright insane, it was a very good way to earn a living. Football's golden age can arguably be traced back to the beginning of the 1960s and the abolition of the £20 per week maximum wage. Even then, it wasn't until stars like Jimmy Greaves and Denis Law decamped to Italy to earn big money that clubs were forced to pay up in order to head off the potential drain of talent to foreign shores. By the end of the 1960s, George Best was earning £1,000 a week, a staggering leap in wages in comparison to what he might have earned at the beginning of the decade. It was the start of the real disparity between the wages of the average footballer and that of their friends from their communities. This ever increasing disparity was firmly entrenched by the mid-1970s, when black footballers were collectively making their way in the game. In addition to the financial rewards, there was the adulation, the very reasonable working hours, the downtime and the myriad off-field distractions. Footballers have lived the lifestyle and black players have been no different in that respect. However, while the lifestyle of a professional footballer has brought great rewards, both financial and otherwise, the experience of black footballers has been materially different from that of their white counterparts. Although some black players firmly attest that they have not faced racism, or that its impact has been marginal, for the vast majority it has been an important feature of their careers as footballers. For those players, whether they played in the top flight and won international caps or spent their careers in the lower leagues, it is their common experience of racism that forged the solidarity that exists between them and it's that which makes their stories so compelling.

CHAPTER 1

PRE-THREE DEGREES

'He was as good as anyone I saw play. As good as Barnes and right up there with George Best. He was the best player I ever played with.' – Cyrille Regis

LAURENCE PAUL CUNNINGHAM was quite simply one of the most talented players of his generation. Possessed of poise, balance and speed, his movement was graceful, effortless and economic. He glided around the pitch and was blessed with great touch, awareness and an ability to play at his own pace regardless of the topsy turvy, helter-skelter nature of the game going on around him. In a remarkable career, he was the first English player to play for Real Madrid and the second black player to win a full England cap. He played for Manchester United, won an FA Cup winners' medal as a prince amongst Wimbledon's Crazy Gang and, at West Bromwich Albion, he made up one-third of the 'Three Degrees', the legendary footballing trio that formed a critical part of the Ron Atkinson side that achieved considerable success throughout the late 1970s and early 1980s. Injuries robbed him of his key footballing faculties while at Real Madrid, and he never fully recovered those key ingredients that made him such a wonderful performer: his easy acceleration and change of pace. While his career declined from its peak of gracing the

Bernabéu, the greater tragedy was the cutting short of his life in a car crash at the age of just thirty-three.

English football could be a dire place if open, attractive football was the kind of thing you wanted to watch. Pitches were often devoid of grass and the first shower of rain would quickly turn them into mud baths. Derby County's Baseball Ground was notorious for being particularly poor. It was covered in several inches of mud throughout autumn and winter, and baked hard in early and late spring as the season drew to a close. Grass seemed to be anathema to the Baseball Ground, as though it were permanently on strike or some grass-based apartheid was at play to prevent it from operating as it should. Coaches valued toughness, grit, determination, work rate and courage over technical ability. Every team seemed to have at least one midfield 'enforcer', who possessed little in the way of technical ability but whose job was to intimidate and brutalise the opposition. Central defenders were typically big, tough-tackling and good in the air, but extremely vulnerable to any kind of pace or speed of turn. Full-backs were often of limited technical ability, but were likewise expected to be tough in the tackle. Up front, target men were often cut from the same cloth as their centre-back counterparts and would typically operate alongside a small, nippy, infinitely more mobile partner to form a big-man/little-man strike force. In midfield, players were expected to get stuck in and display a lung-busting work ethic. As a result, the football served up on a weekly basis often lacked guile and quality and was devoid of anything approaching style. Players would often be covered in so much mud the numbers on the backs of their shirts couldn't be seen. That is not to say that football didn't possess moments of excitement. There were plenty of goal-mouth incidents and the attritional nature of the football on show, while not aesthetically pleasing, had its own unique beauty of a kind.

There were, of course, exceptions to this. Some teams throughout the leagues had supremely gifted individuals of outstanding technical ability, but they were often mistrusted. Viewed often as 'Fancy Dan', maverick types, they were too showy, too ostentatious and over-indulgent for the tastes of all but a few football managers. They were not to be trusted, particularly when the going got tough, and they would often be overlooked at international level. The England national team's wilderness years throughout the 1970s and early 1980s was attributable to this rigid mindset. Successive England managers would ignore or give limited opportunities to flair players, and then all too readily dispense with their services when, with the team set up in a strict, rigid and functional formation, they inevitably failed to perform.

Laurie Cunningham was one of the game's aesthetes. In addition to the fluency and grace of his movement, he had an array of tricks, flicks, drag backs and general ball skills that were simultaneously baffling for defenders and breath-taking for spectators. Traditionally, in-swinging corners were performed by left-footed players from the right-hand side and vice versa. Cunningham took in-swinging corners from the right with the outside of his right foot. He also had two good feet and was a deceptively good header of a ball, but his hallmark was his ability to run with the ball at opposing defences. Picking up the ball from deep, he could turn defenders inside out and, with a drop of the shoulder and a change of pace, could beat them from a standing start.

West Bromwich Albion's Three Degrees marked a watershed in the development of black professional footballers in the UK. Until the 1970s, black footballers tended to exist as isolated examples. Albion's larger-than-life manager Ron Atkinson, however, turned the blackness of Cunningham, Cyrille Regis and Brendon Batson into a somewhat crude publicity drive, dubbing them the Three Degrees after the popular black female vocal trio, who were allegedly Prince Charles's favourite singers.

Atkinson had transformed the fortunes of Albion, and the side had developed into a successful, attractive team. From the beginning of the 1970s, the club had struggled to maintain its First Division status and suffered relegation in 1973. It had gained promotion in 1976 and had performed well, but under Atkinson's stewardship they began to challenge for trophies and titles. Cunningham, Batson and Regis formed an integral part of the team's transformation and Albion was the first high-profile club of the era to play so many black players in the same side. The Three Degrees were distinctly of their time.

Regis and Batson were born in the Caribbean and Cunningham was born in north London. Their parents were of the generation that had come to the UK during the postwar period. Many migrated to Britain without any real plans other than finding work and getting settled, and many others came with the intention of staying for a few years and then returning home. Those whose initial plan was to return home often found that employment, settling into a community and, in particular, raising their children in a new country all acted as impediments to their moving back to their countries of birth.

The second generation had a distinctly different attitude to that of their parents, but players such as the Three Degrees learned, in the rarefied atmosphere of English professional football, to adopt some of those characteristics of determination and stoicism that formed a critical part of their parents' experience. Their parents had faced unparalleled levels of discrimination. Many skilled workers were forced to take jobs several rungs beneath their levels of expertise and competence. Their employment opportunities were characterised by low pay, low status and semi- or unskilled work and they were barred access to promotion, equal pay and often basic employment protection. In housing, the deliberately discriminatory policies applied by local housing authorities and estate agents conspired to consign black communities to the worst housing available, and they suffered discrimination in all other aspects of the social life of Britain, including in shops, pubs and clubs. Racist taunts and abuse in the streets and physical attacks and beatings were a common experience, particularly for young men. Even places of worship were often off-limits for fanatically Christian West Indians, as men of the cloth applied their own rather unique take on Bible teachings of 'Love thy neighbour as thyself' and politely, and not so politely, refused them admittance to church. Their children, mainly born and raised in the UK and without the perspective of immigrants and new arrivals, were not prepared to put up with the indignities their parents were subjected to, and resisted this treatment in more overt ways. Discriminated against in a range of social spaces, including the streets of their own communities, often by right-wing activity or the police-enforced 'Sus' (stop and search) laws, they began to develop both organised and spontaneous forms of resistance.

The Three Degrees were of this generation. All had spent their formative years growing up in London; Cunningham had been born there. Their impact was little short of phenomenal for a number of key reasons. Firstly, they could all play. Regis and Cunningham went on to become full internationals and Batson represented England at B level. Secondly, they were members of a successful side that played free-flowing, attractive football that brought Albion some success before Atkinson departed for Manchester United and the side he had built broke up. Thirdly, as a consequence of the team's success and their manager's eye for publicity, the novelty of three black players in a top-flight side at a time when black players were still rare proved to be too good an opportunity to resist for the press, who competed with each other to come up with the most offensive headlines and ways of peddling lazy stereotypes. The final reason was related to the level of hatred and abuse they received during games. At a time when the existence of racist abuse from the terraces often went unreported by match commentators, even when it was evident from *Match of the Day* or the regional football programmes shown on ITV, the level of venom was such that Granada TV's Gerald Sinstadt commented on the 'unsporting' treatment of the trio by Manchester United supporters in a league game that Albion had won 5–3 at Old Trafford in December 1978. The three had played brilliantly and Cunningham in particular had given United's defence a torrid afternoon. Uniquely, Sinstadt had commented on their treatment at a time when the media routinely ignored instances of racist abuse towards black players.

However, their impact on the generation of black footballers who aspired to play the game professionally, and those professionals already plying their trade as footballers, would prove to be inspirational. Their contribution marked the point at which the experiences of black players moved from the individual to the collective, more generalised experiences. The Three Degrees marked the point at which any young black professional entering the game knew they could expect to receive torrents of racist abuse, but also knew that, given attitudes within the game, they would be forced to deal with this largely by themselves. It is conceivable that for some black players considering a football career, the poisonous environment in which they had to earn a living would have acted as a serious impediment.

West Ham had been the first top-flight club to field three black players at the same time when Clyde Best, Ade Coker and Clive Charles turned out for the Hammers in April 1972 for a game against Tottenham. Before the mid-1970s, black players had suffered racist abuse to a certain degree, but their involvement in the professional game had been different. They were largely viewed as an exotic novelty act. What changed – and the Three Degrees epitomised this sea change – was the numbers of players coming into the professional game, and the subsequent response from the terraces: a concerted campaign to abuse black players, often involving organised racist groups. Their presence was no longer an anomaly; this was a movement. Viv Anderson was winning titles and European honours under Brian Clough at Nottingham Forest. Tunji Banjo and John Chiedozie were at Orient. Luther Blissett was terrorising defences as part of the Watford team that had a meteoric rise through the divisions to finish as runners-up in the then First Division. George Berry and Bob Hazell formed a tough-tackling, physically intimidating centre-back partnership at Wolves. Garth Crooks was top-scorer for his home town team of Stoke City.

The participation of these players and others was an affront to those who viewed the game as the preserve of whites. For the far right, who used football to promote their ideology and recruit followers, here in microcosm was the expression of the narrative that the country was being, or had been, taken over by blacks, and no area of society was safe, including the game that Britain had given the world.

Laurie Cunningham's introduction to the professional game was a baptism of fire. Shortly after making his debut, playing for Leyton Orient, Cunningham played against Millwall at their home, the Den, in December 1974. In May of that year, the National Front had achieved 11.5 per cent of the vote in a by-election in the London Borough of Newham and were claiming to have 20,000 members.

In addition to Cunningham, the Orient side included another black player in Bobby Fisher, and an Asian player, Ricky Heppolette. As the team arrived at the Den, they were met by National Front members, distributing racist propaganda. As they emerged from the tunnel and entered onto the pitch, as well as the usual vitriol, they were greeted with bananas and a carving knife that were thrown onto the pitch. Cunningham and Fisher, in imitation of the 1972 US Olympic athletes John Carlos and Tommie Smith, made black power salutes as an act of defiance.

The game had given the eighteen-year-old Cunningham a taste of the racial prejudice he would face throughout his career. He also recognised his position as a trailblazer and role model, realising that he couldn't be seen to allow the abuse to affect him because of the impact it might have on other black players. Cunningham reasoned that if he could find a way of dealing with the abuse and the other forms of racial prejudice he faced, it would be easier for others to get a fair chance. He understood that he was going to need to put up with the intimidatory tackling, not only because he was a young, skilful winger, but also to prove that, as a black player, he possessed the necessary 'bottle' – the mental fortitude that casual prejudice dictated was a key trait lacking in black players.

Cunningham was shown remarkable patience by George Petchey, his manager at Orient, who was to remain a friend of Cunningham's throughout his life. He was a man prepared to go against the popular and often populist ideas about black players. He was not alone in this regard, but few within the game appeared to be prepared to actively challenge conventional wisdom at this stage. The clubs and the FA appeared impotent and unsure as to how to respond, preferring instead to remain silent, with only a few honourable exceptions. Not wholly convinced that football was to be his chosen career, Cunningham was torn between a career as a dancer (he had an offer to join the renowned Ballet Rambert Dance Company) and football. He'd developed a reputation as a somewhat indifferent time-keeper with a penchant for fashion and nightclubs. However, he also displayed a canny sense of the political and social environment in which he lived, and embarked on a political journey in order to make sense of his experiences and those of other people in black communities. Assessing his time as a young professional at Orient, he remarked:

There have been times when I've been mixed up about the race thing. A couple of years ago I thought that to be black in England was to be a loser. You know, back of the queue for decent jobs. Suspicion on you before anyone knew what you were about.

He continued:

> I did have a feeling for 'Black Power'. It seemed to meet the
> mood of frustration. It could give you some pride. Then I
> changed. It sort of struck me that the great majority of
> people, black and white, are in the same boat, fighting for a
> decent living. It also struck me down at Orient I was getting a
> very good break. I got on well with George Petchey. It didn't
> matter to him whether I was black, white or Chinese just as
> long as I could play.

For Cunningham, the footballer's lifestyle could elevate
him above the economic effects of racism, but couldn't
protect him from its psychological and emotional impact.
It's uncommon for footballers to take a political stance, but
Cunningham had one. How could he not, given the harsh
realities of racism in the game and wider society?

At the beginning of the 1976/77 season, a singular event en-
capsulated the tense relationship between the police and the
black community, something Cunningham no doubt had in
mind when he was analysing the way that black people were
treated with suspicion as a matter of course. Two hundred
and fifty thousand people had attended the 1975 Notting
Hill Carnival, the biggest ever turn-out. Capital Radio had
broadcast live from the event, encouraging attendance from
across London. The carnival had become Europe's biggest
street event and was being established as a must-attend at-
traction for people from the black community from London
and beyond. Middle-class residents in north Kensington had
organised an anti-carnival petition, signed by 500 people
in March 1976. Tension rose throughout the spring and

summer of 1976 in the run-up to the carnival, and the Metropolitan Police had stated there was to be a heavy presence in response to incidences of pickpocketing the previous year. Three thousand police officers were to be deployed, ten times the numbers from previous years. Pressure was placed on carnival organisers to cancel the event or hold it elsewhere. By the August bank holiday, the scene was set for clashes. Disproportionate and aggressive policing, designed to intimidate or to establish superiority, was met with resistance. In the fighting that followed, 325 police were wounded and sixty people were arrested and charged. Later that day, the police, by way of some kind of poorly conceived vengeance on the black community, arrested eighteen young men in Islington, far away from Notting Hill. These young men were first accused of 'suspicious behaviour', then arrested and questioned in custody. While in custody, according to the police accounts, all eighteen young men voluntarily confessed that they had gone to the carnival in order to steal and attack the police. The police case hinged on these 'confessions' of these eighteen men, seventeen of whom provided evidence that they had been assaulted in police cells. In spite of the best efforts of the prosecution to secure convictions, the jury came up with forty-three not-guilty verdicts, eight guilty and twenty-eight undecided to the range of charges that had come to court. The media response was, as usual, to back the police version of events, even in the face of the evidence as to how the 'confessions' had been obtained; there was nothing by way of media or basic journalistic investigative scrutiny of this event. The incident illustrated not only the tense relationship between black communities and the police but, critically, the media's attitude to black communities.

The press, particularly the tabloids, were busy demonising black communities and especially black youths, portrayed as criminal, job-stealing, slum-dwelling immigrants rather than the disadvantaged, criminalised and exploited section of British society that, by and large, they were. The press and media in general did not routinely condemn incidences of racism in football until some two decades later and in fact actively contributed to spreading the stereotypes and myths that were routinely ascribed to black footballers.

The era was also a time of increasing activity from the National Front and the British Movement. The far right had first targeted football as potentially fertile ground in the mid-1960s and again made a concerted effort in the 1970s. Far-right literature cynically contained football-related material in a direct attempt to appeal to fans, with *Bulldog*, the youth paper of the National Front, even having a league table of the most racist fans. While the level of racism in the 1970s was often of a horrific kind, and at clubs where the level of hatred was at its most venomous there existed a significant far-right presence, not all fans who indulged in this behaviour were members of far-right groups. Some indeed were; others had a loose association or alliance; others had no involvement at all but were heavily involved in racist behaviour. Other fans, of course, wanted nothing to do with the behaviour of their fellow travellers. Inevitably, racism coupled with the increase in incidences of football violence turned many off attending games.

There were other developments taking place within the game that were beginning to affect the behaviour of spectators at football matches, too. By the mid-1970s, players' wages were on the rise, which precipitated an increase in revenue. This increase was, at least amongst the top clubs, paid for by an increase in admission prices. The increases weren't significant enough to deter the large bulk of supporters, but they had the effect of pricing out supporters at both ends of the supporter age spectrum: pensioners and those of school age no longer attended matches in the numbers they had previously. These two groups generally had a civilising effect on fan behaviour. Older fans – fathers, grandfathers, older relatives – would actively deter bad behaviour, usually by their presence alone. Young children, mainly boys, would often be taken to games by older relatives, but many would also attend together in small groups. The Merseyside giants, Everton and Liverpool, both had a 'Boys' Pen': an area of the ground set aside specifically for under-12s. When crowd crushes or surges occurred on the terraces (which was often), these young fans would be removed from the affected areas or otherwise 'looked after' by other spectators concerned about their safety. The absence of these two groups of supporters meant that there were greater proportions of young men and teenage boys – precisely those supporters most likely to participate in football violence – and while this didn't on its own lead to racist behaviour, the combination of football-related violence and racist behaviour served to make the atmosphere at football grounds more poisonous.

Elsewhere, the start of the 1976 season saw Cunningham continue to produce stellar performances for Orient, but the side struggled both on and off the pitch. Performances and results were poor and the club was crippled with debt. As the season dragged on, it became clear that due to the club's huge debts and poor form, it was a case only of when, not if, Cunningham was to be sold. There was speculation about where he might go. Johnny Giles, the player-manager of West Bromwich Albion who had taken the Baggies to the First Division, contacted Orient, a fee was agreed and Cunningham was eventually sold, the first of the legendary Three Degrees to join the West Midlands outfit in March 1977.

A few months later, Cyrille Regis joined him. Regis was born in French Guiana and arrived in England, aged five, without being able to speak any English. A good sportsman, his first love was cricket, at which he represented his county at school level, and although he played football like any other boy of his age, he didn't excel. At secondary school, he wasn't good enough to get into his school football team until he was thirteen. He first played on the right wing and then moved to the striker's position, where he found that he could score goals. His strength was his speed and he blossomed into a prolific striker and was selected to play representative football for the Borough of Brent. Along the way he had played for a team called Oxford & Kilburn with future England cricket captain Mike Gatting and Mike's brother Steve, who later played for Arsenal and Brighton. However, it was Cyrille's performances playing Sunday league that got him noticed and he signed for Moseley in the Athenian League in 1976.

The Athenian League was developing a reputation as a decent source of black footballing talent. The previous year, Phil Walker and Trevor Lee had left Epsom & Ewell to begin a successful stint at Millwall. The eighteen-year-old Regis scored twenty-four goals in his debut season, earning him a transfer to semi-pro outfit Hayes Football Club. Combining work on building sites as an apprentice electrician with playing non-league for Hayes, he scored another twenty-five goals in his first season for them. Fifty goals in two seasons alerted a crop of scouts from league clubs. Eventually it was

Ronnie Allen, chief scout at West Bromwich Albion, who persuaded his bosses to pay the £5,000 transfer fee Hayes wanted. Legend has it that Allen offered to pay the transfer fee for the young Regis himself. As Cyrille put it:

> Story goes that they weren't sure about me, not that they'd seen me play or whatever, but it came down to money. Five grand and another five grand and Ronnie Allen said, 'Well, I'll buy him with my own money and when he makes it, give me my money back.' But there's also another story that what persuaded him to buy me was he came down to watch me play at Hayes ... The ball came across from a corner and I went up for a header ... Myself, the goalkeeper and two defenders, and the ball ended up in the net and so that persuaded him to buy me.

Along with his capacity for scoring goals, one of the key criteria that had persuaded Allen to bring Regis to Albion was his strength, which was to earn him the nickname of 'Smokin' Joe' due to his alleged similarity to former heavyweight boxing champion Joe Frazier. The name epitomised the somewhat crude depiction of black players at the time, which chose to focus almost exclusively on their physical attributes. Undoubtedly, Regis was strong and powerful and he was also quick, but this description belied his other attributes. Regis would not have been able to play in the top flight for so long and represent England at international level had he been simply a battering ram of a striker. His hold-up play was intelligent and cunning. His ability to bring others into play was exceptional. His movement was clever and incisive and his finishing was as good as any of his contemporaries. These more cerebral attributes that apply to Regis as well as other black players were rarely analysed in any great detail by a media constrained by a distinctly nineteenth-century perception of black people – and, by extension, black footballers – as 'exotic'.

Football, like many sports, is a game where clichés are in abundance, and within English football they are rife. These clichés often act as a convenient shorthand to convey ideas and concepts. However, in the case of black footballers from this era, the clichés served to present information in a way that not only offered a limited version of the truth but also suggested that the style of play that black players brought to the game was purely and exclusively physical and therefore of limited merit. Bobby Robson, in assessing Johnny Miller, said, 'Miller had potential without ever really fulfilling it … He didn't seem to have the aggression and commitment that I was looking for … At the time there was this feeling in the country that coloured players lacked heart. I must admit that I asked myself a number of times, could it be right?'

Germans may be efficient and ruthless, which provides a useful explanation for their prowess at penalty shoot-outs, but this doesn't preclude admiration for their technical ability. Brazilians possess a rhythmic, samba-inspired footballing style and although popular wisdom often fails to appreciate that the technical ability of Brazilian footballers is rooted in their country's cultural notions of how football should be played, combined with hours of practice to hone that technique, it's at least admired for its beauty and success. The clichés surrounding black footballers were never juxtaposed with an appreciation of their intelligence and their tactical discipline and awareness. If speed were the only attribute required to play on the wing, that position would be dominated by Olympic sprinters. If strength were the only attribute required to play as a target man, that position would be dominated by powerlifters. Good defensive tactics can often negate speed and strength, and the challenge to overcome this requires a level of strategic thought and planning that often goes unappreciated, even by those who have been involved in the game at the highest level. Knowing how to make the best use of your speed or how to best utilise strength has been a key challenge for generations of footballers, but in spite of achieving this week after week and season after season, the same lazy clichés dominated the perception of black footballers for several decades.

• • •

'I was like, where's West Brom? You hear it in the scoresheet, but I didn't know where West Brom was.' – Cyrille Regis

The timing of Regis's shot at the big time couldn't have been better. He had just completed his exams and was now a fully qualified electrician. Albion offered him a one-year contract. His employers wished him well and offered him his job back if it didn't work out. Although he had absolutely no idea where West Bromwich was, he was both excited and apprehensive at the prospect of becoming a professional footballer. Staying in club lodgings in Handsworth, an area of Birmingham with a large Caribbean community, the nineteen-year-old Regis began his professional career. Laurie Cunningham was already at the club, but as Cunningham trained with the first team, Regis, on the reserves, didn't have a great deal to do with him at this stage.

Regis's career at Albion began well. Chief scout Ronnie Allen had taken over as first-team manager after Johnny

Giles had resigned and Regis had played regularly for the reserves, scoring on his debut. He scored twice on his first-team debut, in a League Cup game against Rotherham, and again on his league debut in a victory over Middlesbrough. In his own words: 'I'd settled well. I was living in Handsworth, where I felt comfortable, even though I was far from home and I'd had a great start to my career. Strikers are judged on scoring goals and it's so important to get off to a good start.'

He was blossoming in his quest to make the big time, but something else was happening as well. 'It was great having him around,' Regis said of his new-found friendship with Laurie Cunningham.

> He kind of took me under his wing and we became friends almost immediately. It was good that one of the first-team players took an interest in me and, with him being black and from London, made it more important. I looked up to him and it's only when I think back now that me being there was as good for him as it was for me.

Regis highlights the two factors that were key to his initial development at West Bromwich Albion. Of course, he was hungry. As a raw nineteen-year-old, he was keen to show what he could do in the top flight of English football. Although it's a matter of conjecture as to whether Ronnie Allen had paid for Regis's transfer out of his own pocket, the manager nonetheless had some form of investment in him and was prepared to give him an extended run in the side. His hunger and the belief of his manager were important factors, and these alone may have been enough to guarantee his success at Albion, but equally important were his friendship with Cunningham and his residency in Handsworth. Regis remembers: 'We'd be seen in and around Handsworth and we soon became popular in the black community. People would come up to us and you started seeing black kids taking a real interest in going to football matches.'

His friendship with Cunningham was an important part of his initial experience and, ultimately, with the arrival of Brendon Batson, was to define his career at Albion. Playing up and down the country, suffering the taunts together, created an important bond in helping the two players to deal with the abuse they received. For Cunningham, this was equally important. Up until then, he had been the only black player at the club. Here was someone who was able and willing to share the load.

Handsworth was also an important part of Regis's 'settling-in' period. Becoming a part of a black community provided him with an opportunity to escape from the pressures of justifying his blackness. In Handsworth, he could just be himself. In turn, he became an instant hero amongst the black community. The ability of black players to deal with racist abuse and use the experience as a source of motivation gave inspiration to black communities not only in Birmingham but throughout the country. The experiences of black players in suffering racist abuse mirrored their own experiences, but differed in an important dimension. The dehumanising effects of both racist abuse and racial discrimination offered very few opportunities to resist their impact. Football provided an opportunity to hit back. Here were players who not only took the abuse but turned the taunting of their abusers on its head in order to perform well on the pitch. For black communities therefore, black players who were scoring goals, making goals, tackling and playing well were resisting and fighting back in the only way they were able.

As Regis put it, 'Black people of all ages would just want to talk to us or just wish us well. I suppose in some way they wanted us to know that we had their support and we weren't doing this on our own.'

Regis had quickly established himself as a first-team regular. However, before 1977 had ended, Ronnie Allen had taken up an opportunity to manage the Saudi Arabian national side and Albion were on the hunt for a new manager. Veteran defender John Wile was installed in a caretaker role, but Albion appointed a young and hungry manager who'd done very well with unfashionable Cambridge United. Ron Atkinson was to change Albion's fortunes and play a pivotal role in changing the way that black players were perceived and the way in which incidents of racism were handled.

• • •

Arsenal had won the historic league and cup double in 1971. Their domestic dominance was further underlined by the fact that their youth team, containing Brendon Batson, had won the FA Youth Cup the same year. Batson was born on the Caribbean island of Grenada and had arrived in the UK at the age of nine. He was spotted as a thirteen-year-old playing representative football for his district and signed as an apprentice at fifteen. First-team opportunities had eluded Batson and he made only ten appearances in three seasons. He moved to Cambridge United in 1974 and joined a team in the fourth tier of English professional football. United had only been a league outfit since 1970 and there was an amateurish quality to the whole club. For Batson, this was a far cry from his beginnings at Arsenal: 'At Arsenal the apprentices were raised to be gentlemen as part of our development. We were introduced to fine food, told to dress well, taught good manners and taught discipline. When I went to Cambridge, I wondered what have I got into here?'

However, a few months later, Ron Atkinson was appointed manager and transformed the club. Many of the older players were replaced by youth team players and free signings, and the team began to do well. Atkinson obviously rated Batson highly – and why not? He had played in the top tier of English football for Arsenal and was a fine if very underrated footballer. Batson was a cultured right-back. He was a good solid defender, had good positional sense, was strong in the tackle and good going forward. Quick and athletic, he wasn't blessed with blistering pace, but was rarely exposed by even the best of attackers. Atkinson had made him team captain as United improved considerably and achieved promotion to the Third Division in 1976/77.

Early in his United career, Batson had been sent off for retaliation after being continually called a 'black bastard' by an opponent. He recalled later, 'The ref actually apologised for sending me off and supported me at the disciplinary hearing. It meant that I wasn't suspended.' Atkinson had tough words for Batson and told him in no uncertain terms that he'd need to find a way of dealing with the abuse. Batson learned the necessary lesson and never allowed himself to resort to retaliation throughout the rest of his career. The referee in that incident, however, had shown a level of sympathy for Batson that was entirely out of keeping with the prevailing attitude of football officials. Racist abuse from fellow professionals was commonplace and given free rein. Retaliation would be punished, but there were no sanctions for racist abusers. While black players were often subject to abuse from 30,000–40,000 spectators, in addition to abuse from their fellow professionals and managers, it was far preferable to the experiences of friends and family in the workplace. Batson recalls:

> I had friends who worked at Ford's at Dagenham. That was a terrible place for black people to work. There was NF [National Front] in there selling their stuff on the factory floor. They'd have all kinds of racist stuff written on their lockers and would get all kinds of abuse. You'd have foreman right in their face, calling them nigger this, you black bastard that, you'd have people spitting at you and all kinds and you couldn't do anything. You have to remember that fighting meant instant dismissal at Ford's, so all my mates had to just take it. So it never really bothered me, I felt safe, we were protected. Of course you might have 40,000 fans giving you dog's abuse, but I was much better off playing football. Compared to other black people, we had a good life.

United's improvement under Atkinson had brought the club the kind of success that the relatively new league members could only have dreamed of, and at the start of the 1977/78 season, the newly promoted outfit had made a good start and were in a healthy position when Atkinson left to join West Bromwich Albion. A few weeks later in a £30,000 deal, Batson joined Atkinson at Albion. The Three Degrees had arrived at The Hawthorns.

CHAPTER 2

THE LEGEND OF CES PODD

*'I think the only thing that gets you through things ...
events as it was at the time ... was being surrounded by the
right people and how you handled that, and at the time,
Bradford was a safe haven for me. I had coaches who liked
me ... I'd proved that I could play and the fans were great
so that was enough for me.' –* Ces Podd

BEFORE REGIS, CUNNINGHAM and Anderson, there
was Ces Podd. Footballing club culture dictates that the
player who has made most appearances for the first team
is automatically and inalienably afforded the status of club
legend. Between 1970 and 1984, Podd made 502 appearances, more than anyone else in Bradford City's history, but
his influence on the progress of black footballers was down
to more than merely his record number of appearances. At
age nine, Podd had arrived from St Kitts with his family and
settled in Leeds. As a pacy winger, he'd had trials with Manchester United and was invited to sign professional forms
that the club had posted to him. He'd signed the forms, and
on them indicated his Caribbean birth, at which point he
never heard from United again. He was then invited for a
trial at Wolves. He travelled from Leeds to Wolverhampton and assembled along with other trialists in the hope of

impressing enough to secure a professional contract. At the trial, two teams were picked and Podd was told he'd have to come back another time. He was the only black kid there.

As a result of this second knock-back, Podd decided instead to enrol on a graphic design course at Bradford College of Art. Soon after starting his course, he was invited to attend trials at Bradford City. At the trial, the same chain of events that had occurred at Wolves began to play itself out in similar fashion. Two teams were selected and once again, as the only black kid at the trial, he was told there wasn't space for anyone else.

And then the first-team manager was there, and he said, 'We're short of a left-back, anybody play left-back?' And I put my hand up, and I got on the pitch, and at half-time he said, 'Right, we want to see you again.' And that's how my career started. I went home that night and practised kicking the ball – I'd never used my left foot! I played the whole season without them knowing I was right-footed, I was that scared they'd find out.

Eventually Podd moved to right-back, where he played for the majority of his career. Playing entirely within the bottom two divisions of English professional football, he was never afforded the kind of recognition that many of his contemporaries – the Three Degrees, Anderson, Crooks etc. – received, but as one of a handful of black players plying their trade in English professional football he endured the racist abuse that was a key feature of the experience of black footballers throughout the 1970s and '80s. His experiences of racism would have a profound effect on him, his family and his career choices.

Podd's mother couldn't bear to watch her son receive so much racist abuse. After the first game she attended, she refused to watch him play. His father, however, continued to attend, travelling to away games on the official supporters' coach, where he was treated, as Podd puts it, 'like family'. Podd's commitment and no little skill had endeared him to the club's supporters, and it was the supportive atmosphere they created that provided Podd with an important anchor as he sought to deal with the racism that plagued the game.

Indeed, such was his gratitude that despite being courted by several clubs, he refused to leave Bradford City. In 1974, four years into his tenure at Bradford, he was informed by his then manager that the mighty Liverpool had expressed an interest in signing him and asked if he would go if they made an offer. He said no. Liverpool instead signed the virtually unknown Phil Neal from Northampton. Podd was also offered an opportunity to sign for Portsmouth for far more money than his wages at Bradford, but again refused to leave. His gratitude to the club for providing him with the opportunity to play professional football after so many disappointments elsewhere was a factor, but the biggest issue for Podd was the psychological impact of dealing with racist abuse.

For a large part of his career, Podd rarely encountered another opposition black player, but in 1971 he was joined in the City team by Dominican-born and Bradford-raised forward Joe Cooke. At a time when there were a handful of black footballers, when Podd and Cooke could go weeks and months on end without ever seeing another black player, and when racism from terraces and from opponents was commonplace, Bradford City provided something that money and First Division football couldn't buy. That luxury item was security. Podd was secure at City. He was adored by the fans. His fellow professionals, his managers and indeed everyone at the club treated him not only with respect but with warmth. That comfort and security proved to be irresistible as bigger and better offers to further his career came in. Podd refused them all and it was his experience of racism that fuelled his resistance to a move away from Valley Parade. He had of course played at grounds all over the country and had been subjected to vicious abuse from both fans and opposition players. He cited many southern football venues as places where he received the most hostile of receptions, in stark contrast to the experiences of many black players after him, who described their trips to northern grounds as some of their worst experiences of racism. The security of Bradford City, combined with Podd's thorough and absolute enjoyment of playing professional football, provided him with a shield against some of the worst experiences he encountered. Moving elsewhere could put his love of the game in jeopardy. Dealing with less enlightened and possibly hostile supporters, managers, club officials and teammates was too big a chance to take, so he stayed at City and amassed games, wholehearted performances and his legendary status.

Events in March 1981 perfectly illustrated his standing both at City and amongst his fellow black professionals. He was granted a testimonial match, the first black footballer to be granted such an honour. It was a reward for his commitment, his attitude and above all his loyalty. Amongst supporters, loyalty is revered; disloyalty, or even its impression, is reviled. Long-serving players are described as 'loyal servants' and Podd had stayed loyal in spite of overtures from some very attractive suitors. His record is likely to stand for 100 years. In today's climate it seems impossible that a player in the lower leagues could ever stay at one club for so long. Instability, short-term contracts, poor financial performance and high managerial turnover militate against the one-club longevity of any professional working in the lower leagues. It would be difficult enough at Premier League level; lower down the league ladder, it would be the stuff of fiction.

If the granting of Podd's testimonial made history, the game itself proved to be a significant milestone for other reasons. After writing to a number of league managers, Podd had put together a 'Black All Stars' team to play in his testimonial at Bradford City's Valley Parade ground. With unanimous support from their clubs, almost everyone he contacted agreed to participate. The side included Garth Crooks, Luther Blissett, Alex Williams, Vince Hilaire, Terry Connor, Justin Fashanu and Cyrille Regis as well as teammate Joe Cooke, amongst others. For the first time in the game's history in Britain, the number of black footballers playing in English professional football had grown to such a degree as to make this historic event possible. When Podd had made his professional debut, and for some time after, he could count the number of black players on one hand. As the numbers increased, he wanted to do something to bring the disparate group of black players together, to do nothing more than chat, have a game of football and bond over their shared experiences.

The game on 30 March wasn't the first of this type. A similar match had taken place two years earlier, organised by Batson, Cunningham and Regis, on the occasion of a testimonial for their West Brom teammate Len Cantello. A Black XI took on a West Brom side minus the Three Degrees, who all played for the Black XI. The Black XI side, managed by Ron Atkinson, also contained Garth Crooks, George

Berry, Bob Hazell and Remi Moses, in a game that was to be reprised at Podd's testimonial.

Although Crooks had travelled to Valley Parade to support Podd's testimonial, he hadn't been given permission to play. He had been due to appear three days later in an important league game for his club, Tottenham. In the dressing room, before the game, Crooks stripped off his clothes to reveal his football kit. Ignoring his manager's instructions, he participated in the game, albeit briefly before being substituted early in the first half, such was his determination to participate.

The game proved an important opportunity for black footballers to share stories. Justin Fashanu's brilliant strike for Norwich in a defeat to league champions Liverpool was the current 'Goal of the Season' winner. A silver salver presented in recognition of the achievement was sitting in pride of place on the sideboard of his adoptive parents' Norfolk home. The assembled players had discussed the significance of the goal and debated whether black kids playing football would, rather than pretending to be Keegan or Dalglish, be Justin Fashanu.

Fashanu's legendary status never materialised, but that would prove to be a moot point. The game provided an opportunity for black players to discuss their impact on the black community in Britain and the wider game. They could discuss their experiences at clubs, at grounds, with managers and fellow professionals. As an event, it cemented the bonds between black professional footballers, which were further tightened at Professional Footballers' Association (PFA) dinners, under-21 get-togethers and charity events. These opportunities to bond would prove to be invaluable.

CHAPTER 3

VIVA ANDERSON!

AUDLEY ANDERSON HAD arrived from Jamaica in 1954. His wife Myrtle joined him a few months later to make Nottingham their home. Their son Viv was born in the summer of 1956. Competition for the most important of resources – jobs, homes and social spaces – had created serious racial tension in the city between its newly arrived immigrant population – some 2,500 West Indians, almost all of them, like Audley and Myrtle Anderson, from Jamaica, plus around 600 Asians – and the local British-born whites.

The simmering tension exploded into violence and, as is often the case in these matters, the thorny subject of inter-racial relationships – or, more explicitly, inter racial sex – proved to be the combustible material that exploded into all-out warfare between blacks and whites. The seemingly innocuous sight of a West Indian man enjoying a drink with a blonde British woman in a pub in the St Ann's area brought things to a head. The man was assaulted and soon a crowd gathered. Contemporary reports at the time said that the police and local whites were surprised at the speed of the West Indian response as blacks took their revenge on 'local teddy boys' and, over a period of several hours, fierce battles were fought in which there were several beatings and stabbings. The police finally gained some control and, over the following week, word of a massive once-and-for-all showdown between blacks and whites culminated in some 4,000 angry and up-for-it white people gathering in St Ann's to put the blacks in their place and show them decisively who was in charge. Unfortunately for the racists, in all the excitement no one had bothered to invite the blacks to the battle and, fuelled by adrenalin and spoiling for a fight, the crowd turned on each other; dozens were arrested.

Vivian Alexander Anderson was two years old during that long, tense Nottingham summer. He would go on to make history. Like most boys, black or white, Viv Anderson wanted to be a footballer. Eschewing support for Forest or Notts County, he was seduced by Best, Law and Charlton into supporting Manchester United. He'd attended the biggest secondary school in Nottingham and they dominated football in and around the Nottingham area. Included in his school side were Peter Wells, a future Forest and Southampton goalkeeper, and Glyn Saunders, who would later also play for Forest.

Nottingham has produced its fair share of black footballers. As well as Viv Anderson, pioneering football manager Keith Alexander was born in the city. Record-breaking goal scorer Andy Cole hails from Nottingham, as well as Calvin Plummer, Michael Johnson, Chris Fairclough, Ian Benjamin, Tristan Benjamin, Jermaine Jenas, Jermaine Pennant, Leon Best, Wes Morgan, Tom Huddlestone, Martin Carruthers, Julian Bennett and Devon White, all of whom began their footballing journeys in the streets and parks around Nottingham.

In the 1960s, the city went through a process of slum clearances. The West Indian community were dispersed to council estates in and around the city itself. With few alternatives, many boys and young men gravitated towards football, and a network of teams and clubs sprang up around the Nottingham area. It became something of a rite of passage for black boys to join clubs and teams in the area, and the early success of Anderson and others like Tristan Benjamin and his brother Ian provided the role models for the tight-knit community. Anderson's father was well known in the city as a swimming instructor and was a popular figure both in the local area and within the black community. Jermaine Jenas's father was a well known footballer and coach who helped nurture the career of his son and others, working as a coach at Nottingham Forest.

At fourteen, Anderson was signed on schoolboy forms by Manchester United. On a separate pitch, yards from where he trained, he would see Best, Law and Charlton, as well as the rest of the first team, being put through their paces. He spent a year at United before being released. Devastated, he returned to Nottingham to play local football and found work as an apprentice silk-screen printer. The job lasted some five weeks before he was offered a chance to sign for Forest as an apprentice. At the time, he was the only black player or indeed employee at the club. However, his school friends Saunders and Wells, who also lived on the same council estate as Anderson, helped him settle in.

While still an apprentice, he made his first-team debut in a pre-season friendly in August 1974 and made further sporadic appearances as the season progressed. Results that season were poor. The Forest side was a mediocre outfit, languishing in the lower reaches of the Second Division and embroiled in a relegation battle. In January 1975, manager Allan Brown was sacked, to be replaced the following month by Brian Clough. As the saying goes, the rest is history.

As a young player, the worst racist abuse Anderson received was at Newcastle, which he remembered vividly because it was the first time he'd been subjected to such hatred. In a midweek League Cup game, he got what he described as 'dog's abuse'. He was accustomed to being racially abused: it had occurred several times during games as part of the cut and thrust. A misplaced tackle or hefty challenge would usually be the trigger for some foul-mouthed racist invective, but this was the first time he'd heard such wholesale abuse in a stadium environment. The game hadn't even started; he'd only gone out to inspect the pitch.

Shaken, he told Clough he didn't think he could play. 'You're playing' was Clough's gruff response. The following Saturday, they'd played Carlisle in a league game. Anderson had been named as substitute and part way through the second half was instructed by Clough to warm up. Going through his routine, he was showered with bananas and other fruit. After five minutes he sat down. Clough said, 'I thought I told you to warm up', to which Anderson responded, 'They're throwing bananas, apples, pears and everything at me.' Clough was firm: 'Get back out there and get me two bananas and an apple.' Anderson finished warming up and eventually got on the pitch. However, Clough didn't leave it there and gave Anderson the most important advice in his young career to date, words that were to shape the rest of his career.

He pulls me afterwards and says, 'The reason I made you go back out there is because, if you're going to worry about what people say, you aren't going to make a living. You ain't going to be good enough for my team because you'll always be worried about what people say and you're good enough to play in my team, but if I think you're not going to be good enough to play in my team because you're worried about what people are saying, I'm going to pick somebody else ... So you get back out there, show them what you can do and forget it completely.'

A combination of instilling the young Anderson with self-belief and warning him to focus on football or he would jeopardise his career before it had got going did the trick. It was the advice that the young Anderson needed if he was to become a professional footballer.

At the end of Clough's second full season, Forest finished third to win promotion to the First Division, where, implausibly, they were to go on to win the title and the League Cup and, impossibly, then went on to win the European Cup the following season, knocking out cup holders Liverpool along the way.

After the European Cup triumph, veteran left-back Frank Clarke, an all-knowing, all-seeing oracle who would later manage Forest and head up the League Managers Association, had told Anderson and his fellow youngster Tony Woodcock to enjoy the moment. 'You haven't a clue, it doesn't get any better than this.' Clarke was right, to a point, but the following season they retained the European Cup, winning a tight game against Kevin Keegan's Hamburg.

In the years preceding Anderson's historic debut for England, the question of who would be the first black footballer to play for the full England side had been the subject of media attention for some time. Laurie Cunningham had been touted as the favourite and had cemented this status during a scintillating performance for the England under-21 side against Scotland. Cyrille Regis had been mentioned along with Stoke's Garth Crooks, but Anderson wasn't really in the running. The others had strong under-21 credentials and Anderson didn't. However, Forest's meteoric rise had brought him attention, trophies and experience. By 1978, he had racked up a league title, a League Cup and a European Cup. Cunningham was to make his own England debut a few months later, but when Ron Greenwood's squad for England's game against Czechoslovakia in November 1978 was announced, it was Viv Anderson's name on the list.

The significance of the achievement didn't go unnoticed. The media seemed to regard it as part historic event and part novelty as they reported on Anderson's selection. In the run-up to the game, he received a telegram from the Queen and also one from Elton John. East Midlands television visited his parents' home in Nottingham and broadcast a feature to mark the historic event. Before the game, seasoned internationals Trevor Brooking and Kevin Keegan had given him encouragement and advised him to play his normal game. Running lengthways, one half of the pitch was icy and the other half was soft, so he had to change his boots at half-time. He had a hand in the move leading to the goal that proved to be the winner as England won 1–0. His England career was sporadic, winning him thirty caps over a nine-year period. He went to four tournaments including two World Cups, though he never played in either. He lost out to the experienced Phil Neal and Mick Mills and, later in his career, had to contend with the emergence of the youthful, dynamic Gary Stevens, who'd won titles both north and south of the border and earned European glory with Rangers and Everton. He was never able to get a run in the England set-up, his longest consecutive run of games being four.

Of that legendary Forest side, Anderson was the last one to leave. He joined Arsenal in 1984, winning the 1987 League

Cup in the process. He became Alex Ferguson's first signing
for Manchester United, finally getting the professional contract for United that had been denied to him at age fifteen.

Anderson didn't conform to any of the stereotypes that
characterised the image of black players. He wasn't a fast,
skilful winger or battering ram centre-forward who lacked
bottle and couldn't play in the cold. He wasn't in possession
of natural athletic flair but lacking the intellect that white
players possessed.

Significantly, of the players who had been in the running
to be the first black player to represent England, Anderson
was the only one who wasn't an attacker. As for the cold, he
always wore short sleeves, and, as for bottle, he was always a
tough and resilient defender. As he put it, his job was to kick
wingers and anything else was a bonus, but he does himself
a disservice with that description. He was far classier than
he gives himself credit for. He was very quick, got forward
extremely well and scored with a few spectacular strikes,
and his distribution was excellent. After playing for Manchester United, he reinvented himself as a centre-back, where
his experience, intelligence and positional sense allowed him
to make the successful transition.

Anderson had opened the door to allow other black English footballers an opportunity to represent the national side
and, over the next few years, the inclusion of black players
representing England became increasingly commonplace.
His appearance cemented the belief amongst black footballers and fans that the presence of black players within
the English game was no longer something of a novelty,
but evidence that they had arrived and were here to stay.
The impact of Anderson's debut also represented a significant milestone at a time when the notion of ethnicity and

national identity was being fiercely debated and when parties advocating repatriation of people of colour were gaining significant electoral success.

CHAPTER 4

THE THREE DEGREES
GET HOT

OF THE VERY few statues or memorials that commemorate the achievements of black people in the UK, three are of footballers. There is one of Arthur Wharton, considered to be the first black professional footballer in the world. He was inducted into the English Football Hall of Fame in 2003 and a statue of him was unveiled in October 2014 at St George's Park, the National Football Centre. There is a second of Walter Tull, who played inside forward for Tottenham and Northampton Town. He was the first black outfield player to play in the top division and the first black person to be commissioned as an officer in the British Army in May 1917, despite the *Manual of Military Law* specifically excluding 'Negroes and Mulattoes' from serving as officers. He was killed in action in March 1918 and a memorial to him can be found at Sixfields Stadium, the home of his former club, Northampton Town. The third is at the home of West Bromwich Albion, The Hawthorns. Entitled *Celebration*, the bronze statue is of Brendon Batson, Laurie Cunningham and Cyrille Regis and is a fitting tribute to their achievements and legacy.

The West Brom team they played in certainly had more about it than just the Three Degrees. The side included

Bryan Robson, who would go on to captain England and become a Manchester United legend. On the opposite flank to Batson was Derek Statham, a talented full-back who never fulfilled his early promise but was an important part of the side. However, the Three Degrees were critical to the team's success. Batson added steel, composure and class and he marauded forward at every opportunity. Cunningham provided flair, grace, creativity and attacking menace and pitched in with a few goals. Regis offered strength, pace and great movement and regularly found the back of the net. 'He is all muscle, all black power,' as *Sun* journalist Brian Woolnough said of him.

They were all highly intelligent, not necessarily in an academic sense (although there is no doubt that had they had the opportunity and inclination they would have been good students), but they were intelligent in a footballing sense. They were able to ally their technique and skills to an acute understanding of when and how to use them.

At the time the Three Degrees were the toast of The Hawthorns, there were perhaps fifty or so black professional footballers in total, compared to an estimated 900–1,000 today. The decision to have three black players playing in one side was therefore met with a large degree of curiosity and bemusement by some, indignation by others, and, for those who really couldn't handle it, outright hostility.

Britain under the Labour government of 1974–79 saw living standards fall for the first time in real terms since the 1930s. Unemployment had risen from 500,000 to over 1.5 million, while inflation eroded the wages of those still in work. Health, education and welfare services were being savagely cut. Traditional industries such as dock work and

shipbuilding, which had provided employment opportunities for generations of working-class communities, were
being modernised or lost altogether, threatening the security of families and communities all over the country. Black
youths in particular were struggling to find employment and
found themselves on the dole in an increasingly competitive
and discriminatory job market.

In this economic climate, a new racist offensive was taking
place, something that hadn't been witnessed since the arrival of large numbers of migrants from the West Indies and
Indian sub-continent in the 1950s. This offensive contained a
number of key elements: far-right activity; the appropriation
of racist ideology and language into mainstream politics; an
increase in racist murders and attacks; and an increase in
respectability for popular racist ideas.

In 1976, the National Front had won 20 per cent of
the vote in local elections in Leicester. In May 1977, they
had achieved 17.4 per cent of the total vote in the Greater
London Council (GLC), polling 119,060 votes and beating
the mainstream Liberal Party in thirty-three out of ninety-
two constituencies.

Brimming with confidence from their election result, in
August they announced a march through the ethnically diverse area of Lewisham in south London. Seeking to intimidate and harass the local black community, they marched
under an inflammatory slogan claiming that 85 per cent
of muggers were black while 85 per cent of their victims
were white. Calls for the march to be banned fell on the
deaf ears of then Metropolitan Police Commissioner David
McNee, who declined to make an application to the Home
Secretary for a ban to be imposed on the NF in favour of
the local black community and anti-racists, claiming that a

ban would lead to 'increasing pressure' to ban similar events and he would be 'abdicating his responsibility in the face of groups who threaten to achieve their ends by violent means'.

The NF's confidence was checked, if not shattered, in the wake of the so-called 'Battle of Lewisham'. The NF planned to march from New Cross to Lewisham, but never reached their final destination. Two hundred and seventy police-men were injured and fifty-six hospitalised, while over 200 marchers were injured, with seventy-eight hospitalised. Riot shields were used for the first time in the UK outside Northern Ireland as the police and racists on one side and local black youths and anti-fascists on the other side were involved in violent clashes.

Fearing similar violent clashes, Greater Manchester Police banned an NF march through Hyde in October 1977, but were defied by NF guru Martin Webster, who marched alone carrying a Union Jack and a sign reading 'Defend British Free Speech from Red Terrorism'. In spite of the ban, Web-ster was protected by some 2,000 police as he marched, since 'one man' did not constitute a breaking of the ban.

The NF was the predominant Nazi organisation of the 1970s. They adopted an opportunist approach to politics by campaigning aggressively against non-white immigra-tion, particularly highlighting supposed competition for jobs and housing, and preyed on the fears of British-born whites by emphasising black youths' alleged propensity for crime. An unashamedly racist membership organisation, it actively tried to recruit amongst white football supporters and engaged in highly provocative actions such as marching through black and Asian neighbourhoods and communities, therefore deliberately provoking a violent confrontation with black and Asian youths and white anti-racists. Invariably this provocative behaviour was supported by local police forces, who took the side of the far right, as illustrated in Lewisham.

As a matter of operational policy, the police systematically misappropriated Section 4 of the Vagrancy Act 1824 in order to harass, intimidate and criminalise black communities, particularly young black men. The 'Sus' law, as it was referred to in common parlance, enabled police to stop and search certain individuals they suspected of frequenting or loitering in a public place with intent to commit an arrestable offence.

This hated law had provoked drives for greater police accountability in the use of stop and search, as black communities increasingly took exception to the manner and frequency with which young men were being harassed. The law illustrated the overwhelmingly tense and suspicious relationship that was the dominant feature of relations between the police and black communities, which occasionally spilled over into violent clashes. In 1975, a Bonfire Night celebration in Chapeltown, Leeds, where Ces Podd grew up and where he would later undertake some outstanding community work, ended in a violent confrontation between black youths and police in which police cars were stoned, severely injuring two officers, and pitched battles were fought with police who arrived to rescue their colleagues. The much larger and higher-profile disturbances at the Notting Hill Carnival over the August bank holiday weekend in 1976 provided a further example of this fraught relationship.

In mainstream politics, Margaret Thatcher, then leader of the Conservative opposition, had told ITV's *World in Action*, when speaking on the subject of immigration in January 1978, that 'people are really rather afraid that this country might be swamped by people with a different culture'.

Her comments didn't represent a shift in policy. The Conservative Party had taken a hard line on immigration since she had been elected as party leader in 1975, and she had reintroduced a racist discourse to mainstream politics not heard since Enoch Powell's infamous 'Rivers of Blood' speech in 1968, which had seen him dismissed from the shadow Cabinet – a discourse that had been confined to the far-right fringe for a decade. Shortly after her comments, a National Opinion Polls survey recorded an increase in support for her party, who jumped to an eleven-point lead over Labour, whom they had previously been trailing by two points, followed by the general election victory a year later.

Between 1976 and 1981, there had been thirty-one racist murders and countless racist attacks on British citizens of black and Asian heritage. These included the murder of ten-year-old Kenneth Singh, who was stabbed to death yards from his east London home on 21 April 1978. The killers, who were never found, left eight stab wounds in the back of his head.

Even popular musicians were willing to express openly racist ideas. In 1976, Eric Clapton had praised Enoch Powell, and warned against Britain becoming a black colony, in a drunken rant during a performance in Birmingham. David Bowie had expressed his admiration for Hitler and fascism. Ironically, both artists had enthusiastically embraced black musical forms throughout their careers, but this paradox was seemingly lost on them. In addition, crude racist stereotypes and ideas were regularly evoked within British popular culture by comedians and in TV dramas.

It was in this climate – with the rise of the far right, the racist discourse in mainstream politics, increased racist attacks and murders, hostile relationships between black communities and the police, the willingness of prominent public figures to align themselves with racist ideas and the widespread use of casual racism in popular culture and the press – that Brendon Batson joined Cunningham and Regis at West Bromwich Albion. The area itself was no stranger to racial tension. In May 1973, in a by-election in West Bromwich West, the National Front candidate, Martin Webster, polled 4,789 votes (16.2 per cent).

The racist abuse suffered wherever Albion played was so prevalent as to be a normal occurrence. Batson remembers the noise and volume of abuse at some grounds being deafening. Upton Park, the home of West Ham, Chelsea's Stamford Bridge, The Den at Millwall and St James' Park, where Newcastle United played, were amongst the most hostile and vicious places to be a black footballer. As Batson later recalled:

> We'd get off the coach at away matches and the National Front would be right there in your face. In those days, we didn't have security and we'd have to run the gauntlet. We'd get to the players' entrance and there'd be spit on my jacket or Cyrille's shirt. It was a sign of the times. I don't recall making a big hue and cry about it. We coped. It wasn't a new phenomenon to us.

The three regularly received hate mail and death threats. An Everton fan regularly wrote them abusive letters and on one occasion had urged Atkinson not to select 'monkeys' for an upcoming game against the Merseysiders.

Cunningham in particular received more than his fair share of hate mail. His high-profile relationship with his fiancée, whom he had known since the start of his career at Orient, was often the subject of tabloid titillation and curiosity. It was this relationship that invoked the most opprobrium, since, in the eyes of the racists, he had broken that most solemn of taboos: he was having sex with a white woman. Death threats were sent to their home in Birmingham and on one occasion Cunningham was forced to stamp out a petrol bomb that was thrown through his front door.

During games, bananas were pelted in their direction and they were booed and abused horrendously every time they touched the ball. When they did something good, which wasn't uncommon, the level of abuse would be cranked up several notches, particularly when they played at those hot-houses of Upton Park, Stamford Bridge, Elland Road and St James' Park.

In addition to the racist abuse they received from the terraces, they would be routinely abused by their fellow professionals. A mistimed tackle, a fifty-fifty challenge, indeed any minor altercation would be the trigger for racist abuse. Sometimes it took far less than that. Opposition players would regularly abuse them for no apparent reason. However, it would be churlish to suggest they were passive recipients. They would talk back: a racist remark about the size of black men's sexual organs (racists appear seemingly obsessed with sex) would be countered with an invitation to allow the player's wife or girlfriend to spend a night with them or some other unspecified black man. However, this was no tit-for-tat exchange of petty insults: it was a conscious attempt to turn the racists' arguments on their head by playing up the racial stereotypes to invoke some deep, dark sexual fear on the part of their antagonists. This kind of retort would often invoke fury from the abuser, raging about the unfairness of the remark and how some line at the summit of some moral high ground had been crossed. But sometimes the insults were so hateful there was no possible response.

Their sense of isolation was palpable. There was little chance of any recourse from teammates or the media, the FA or the police. Brendon Batson, speaking to Paul Rees for his book *The Three Degrees*, said:

> From when I came to England, I was familiar with people shouting at me from cars or on the Underground in London. With the other players in the side, it was none of their business. It didn't concern them and they weren't sensitive to it. I also remember speaking to the BBC and confronting them about when they were going to say something about it. They told me it wasn't possible to make out what was being shouted. What a load of bollocks that was. All of the excuses I got were a joke.

However, they drew strength from each other, three black men joining together to share experiences. They bonded on a number of levels. Three black Londoners, living and working in the Midlands, facing abuse every time they went out to work. They would exchange stories and observations about particularly abusive crowds, about comments from and altercations with particular players, and they would discuss the attitudes of teammates and opponents alike. They would bond in hotel rooms and at social occasions, drawing mutual support from each other, comfortable that they were all walking in the same shoes.

If they didn't know they were role models, the black community in Handsworth soon showed them. They were familiar visitors to the area and, indeed, were local celebrities. In fact, Regis had lived there briefly upon his arrival in the West Midlands. Albion's Hawthorns ground borders Handsworth and, as a result, Albion began to attract a significant following of black supporters.

Empire Road was a BBC soap opera that ran for two series in 1978 and 1979. It was notable for being the first British television series to be written, directed and acted predominantly by black artists. It depicted the life of black and Asian individuals and families in a racially diverse street, set in Handsworth. Cyrille Regis had appeared in an episode that featured two young black characters who were attempting to meet their hero and had unsuccessfully tried to get into a game at The Hawthorns. Regis's acting wasn't going to win him any awards, but the episode illustrated the esteem that he and the other two members of the trio were held in. The impact the trio had on the black community in Handsworth and on other black communities across the country cannot be underestimated. The discrimination and prejudice they suffered echoed the experiences of members of those communities. The fact that they faced horrendous abuse, suffered it with dignity and then performed brilliantly won them the admiration and respect of black people way beyond Handsworth and the West Midlands. They became role models, not just to young black men who had dreams of playing professional football, but to ordinary black people who were factory workers, health service workers, transport workers, school kids and the unemployed. They were admired because they were experiencing something that most people in the many beleaguered black communities would have struggled to survive with their dignity and sanity intact. They were respected because, at a time when the media and popular culture portrayed black people in an almost exclusively negative light, here were black men playing the national sport and winning in the face of unimaginable and constant hostility. Although it wasn't their intention, theirs was an act of defiance and therefore deeply political.

Together, the three wreaked revenge on the racists in the one area they could control: on the pitch. Cunningham had progressed to the England under-21 squad within a year of joining Albion in April 1977, and in so doing became the first black footballer to represent England at this level. His brilliant debut saw him terrorise the Scottish defence, pick up the Man of the Match award and bag the winning goal into the bargain. The press speculated as to how long it might be for him to win a full England cap and become the first black player to achieve this honour.

Their first full season together proved to be a stellar one for both Albion and the Three Degrees. Regis made his England under-21 debut in September 1978 and two months later appeared for the England B side in a 1–0 victory against Czechoslovakia, ending the season as PFA Young Player of the Year, the first black player to win this accolade. Cunningham ended the season by becoming only the second black player after Viv Anderson to win a full England cap, in a Home International fixture against Wales. As for Albion, they finished a successful season in third place in the league and got to the quarter-finals of the UEFA Cup.

Cunningham, now an England international, had attracted the attention of some rich suitors. His performances in Albion's UEFA Cup campaign had given him a European-wide platform and the legendary Real Madrid signed him at the end of the 1978/79 season for a then massive fee of £950,000.

So ended one of the most important periods in the history of British football, and in the history of West Bromwich Albion. The Three Degrees had been in existence for only a season and a half, which constituted some eighteen months, but they had made an indelible impression in the West Midlands and beyond. They elevated themselves to hero status amongst black communities in all parts of the country and became role models for their response to racism. Their historic role as the first trio of black footballers to become regular members of a professional football team, let alone one in the top flight, paved the way for future generations of black athletes to earn a living by playing professional football. Their response to racism, both defiant and dignified, set the blueprint for how black players were required to deal with the issue for the next twenty years.

CHAPTER 5

UPRISING

'I had no problems in being able to look after myself, but it was important to know that Bob had my back.'
– George Berry

THEY HAD VISITED the seething cauldron of hate that was Elland Road and had come away with the points. At the heart of the Wolves' defence were Bob Hazell and George Berry. Getting a hostile reception at grounds was a normal occurrence for black footballers but Elland Road was of an altogether different magnitude. Even though they had been warned to expect hostility, black players were regularly taken aback on their first visit to the ground. As Berry himself says, 'They were the most racist set of fans I've ever come across in my life. They had it to a fine art. The chanting and everything and the intimidation was like nothing you'll ever hear anywhere on earth.'

This game had been no exception. 'Fucking niggers, black bastards, fuck off back to Africa, you fucking ape' had greeted them when their names were announced before kick-off. From the first minute to the last, there was no let-up. Every time they touched the ball, Berry and Hazell were greeted with boos and monkey noises from all parts of the ground. If the play took them over to the touchline, the noise levels rose. Men, women and children, with their twisted, contorted, furious faces, spitting, gesturing, throwing bananas, threatening death, urging their own players to maim, hurt and kill.

But Berry and Hazell were ready and were right up for the game. The two had been immense throughout. They'd been tough, menacing and intimidating. Their philosophy that day was: 'The ball can go past. The man can get past, but not both together, not today.' They relished the poisonous atmosphere, even wallowed in it. If any of the opposition were going to indulge in racist abuse, that was great, because the two were going to give some back and they were going to give it back with interest. They were switched on to bad boy mode. Swaggering, shouting and cursing in the Jamaican patois of their parents, nobody could understand what they were saying. At one point, Clive Thomas, an arrogant, officious referee from south Wales, had spoken to the two of them, telling them that although he didn't understand what they were saying, he knew it was bad, and if they continued, he would book them.

A tough victory had been earned that day and Berry and Hazell had been key in securing the win for their side. After the game, most of their teammates and coaching staff were already sitting on the coach and they were amongst the last to make their way from the dressing room to their waiting transport, only to be met by forty or fifty baying Leeds fans, the pride of West Yorkshire's NF, who circled the two players and prevented them from getting to their coach.

They quickly weighed up the situation and located the person who appeared to be the ringleader. Next to him was his henchman and they decided that these were the two who needed to be taken on. Hazell agreed to take out the ringleader; Berry was to deal with his henchman. Agreeing that under no circumstances could they initiate an attack, they waited for the Leeds fans to make the first move. From nowhere, Berry's brother arrived on the scene and pushed his way ahead of his brother and Hazell. Berry's brother, who, like their father, had served in the army, spoke directly to the ringleader, telling him that if the mob wanted to attack the two players, they were more than welcome, but they would have to go through him first. To describe the situation as tense was a gross understatement as the racists seemed to take an age to consider the odds. Reckoning that forty defenders of the master race against three young, fit, athletic black guys was too much of a gamble, they backed off and let them through. It had been a close call, but Berry and Hazell were able to escape to the comfort of the team bus and Berry's brother was allowed to go about his business.

The experience of Berry and Hazell at Leeds was a marginally more extreme example of the kind of thing that happened to black footballers on a regular basis. At many grounds across the country, however, the number of black players was increasing as a new decade emerged from the embers of the 1970s, and the tide was slowly, but inexorably, beginning to turn in terms of how these players were viewed. The early pioneers had been largely looked upon as exotic embellishments to what had always been considered a white working-class game. Their novelty status was now starting to shift as a new generation began to add to the ranks of black footballing talent. They would be drawn from football's traditional heartlands, the towns and inner cities, where black communities were overwhelmingly located. Making his debut in 1980, Bobby Barnes from east

London began to make his name at West Ham. In the same year, south London boy Paul Davis became the first black player to play for Arsenal since Brendon Batson. Making their respective debuts in the 1978/79 season, Dave Bennett and Roger Palmer from Manchester were breaking through into first-team football at Manchester City. Howard Gayle from Toxteth made his debut in October 1980 for European powerhouse Liverpool, and Chapeltown lad Terry Connor was making a massive impact at his local club, Leeds United, scoring the only goal on his debut against West Bromwich Albion, as a seventeen-year-old in November 1979. In addition to the young black players beginning to take their first steps in the professional game, more established stars were also making an impact. One of the most significant examples was that of Justin Fashanu, who in 1981 moved from his local club, Norwich City, to Nottingham Forest and in so doing became the first million-pound black footballer. In 1980, Garth Crooks made a big-money move to Spurs, from his home-town club of Stoke City.

As Cyrille Regis opined, as more clubs began to field black players, the racists had something of a dilemma. How could they hurl abuse at black players on the opposition team when they had black players within the ranks of their own side? Furthermore, if opposition fans abused black players playing for the side they supported, the tribal nature of football support dictated that they couldn't side with the opposition's fans. Therefore, as more and more black footballers became established within their sides, the level of terrace abuse subsided and eventually disappeared altogether at some grounds.

That was certainly the case at Arsenal. During the 1970s, the club had acquired a certain reputation for terrace racism, a reputation that lasted until Paul Davis appeared in the side. The famous 5–3 victory for West Brom against Manchester United in December 1978 was significant for the brilliance of the Three Degrees and the sickening racism of the Old Trafford support that had forced commentator Gerald Sinstadt to condemn sections of the crowd. The arrival of Remi Moses, ironically from West Bromwich Albion, seemed to bring an end to the terrace racism that had been prevalent at the ground. However, this trend was general, rather than a cast-iron law. Some teams fielded black players yet large sections of their support still indulged in racist abuse; the irony of abusing the opposition's black players while cheering black players on your own side had not been adequately grasped. Where the nature of racist abuse could be characterised as largely casual, it gradually fell away, but where racism was organised and where the far right were able to have an influence, it remained a pernicious feature at those clubs.

Away from football, the far right continued their attempt to intimidate black communities as campaigning for the 1979 general election took place. The NF, confident of making an electoral breakthrough, held their St George's Day meeting in Southall Town Hall. Paul Canoville grew up in the area and reflected on what it was like around the time.

Lots of racism in Southall, it was a very terrible time, scary time ... I remember times going to little youth clubs ... You know, your mum gives you a precise time, you got to be back at that time, no minute, no second after ... You're running late ... Then you notice that this car slows down with four white guys in ... So you stop and they stop, and that decision now, you got to go the long way round and obviously you're

going to be home late, but don't explain any of that to your
mum, she don't want to hear that. That's how bad it was at
that time.

Canoville had every right to be apprehensive. There were
many racist attacks in and around the area and in 1976,
seventeen-year-old Sikh schoolboy Gurdip Singh Chaggar
was brutally stabbed to death in a racist murder outside a
Southall pub. The murder had galvanised the local community to resist the activities of the far right and as the NF
gathered in Southall, they were opposed by demonstrating
anti-fascists. Blair Peach, an anti-racist campaigner, died
from head injuries sustained by a police truncheon.

The NF's confidence that they could make a significant
impact on the general election proved to be misplaced, as
the Conservatives won with a landslide. Adopting elements
of the far right's rhetoric, the Tories had given racism an air
of respectability. The commitment by the party to tackling
immigration once in government, by introducing legislation
to curb the movement of black and Asian people into the
UK, had left the NF wrong-footed, given that the issue was
more or less all they had. So, over the next few years, the NF
and other far-right parties experienced splits and divisions
within their ranks. However, as the decade began, they were
far from finished and continued their strategy of harassment
of black communities.

The activities of the far right and other racists who associated with or were inspired by them didn't uniformly affect
all black communities. While their presence in some communities was extensive, in others it was more of an irritation
and in others still, virtually non-existent. Sus was the constant issue that impacted upon black communities and the

issue that characterised the relationship between them and the police. The use of the law continued to cause bitter resentment, and while harassment by the police was a regular occurrence, their response – or lack of response – to racist attacks, racist abuse and racial harassment constantly reinforced the message that the law, and in particular the way in which it was applied, was far from being even handed and without prejudice; in fact, it was deeply racist. For black footballers, the idea that they should report to police the racist abuse and harassment they received from crowds, and the taunts, spitting and gesturing from individuals, which was actually illegal under incitement to racial hatred legislation, would have been laughable. The racist behaviour occurred at grounds where there was almost always a sizeable police presence.

While the inner-city disturbances that occurred within many black communities had as their cause a complex set of interrelated factors, at their heart was the issue of police harassment. On 2 April 1980, a raid on a Bristol café, the Black and White, that was popular with local black youths, set off several hours of battles between local youths and the police. Ignoring any kind of context or the fact white youths had also been involved in the battles with police, the next day the *Daily Telegraph*'s crude headline read '19 Police Hurt in Black Riot'.

The combination of media and political indifference and downright hostility to black communities was best illustrated in events in New Cross in south London. The NF had been active in the area and there had been a large number of racist attacks. Paul Davis grew up in that part of London and remembers it as an area where, as a black kid, he had to be extremely careful where he travelled, especially at night, but he also remembered that areas such as the Old Kent Road, amongst others, were no-go areas for blacks. On 18 January 1981, thirteen young people aged between fourteen and twenty-two died in a house fire in New Cross at the birthday party of one of the victims, sixteen-year-old Yvonne Ruddock. The cause of the fire has never been firmly established. There were some suggestions of a racist attack and some suggestions the fire was accidental. These lines of enquiry were never fully investigated: the police insisted in pursuing the sole line of investigation that the fire was started after an argument, forcing statements from people in order to support this notion and generally pursuing a lacklustre investigation. They caused additional resentment by interrogating partygoers as if they were criminals rather than victims. The media reaction was largely unsympathetic. Four weeks later, a fire in a Dublin disco killed forty-eight young people. The victims' families received a letter of condolence from the Queen, something the New Cross fire victims' families never received. One of the victims' parents was sent an anonymous letter stating that 'it was a great day when all the niggers went up in smoke'. At the Den, the home of nearby Millwall, in the wake of the fire, the chant from the terraces was, 'We all agree, niggers burn better than petrol.'

Understandably, the anger from black communities in London and elsewhere was at an all-time high.

In response to the fire, on 2 March, 20,000 black people marched from New Cross to Hyde Park, with several in school uniform. As the march progressed along Fleet Street, the marchers' ire was directed at newspapers, due to their lack of sympathy and their hostility to the victims' families. The previous day, the *Daily Mail* had reported that several partygoers had been arrested and that charges would follow.

It was completely untrue. Journalists and staff from *The Sun*, amongst other titles, shouted racist abuse at the demonstrators and, in the following day's reports, proceeded to completely misrepresent the march, suggesting there had been a riot.

As these incidents showed, the negative stereotypes ascribed to black people weren't confined solely to football. The characterisation of black footballers as strong, brutish and aggressive extended to black communities and, in particular, their young males, although footballers occasionally assumed a kind of above black status. Speaking of Cyrille Regis, Woolnough wrote, 'He doesn't go round in flash cars and white suits and has no ambition to force the black man's claim on society.'

Policing of black communities and the use of Sus was largely viewed by mainstream media as necessary to keep black communities in check. Two weeks after the New Cross march, the Metropolitan Police launched Operation Swamp, in which almost 1,000 youths, overwhelmingly black, were stopped and searched in Brixton over a six-day period. This proved to be the spark that ignited a summer of disturbances, largely prompted by discriminatory policing methods. Unrest took place in Brixton on 9–13 April, Finsbury Park on 20 April, Southall on 3 July and Toxteth on 3–8 July. Over the weekend of 10–11 July, further disturbances took place in Moss Side, Handsworth, Chapeltown and over thirty other towns and cities across the country, many of which had very few black youths residing within their areas.

In the media's reporting of the disturbances, little emphasis was placed on the fact that thousands of white youths were involved in the summer's unrest. Racism as an underlying reason for the disaffection of black communities was given

rather short shrift. Where racism was reported, it was confined to the activities of the lunatic fringe. Thus, perpetrators
of racism in football could expect a more than fair hearing.

For England right-back Viv Anderson, the decade had
begun well. He was to finish the 1979/80 season with that
historic England appearance and added a second European
Cup medal to the one he'd picked up the previous season.
Wolves had prevented Anderson from picking up a second
medal in a year by defeating Forest in that season's League
Cup final. At the heart of the Wolves defence was George
Berry. Berry had been born on a military base in Germany,
where his Jamaican father was stationed. His family had
moved briefly to south Wales, where his mother was from,
before settling in Blackpool. Berry had been a keen sportsman. He was a very good tennis player and had been invited
to a tennis academy run by the All-England Lawn Tennis
Association to receive specialist coaching. Berry's father was
keen on sports, although he wasn't a football fan and, like
many from the Caribbean, loved cricket. Berry's secondary
modern school didn't have the space or grounds to support
the game, located as it was in a tight, densely populated area
of Blackpool. Cricket was for the grammar schools in the
area, so Berry, like many boys, became a member of the generation that broke the dominance of cricket as the premier
sport of communities of West Indian heritage in the UK. Although school wasn't of any real interest to Berry, his father,
like many West Indians and indeed all migrant communities,
valued education highly and wanted his son to get his qualifications. He insisted young George could only play football
in return for working hard at school and had, on one occasion, hidden Berry's football boots as punishment for a lack
of academic application. George signed for Wolves the day

after completing his O levels and moved to Wolverhampton, where he started his football career as an apprentice. Berry's duties as an apprentice were to clean out the first-team dressing room and what he learned while undertaking his duties shocked him. Wolves had been a traditional powerhouse of English football and were one of the leading English teams of the 1950s and early '60s. They had won the League Cup in 1974 and the majority of that side formed the basis of the first team.

At many clubs at the time, apprentices did a variety of menial tasks such as cleaning the boots of first teamers, sweeping the terraces and cleaning the changing rooms. It was a good grounding and far removed from today's academy set-up, where young footballers have everything done for them and are rewarded well financially. Dressing room culture at the time dictated that apprentices were often treated with disdain by seasoned professionals. Berry was expected to carry out his cleaning duties in relative silence and certainly would not be expected to speak to a member of the first team unless he had been spoken to. As such, Berry carried out his cleaning duties in apparent invisibility to first teamers, while a young black forward named Noel Gardner, who was on the fringes of the first team, was bullied mercilessly and suffered racist abuse by established first-team stars. Gardner took the abuse, but the young Berry vowed he wasn't going to stand for the same kind of treatment.

George Berry was a physically imposing figure. He had grown up in an almost exclusively white, tough area of Blackpool where, as one of the few black kids around, he understood the importance of being able to fight. His father had encouraged him into boxing, where he excelled enough to represent Lancashire at schoolboy level. It was safe to

say that George knew how to look after himself. His first
love, however, was football, and the choice as to whether to
pursue football or boxing was made for him by a brawny
but technically limited Scouse kid who had caught Berry
cold at the opening bell of a bout and had landed a wild
haymaker that dropped him for a count. The intervention of
the big Liverpudlian had provided Berry with some excellent
career advice and from that point on he decided to hang up
his boxing gloves and concentrate fully on football.

Of all the stereotypes ascribed to black players, Berry
shattered many of them. He had strength but he also had
'bottle', that somewhat slippery terminology that indicated
a combination of bravery, courage, strength in adversity and
stubbornness that common stereotypes dictated was a quality lacking in black players. In fact, he was a very typical
British centre-half: strong in the tackle, good in the air, imposing, but limited with the ball at his feet. His wholehearted
displays saw him progress into the Wolves' first team, where
it wouldn't be long before he got a chance to banish the
legacy of Noel Gardner's treatment once and for all. Hours
before a vital league match, Berry and his teammates were
sitting around a table having their pre-game meal. From the
opposite end of the table, one of the senior pros shouted to
Berry, 'Hey, pass me the nigger lips', nigger lips being rhym-
ing slang for chips. A few sniggers came from around the
table and the room fell silent as everyone turned to Berry
to see how he would react. Berry knew it was an important moment. How he responded would dictate the fate not
only of himself, but of future black players coming into that
environment. Not shirking the responsibility of changing
the culture in the dressing room, Berry told the player in no
uncertain terms that if he repeated the racist slurs, he would

kill him. Despite being severely admonished by the coaching staff for his reaction, while the racist was left alone, the young Berry had taken a brave step and had let the whole dressing room know that he wasn't going the way of Noel Gardner, whose confidence had been shattered and who had drifted out of the game.

A year or so after breaking into the first team, Berry was joined by Bob Hazell. Although he had paved the way for black players to gain a smoother entry into the Wolves dressing room, Berry said of Hazell, 'Bob didn't need looking after. He was militant and he was a big lad. He was a bad boy from Handsworth.' The two instantly formed an imposing centre-back partnership and a lifelong friendship. Indeed, Berry went on to marry Hazell's cousin. The two ensured that the culture within the dressing room remained free of abuse and they provided mutual support in the face of terrace taunts and the casual racism of opponents.

On one occasion, Berry had confronted a racist fan. Late in a home cup game against Watford, Berry horribly sliced a clearance, which fell invitingly for Luther Blissett, who promptly dispatched the ball into the top corner to put Watford 3–0 up and confirm Wolves' exit from the competition. The final whistle sounded immediately after the ball went in and a hugely despondent Berry trudged off the pitch to be met with a Wolves supporter giving him abuse: 'Coon, fucking black bastard, fucking nigger ... piss off back to Africa.' As he made his way down the tunnel towards the dressing room, Berry had a change of heart, turned back towards the pitch, jumped into the crowd and punched his abuser. Berry was eventually pulled away, but all hell had broken loose. Both he and his abuser were arrested. The racist threatened to press charges for assault and the next day both Berry and the racist fan were summoned to see the Chief Inspector, who agreed that if both men apologised and shook hands, the matter would be dropped. Through gritted teeth, Berry agreed, and by some kind of 'Gentleman's Agreement', the incident was cut out of TV footage and wasn't reported in local papers. Berry had had a lucky escape. Through the rare intervention of a reasonably sympathetic police chief, not only had he escaped the possibility of criminal proceedings being brought to him, but he would surely also have faced a lengthy ban, at a minimum, if the incident had reached the attention of the national media and the FA.

By the turn of the decade, Berry's partnership had been broken up as Hazell was sold to QPR and, in the same summer, Laurie Cunningham became the first Englishman to play for Real Madrid when he was sold to the European giants for a shade under £1 million, so bringing to an end the exploits of the legendary trio.

If 1981 was the summer of unrest within many black communities, it proved to be a summer of firsts for black footballers. Dave Bennett of Manchester City and Garth Crooks of Spurs became the first black British footballers to appear in an FA Cup final, with Crooks gaining the honour of becoming not only the first black FA Cup winner but also the first black player to score in an FA Cup final, as Spurs ran out 3–2 winners over City, after a replay. Following his move to Real Madrid, Laurie Cunningham appeared for his new side as they were beaten by Liverpool in the final of the European Cup in May 1981.

As for Cyrille Regis, his game had continued to blossom. The additional experience he'd acquired, along with the responsibility of leading the West Brom line, meant he was becoming one of the most feared strikers in English football.

The season proved to be a brilliant one, at least individually. He was rewarded with a full England cap in February 1982 and ended it with the Goal of the Season for a brilliant, thunderous, long-range strike in a cup game against Norwich.

At the end of the 1982 season, the FA Cup final pitted the holders, Garth Crooks's Spurs, against Second Division QPR, whose defence included Bob Hazell. In the semi-final, Hazell had marked Cyrille Regis out of the game to help put his side in the final against hotly fancied Albion. At the end of Wembley Stadium, reserved for the Rangers support, an elaborately made giant banner depicting two black players, one in a QPR kit and one in a Spurs kit, was displayed with the caption 'Bobby Locks Up Crooks'. Hazell did pretty well but couldn't prevent Crooks adding another FA Cup winners' medal to the one he'd received the previous year. Spurs won narrowly, again after a replay, their class in the end seeing them through. That summer of 1982 was also the year that English football would be shamefully linked to the apartheid regime.

One of the enduring images of the struggle against apartheid, and one that helped to bring international attention to the campaign against the regime, is of the limp body of a boy being carried through the streets of Soweto after being shot by South African police. His body is being carried by his friend and flanking him is his distraught sister, Antoinette Sithole. The boy was declared dead on arrival at hospital. He was thirteen-year-old Hector Pieterson.

In June 1976, a number of school students from Soweto boycotted school in opposition to the imposition of Afrikaans as the medium of instruction in schools. Afrikaans was the language of the white minority and the official language of the apartheid regime. The decision by the South African authorities could not be viewed in any light other than as an instrument of oppression and on 16 June some 20,000 students marched in protest to the Orlando Pirates football stadium. Their way was blocked by the South African police, who opened fire and set their dogs on the children. Hector Pieterson was amongst the first to be shot, and by the end of the day twenty-three protesters were dead, almost all of them children. The following day the South African police, in a show of force, occupied Soweto and continued to kill protesters. With unimaginable bravery, the protests continued and, by the end of 1976, somewhere between the official figure of 176 and an estimated 700 people had been murdered by the security services, almost all of them children and young people.

These events, and the image of Pieterson's lifeless body, caused international revulsion and, under pressure from African nations in particular, the Gleneagles Agreement was drawn up by Commonwealth heads of state in January 1977. The agreement, named after the Scottish town where the heads of state met, agreed to impose a ban on all sporting ties with teams and individuals from South Africa.

Over the next few years, there were concerted efforts to break the agreement, mainly in cricket and rugby, the sports that were most closely associated with white South Africa. In 1982, former PFA chairman Jimmy Hill accepted an invitation by South African Breweries, who had bankrolled previous cricket and rugby tours, to organise a six-match series. In order to provide the tour with a modicum of credibility and create the illusion that the purpose of the visit was to bring the races together, it was critical that the tour should include a black player in the squad. A number of players were approached, amongst them Cyrille Regis and George Berry, both of whom declined the invitation.

Nineteen-year-old Calvin Plummer, who had recently made his first-team debut for Nottingham Forest, had been called to his manager's office and naturally wondered why he had been summoned. Speculating as to whether he was to be offered a new contract, he found out that Brian Clough had a proposition for him. Clough explained to Plummer that he'd been in contact with 'James', who was organising a three-week tour to South Africa. He was told that as Viv Anderson and Justin Fashanu had England careers that may have been placed in jeopardy if they participated in the tour, it was unwise for them to go, but that he could go and earn some good money. He suggested that Plummer think about the offer and let him know his decision the following day. Plummer spoke to his parents, who encouraged him to go, and at a later stage he sought advice from Anderson, who suggested it was a good opportunity. Knowing nothing about apartheid, Plummer informed Clough that he was willing to participate in the tour. Clough explained to Plummer that they wanted him to attend because he was a black European and was just starting out in his career. Clough further explained that the Forest coach, Jimmy Gordon, would also attend and that there may be some controversy, but assured Plummer that Gordon would look after him.

As the date of the tour approached, an agent provided Plummer with an itinerary. He was to meet at Heathrow to fly to Jan Smuts Airport, Johannesburg, and it was only when he arrived at Heathrow that he found out who else was to participate in the tour. Most participants were ageing stars who were at the end of their careers. Mick Channon, Dave Watson, Brian Greenhoff and Stuart Pearson were all former England internationals. Milija Aleksic and Gordon Smith were also players in the latter stages of their careers.

Jack Taylor, the former ref who had officiated at the 1974 World Cup final, was brought along for refereeing duties. Plummer realised that not only was he, by some way, considerably younger than other tour participants, but he was the only black player to tour. The other players were all established names and nobody knew who Plummer was, given that at that stage he wasn't an established member of Forest's first-team squad. However, the starry-eyed Plummer was particularly impressed with the identity of the two most exotic names on the tour, namely Ossie Ardiles and Mario Kempes, two of Argentina's 1978 World Cup winning squad.

> I was surrounded by all these guys, so it was a real eye-opener for me, because we were training and then they were telling us what we were going to do, we were going to play against the Kaizer Chiefs, Orlando Pirates. They're going to do these tours here, and play these games and go and sign autographs … It was flippin' brilliant … and with me being, like, the only black guy amongst them all, they've obviously singled me out … Who's this young kid? … They were unbelievable … They were like wanting to carry me bags … I'd say, 'I'll carry it.'
>
> 'No, no, no, Mr Calvin, we'll carry it for you.' … I didn't have to do nothing.

At the Kaizer Chiefs' stadium in Soweto, a massive crowd gave him, as the only black player in the squad, a special welcome. He observed that the crowd was all black except for those in the segregated, expensive seats in the main stand, who were exclusively white. He'd also visited Table Mountain near Cape Town, which overlooked Robben Island, where Nelson Mandela was being incarcerated even as the tour made its way around South Africa. It was only when he

travelled around the country that the bitter truth began to
dawn on him.

> I wasn't aware of the apartheid thing and it's only when
> I went out there, when I saw some of the signs for 'blacks
> only', or 'no blacks', 'whites only', and all that type of thing,
> but when I was walking around in Johannesburg, I could go
> anywhere, and it was only because I was with this party.

Back home, a storm was brewing and, unbeknown to him,
FIFA and the FA had condemned the tour and pressure was
mounting on them from anti-apartheid campaigners to take
action. Plummer received a phone call from a Forest official,
Paul White, saying that he wasn't allowed to play in any of the
games. The FA had announced that anyone who played on
the tour would have their league registration cancelled. This
left Plummer in a strange situation of travelling with the tour
but unable to play in matches. He phoned home, where his
parents informed him there had been plenty of unrest. They
expressed fear about the impact of the tour on his career and
advised him that he should be careful. In South Africa, the
controversy was having an impact as the tour was beginning
to unravel due to the international pressure. A heated meeting was held between the sponsors and the players, whose
sole concern was whether they would still be paid if the tour
was called off. Plummer was receiving what he described as 'a
princely sum'. As he was the youngest and least high-profile
member of the touring party, the other players must have
received a king's ransom. Jimmy Hill assured the players that
they would still be paid if the tour was called off and that
this provision had been included in the contract in the event
that the tour was cancelled. The pressure back home grew

and, after two weeks of a tour in which he hadn't kicked a ball, one of the tour officials told Plummer that Forest had requested that he return to England.

After a fourteen-hour flight from Jan Smuts to Heathrow, he arrived to a media scrum. Microphones were thrust in his face, cameras flashed in his eyes. 'What was South Africa like?' 'How much money did you get?' He'd been told to say nothing and was ushered through the press pack. Accompanied by a Forest official, he flew to East Midlands Airport and went straight to the City Ground, where he was met by Clough. Clough gave him a hug, told him he was pleased to see him and asked him if he'd been paid. Plummer told him that he had, to which Clough replied that he also had received a payment.

After a day or two's rest, Plummer returned to training, where his teammates gave him the nickname of 'Springbok'. As he sprinted during a training exercise, Clough joked that he could run like one. As for the tour, it had limped on but Plummer's departure was the beginning of the end. It was a public relations disaster and after three games the tour was abandoned. Upon the return of Hill and the rest of the party, media interest in the event fell away and the world moved on.

Meanwhile, within Nottingham's black community, Plummer's actions had caused upset. He was invited onto a local radio station to explain his side of the story, which he did, after which his explanation appeared to be accepted and any opposition to him personally melted away.

Clough had placed Plummer in a terrible situation and could have jeopardised his career as well as his standing within the black community and amongst his fellow black professionals. The threat to his league registration could

have ruined Plummer's career before it had fully started. It
was cynical of Hill and Clough to involve a young black
footballer when apartheid money was at stake. That Clough
had informed Plummer he wasn't to play and had brought
him home from the tour early probably saved Plummer's
career, but it was a close call. Plummer had been hung out
to dry by his manager and forced to face the disquiet of his
local black community on his own. It was common knowledge within the game that Clough was fond of finding ways
to supplement his income and earn a few extra pounds here
and there. Alan Sugar, former Spurs chairman and star of
The Apprentice, stated that Clough liked a bung. He had
assisted in organising the tour by getting players and providing the team with the Forest coach. Clough had been one of
the original signatories to the formation of the Anti-Nazi
League in 1977. The league had played a prominent role in
opposing the activities of the far right throughout the late
1970s and early '80s. He was also close friends with Lindy
Delapenha, his Jamaican teammate from his time at Middlesbrough. Clough had compromised his anti-racist credentials and had shamefully exploited a young black man
whom he had a duty of care to protect and support, simply
to please an unacceptable racist regime.

Plummer was a small but quick and skilful winger who
had two spells for Forest and also played for Derby and
Chesterfield. He grew up on a council estate in Hyson Green
in Nottingham, a very ethnically diverse area, and played for
his primary and secondary schools. Playing for Nottingham
Schoolboys and for local teams, he was spotted by a Forest
scout and eventually signed for them after leaving school
in 1979. Plummer recalled many black players being signed
for Forest and other local sides, but they found things very

difficult because of the attitude of coaches at the time. The lazy stereotypes that circulated around the game meant that many black players didn't get the opportunities that their talent merited. When he joined Forest, he and Viv Anderson were the only black players at the club. They were to be joined the following year by others, including future Leeds United legend Chris Fairclough. As an established first-team player and local lad, Plummer looked up to Anderson, who was a great influence not only on Plummer but on all the young players at Forest. On making his first-team debut, away to Brighton, Plummer had shared a room with Anderson, who set about putting the nervous youngster at ease and provided sound advice as to how he should approach the game.

Plummer was taking the place of Forest striker Justin Fashanu. Fashanu had arrived at Forest from Norwich City as the first £1 million black footballer. Plummer had been scoring goals for fun in the reserves; Fashanu was struggling, badly.

Fashanu was very personable and widely considered around the club as a genuinely nice person. He wasn't flash, but was always well turned out. His time at Forest proved to be a difficult one. He had a big price tag and had been playing poorly. At Norwich, his rawness had been harnessed well. He was required to, in football parlance, 'put himself about' and was well served as the focal point of the Norwich attack. A combination of his strength, a decent turn of pace and a more than adequate touch had seen him score twenty-nine goals for a Norwich side that was relegated at the end of the 1980/81 season. He was twenty years old and an England under-21 international and he had his best years ahead of him. The logic of signing him was in no doubt when Clough beat off interest from other clubs to gain his signature in 1981. Fashanu's problem was in how Clough chose to manage him. In training he was a hard worker. He could run all day and was strong and powerful in the gym, but when it came to technique, he struggled. Clough was merciless in his criticism of Fashanu's technique, and instead of galvanising him to improve, as no doubt Clough intended, it shattered the player's confidence. His poor technique in training spilled over into games. For a player, especially for a forward, whose reliance on technique affects a sizeable proportion of their game, when their confidence becomes fragile their touch and technique are often the first aspects of their play to suffer. As a big man, Fashanu's touch would never be described as silken, but as he regularly demonstrated at Norwich and for the England under-21 side, he had two good feet, could dribble and, with his pace, could beat a man when he got up a head of steam. With Clough placing his touch under such high scrutiny, he became over-conscious of the need to control the ball properly. He began to overthink his game, which then went to pieces. On match days, his teammates became frustrated at his poor first touch, his inability to hold the ball up and his clumsiness, and, attempting to compensate, he would try to make challenges and generally put himself about, with the result that he gave away too many free kicks.

Fashanu wouldn't be the first player in the history of football to be badly handled by Clough, or any other manager for that matter. Clough liked to keep football simple and, by extension, training sessions were also simple. There was certainly no room for the kind of individually tailored programme that could have benefited Fashanu.

The lack of confidence in his football was compounded by the issue of his sexuality and his recent conversion to

Christianity, the two of which were seemingly incompatible. His sexuality wasn't widely known to his teammates, his relationship with his fiancée putting his teammates off the scent. His sexuality was known by Clough, whose homophobia, compounded as it was by Fashanu's poor form, had rendered their relationship very difficult to say the least.

So it was that the young Calvin Plummer came to make his debut in the Forest side. He followed up his debut by playing the next game at home against Ipswich and scored his first goal for Forest. At his next game, at home to Middlesbrough, with his parents and his brother proudly watching him, the away fans proceeded to welcome him with monkey chants. His mother, watching her son for the first time, was deeply upset.

The worst grounds he visited were at Millwall, Newcastle, Sunderland and Leeds. Being a winger, and therefore being stuck out on the flanks, he received a lot of abuse but developed some kind of acclimatisation to it. Early in his career, he was named as substitute in a game at Upton Park, the close, hostile and deeply racist home of West Ham United. Clough told him he was going on, so he got off the bench to stretch and warm up. The crowd, relishing their role as tormentors in chief, rained down their racist abuse at him. Going through his routine, but sensing the hostility of the crowd, something hit him on the ear. Looking down, he saw a banana; he picked it up, pretended to eat it, then threw it back on the floor. Cutting short his warm-up routine, he returned to the safety of the dug-out. As he sat on the bench, Clough told him, 'Right then, young Plummer, you get back up there and show 'em that you're not intimidated. And by the way, young Plummer, bring me back a banana.'

It had lightened the mood on the bench and had quashed

his fears. Clough had used a similar strategy with Viv Anderson when he first broke into the side, with similarly positive results. In addition to abuse from opposition fans, Plummer also suffered abuse from opposition players. He found a Birmingham City defender to be a particularly nasty individual. As Plummer said of racist abuse:

> Black this and the black that, not a problem, but the 'N' word ... that was more personal. That was the first time I got the 'N' word from a player ... Every time ... standing at a corner, 'What you doing here?' ... jungle house ... tribal stuff. He was the only one I ever really had a problem with.

While the kind of remarks made were widespread, even within the context of football and wider society in early 1980s Britain, their commonality of usage did not render them socially acceptable. As Mark Walters remarked, 'They would say these things on the pitch, but they would never go up to you and say them in the street.' This tacit understanding of what was known to be appropriate behaviour towards black people rendered football one of the few areas where racists were not only able to indulge in racist behaviour, but could even be afforded protection to do so. Their behaviour was distinctly cowardly. Given the aggressive stereotypes, to racially abuse a black man in the street would be to invite confrontation, in which there was a good chance it could end badly. The unwritten code of street relations would also brook little sympathy if the racist received a good beating, but the experience of many black footballers mirrored that of black people outside the rarefied atmosphere of a football ground. Most racists would rarely indulge in racist behaviour without the protection that being part of a crowd offered. In football, the protection for this racist behaviour was provided by teammates, referees, coaches, the FA, the media, football authorities and in fact the whole culture of the game itself. For racist fans, the culture of the game afforded them similar protection. Very few areas, other than the nastiest of workplaces, offered such protection for racist behaviour.

And, while it was true that racism was used as a motivational tool by many footballers, the picture was far more complex: as Calvin Plummer acknowledged, it could eat at a person's pride and self-respect. When he was playing well and his team were winning, the racism would wash over him, but when he wasn't, it was hard to take.

CHAPTER 6

MOSS SIDE MANIA

*'Compared to West Brom, I think City's record is as good if
not better in giving opportunities for black players.'*
– Alex Williams

WILBRAHAM HIGH SCHOOL in Chorlton had great
football teams in the mid- to late 1970s. With a strong
sporting tradition, its football teams were amongst the most
dominant in Manchester and the surrounding area. From
this school came a crop of boys from in and around Moss
Side who would go on to form an integral part of the Manchester City youth side that got to two FA Youth Cup finals.
Gary Bennett, who went on to play 440 times for Sunderland and become club captain, and future Oldham Athletic
all-time leading scorer and out-and out legend Roger Palmer
both attended the school. Such was the dominance of their
football team that Alex Williams's school team never lost a
single home game in each of the years from age twelve to
sixteen that he kept goal for the team, drawing only once.
In the same school team as Williams and playing on the left
side of midfield was Clive Wilson, who played over 500
times for City, Chelsea, Tottenham, QPR and Chester City.
As well as sharing a place on the school football team, Williams and Wilson shared a classroom, back-to-back places

on the school register and a birthday (13 November). Both played for Manchester Schoolboys and both were offered apprenticeships in City's youth set-up.

City was the team of choice for Manchester's African-Caribbean community. Migrants from the West Indies began to settle in Manchester in the 1950s and '60s and Moss Side was its hub of the community. As well as West Indians, the diverse community included Indians, Pakistanis, Chinese and Irish residents. City had moved there in 1923 and were to remain there for the next eighty years. Alex Williams's parents arrived in Moss Side in the 1950s, along with many others from the Caribbean. Williams was born in Moss Side, but the family moved to nearby Levenshulme when he was two years old, although his ties with Moss Side remained close. Wanting to join the school football team, he wasn't good enough to play outfield but got a chance to keep goal when Wilbraham's keeper got injured. The twelve-year-old Williams volunteered to go in goal, found he was good, got better, kept his place in the team and eventually found his way to City in 1978.

As a strong footballing school, there were often scouts at games. One of the school teachers, Bert Jackson, had strong links with City. Williams played for Manchester boys and the north-west area boys' teams, but for reasons unknown he didn't attract the attention of scouts until two weeks before he was due to leave school, when he was approached by a City scout to go for training. After impressing, he continued to train at City twice per week and to his delight was offered an apprenticeship when he turned sixteen. In the six months between leaving school and signing for City as an apprentice, Williams had worked collecting glasses in the evenings at a club in Manchester's Piccadilly and had worked on a milk round in the mornings.

In City's youth set-up he was joined by Gary Bennett, Roger Palmer and Clive Wilson, whom he knew from school, and by Bennett's older brother Dave. As Williams said,

> It was a great time at City, 'cause we always had quite a few black players, Roger Palmer was there, Dave Bennett was there, young Gary Bennett was in the same squad as me, Clive Wilson came along about eighteen months later. So City always had black players in the team. I think it just made me feel a little bit more at home.

This was a unique experience for black footballers in Williams's era. There was none of the isolation, the sense of otherness, the feeling of being an outsider that had so characterised the experiences of many of Williams's contemporaries. As he says,

> I think that the fact that we've always had black players in the team and the fact that we were in the heart of Moss Side, which at that time was very much an Afro-Caribbean area, and I think that all just helped as well, but the club were great, they never looked at you like that, I never thought of myself as a black player or black goalkeeper, I just thought of myself as a player ... It was just a great place to be.

Williams was a very good keeper, probably the outstanding young keeper of his generation. Not only did he have all the right physical attributes – tall, broad, agile, huge hands – but he was also brave and possessed an astonishing temperament for a young goalkeeper. He showed remarkable poise and incredible self-assurance, and sped through the ranks at City to cement his place in the first team, while also seamlessly working his way through England youth sides. Such was his progress, his debut for City was only a matter of time.

His chance came when regular keeper Joe Corrigan was injured: he made his debut in 1981 against West Brom. Williams made an important save with the game still goalless, City eventually taking a two-goal lead before conceding a late goal but hanging on to win.

So it was that Alex Williams became the first black British goalkeeper to play in the top division of English football and he had made a winning start. It was 1981 and although the number of black players was increasing, the sight of a black goalkeeper caused considerable consternation.

> It was strange making my debut and in particular going to the first half a dozen away games or so, because you could almost, as I ran on, hear people aghast and going, 'Hang on, what's this?' ... You know, some of my early games were the likes of Tottenham away, West Ham away, Leeds away.

In football folklore, goalkeepers are often characterised as loners or eccentrics, as if this state of mind is a prerequisite for being a goalkeeper, and of football's long list of eccentrics, outsiders and the downright bizarre, a fair number have indeed been goalkeepers. This impression is perhaps due to their particular role in the side, but it has often been at odds with the reality of what many teams have required from their goalkeeper. The majority of the successful sides in the game's history have featured a good goalkeeper. As well as athleticism, bravery and agility, keepers need to be solid and dependable; in fact, the antithesis of the wildly eccentric, madcap image that often prevails. Williams was of the solid, dependable, non-eccentric type; at his best, a calm and reassuring presence in City's goal and an excellent shot-stopper when called upon.

Of all the stereotypes that have been ascribed to black footballers, their supposed inability to keep goal is perhaps the most enduring. The first black professional in English football was a goalkeeper, Arthur Wharton, but apart from Williams, Derek Richardson, who had played in Len Cantello's testimonial in 1979, was the only other black goalkeeper of that generation. Richardson had been at Chelsea as a youth player and then at QPR, where he was famously mistrusted as a goalkeeper on account of him having only one good eye. The novelty status that black goalkeepers like Williams were held to began to disappear with the prominence of David James and others like Matt Murray, who would go on to represent England at under-21 level, his Wolves teammate Carl Ikeme, and Jason Brown, who was capped by Wales. What is true, however, is that there have been few black goalkeepers in comparison to players in other positions, and although a number of reasons have been put forward as to why, the germ of the answer is likely to boil down to role models.

The great Brazilian sides of the 1960s and 1970s never had a black goalkeeper, and in fact Brazil never had one at a World Cup until Dida played in goal for the team in the 2006 World Cup, the first black goalkeeper to be a regular for the Seleção since the 1950s. The notion that blacks don't make good goalkeepers remains a feature of Brazilian footballing culture to this day. The stereotypes that many British coaches had, which meant that for many years, black players couldn't be trusted with more central playing responsibilities, along with a lack of outstanding goalkeeping role models, leaving very few black goalkeepers for young black kids to emulate, means that, with the exception of a handful like Williams, James and Brown, very few black goalkeepers have had an impact on the game in this country.

When Williams replaced Corrigan, he expected City to buy another keeper. There was talk of City signing Pat Jennings, the experienced Northern Ireland international keeper, but so good were Williams's performances, they showed tremendous faith in their young keeper, who went on to play over 100 successive games and keep twenty-one clean sheets in one season, still a Manchester City record.

Williams's hero status as a Moss Side black kid made good was further cemented by his regular participation in the Junior Blues scheme, which was a club initiative to connect the club with its younger fans. The genial local boy was forging a good reputation for himself, enhanced by his support for the Junior Blues initiative and by other community work and coupled with his meteoric rise through the youth ranks for both club and country.

However, he was forced to face a series of uncomfortable truths. Although his status as a footballer protected him from many of the worst experiences of other young black Moss Side men in their late teens and early twenties, he was forced to deal with his own uniquely footballing brand of racial discrimination. While home games were largely free from some of the more horrific examples of abuse, it was often a different story away from Maine Road.

At the time I was playing, there was a lot of racial trouble, you know, with the fans and racism in football, and most of the grounds had barriers at the front of the stands to stop people from getting on to the pitch and I was running out for the second half at Everton, and I ran up to whatever the main end is and somebody had climbed onto the barrier and got a programme and made it into a cross and as I ran up to them they lit it, à la Ku Klux Klan … The funny thing about it was I turned round looking for support from the players and all my players were rolling over laughing at it. It was quite funny – it wasn't funny at the time but I can see the funny side of it now.

Like all black players of that generation, Williams had to be mentally tough. As a keeper, there was nowhere for him to hide. The abuse never really bothered him, but he had been surprised by the vitriol meted out at certain grounds, and made a distinction between the types of racism he suffered.

I always thought there was two elements to racism in football, one was the mickey-taking type, which, you know, rightly or wrongly, I class at places like the Everton incident and then like, you know Liverpool, I've had a little bit of stick … But there are some grounds where it's deep-rooted. I played at places like Millwall – I played there in my first FA Youth Cup final … It was a two-legged affair, so they brought about a thousand fans up to the first leg at Maine Road, we drew 0–0 and when we went down there it was just absolutely terrible, about 10,000 in the crowd, I got loads of abuse … and places like Leeds where they threw a load of bananas at me.

Williams distinguishes between a more benign form of racism and more hostile, hateful forms of abuse. As one of the first generation of black footballers, he was forced to rationalise as to which forms of racism were more acceptable than others and to find a way to dismiss them, or literally grin and bear them, as the situation required. Winning over crowds, con-centrating on performances, trying to encourage people to see the player, rather than the colour – this was the experience of Williams and his contemporaries as they navigated their way through the minefield of hatred, casual prejudice, stereotyping and hostility that characterised English football in the 1970s and '80s. Dealing with both subtle and overt forms of racism and determining the most appropriate response was a daily challenge. Could he take a joke, could he stand up for himself, could he ignore it, could he show it wouldn't affect his game, did he have a chip on his shoulder, how should he maintain his dignity? The right response at the wrong time could lead to allegations of not possessing enough mental fortitude to forge a career in the game, so players were forced back to the familiar default responses. These challenges were in evidence even when racism occurred in the dressing room, as Williams recalls:

> I remember we were having a team talk at Chelsea by Billy McNeill and he said at the time, 'I want you to get out there and work like a bunch of blacks' … and I looked at Clive and Clive also looked at me and you know when somebody says something and you think, 'Did they really just say that?', but he was so apologetic and so embarrassed after he'd said it.

One advantage that Williams had was that, at least in his case, there were other black players at the club. It provided an opportunity to talk, to share experiences and knowledge, to discuss strategies and to check in about whether their feelings were mutual.

> You don't really say that much, to be honest. I mean after the game, if the players had spotted somebody saying or hearing something silly, they'd mention it and sometimes it'd be a

serious conversation for a couple of minutes or you might
even make a joke of it ... I think the only time I ever spoke
to somebody, we were in a hotel once in London, and we
were about to play Chelsea, and somebody had sent a parcel
and there was a razor blade inside it. I think Clive Wilson
was there at the time and we discussed it. It was just a parcel,
which obviously I never got, and inside apparently was a
razor blade, but you just get on with it ... You're hoping it
doesn't get to you, but I was never frightened in any way,
'cause you've just got a job to do, you get on with it, but that
was the only ever time or incident I was aware of. There may
have been other things kept from me, which would have been
good of the club, but you just go out and play, at the end of
the day, you know you're going to be in an industry where
you're going to be shot at, not physically shot at but verbally,
people are going to say things, and you've just got to get on
with it, and rightly or wrongly accept it.

While the burden of dealing with racial abuse was shared
with other black professionals at City, Williams was careful
to protect his family from its worst excesses. Williams was
forced to ask his father to stop attending games, fearing it
would aggravate his father's asthma attacks.

You couldn't say anything to my dad about any of the family
or his ethnic origin, he would nip it in the bud straight away
and want to fight people ... but just sticking up for his rights
and stuff like that ... He went to the odd game and I think he
learned to just be quiet and accept what was said in the crowd.

The price Williams's father had to pay in order to watch his
son play the game he loved for the team he loved was to

adopt the 'just got to put up with it' approach to attacks on his pride and dignity. The natural desire to defend his child had to be suppressed by Williams senior, who was forced to keep quiet and bite his tongue in order to help his son's career and allow him to play for his beloved City ... and love the club he did. As a child he had gone to watch both City and United, but gradually developed an affinity with City, which was cemented by their 1969 FA Cup final win. For Williams, playing for City – his boyhood club, who were at the heart of his local community – was a source of immense pride. Like many parents of that generation, his mother and father had no real understanding of football and therefore didn't put any pressure on him, in stark contrast to the experiences of many young players in today's academies.

As a young black man growing up in 1970s and '80s Britain, Williams considered racism to be a normal part of his existence, yet on occasions like his experience in front of 10,000 baying, vitriolic south Londoners at Millwall, even he could be taken aback by its sheer intensity. He could never be described as a militant or as having a chip on his shoulder, but his analysis of racism's subtle intricacies and motivations is crystal clear: 'There's a lot of jealousy, as well, you know, a black kid from Moss Side, doing well, earning a lot of money and having nice cars and living well. There's still a lot of people resent that.'

Alex Williams was never anything other than a model professional in his approach to playing and training, his community work, and the way he dealt with the end of his career. Suffering from a disc problem that affected his right leg, he slowly realised that he was doing himself and his fellow professionals no favours by carrying on. The end came inauspiciously in front of a crowd of 2,500 while out on loan at Port

Vale. He'd gone there after an operation to cure the problem, because Port Vale had a reputation for its expertise in offering the kind of rehabilitation he was going to require if he was to get back to full fitness. Operating at around 20 per cent of his usual fitness level, he'd decided during the game that it was to be the end. The next day, he went to see Port Vale's manager, John Rudge, and informed him that he was retiring. He was twenty-four. Had his career not been cruelly cut short by injury at such a young age, he may well have gone on to be the England no. 1 for a generation.

Williams returned to the club shortly after his retirement to take up community, coaching, charitable and ambassadorial roles at the club, and, after the club secretary, he is the second longest-serving employee at City, with his association with the club enduring for over thirty-five years. He and that first group of Moss Siders paved the way for an astonishing array of black footballing talent.

While Ron Atkinson's West Bromwich Albion were lauded as pioneers for their inclusion of the Three Degrees, City's record then and now is quietly impressive. In addition to Williams and his contemporaries at the club, the list of young black players who began their professional careers by way of City's youth system is certainly impressive. Micah Richards, Daniel Sturridge, Shaun Wright-Phillips, Bradley Wright-Phillips, Dickson Etuhu, Nedum Onuoha, Jeff Whitley and Tyrone Mears all graduated through City's academy and went on to win full or under-21 international caps for their country. In addition, Kelvin Etuhu, Adie Mike, Leon Mike, Jason Beckford, Darren Beckford and Shay Logan all went on to have careers in the game.

• • •

Dave Bennett knew he would need to toughen up not long into his Manchester City debut at Maine Road against Everton on 23 September 1979. Bennett had picked up the ball and tricked his way past an Everton midfielder. Comprehensively beaten, his opponent scythed Bennett down and, as he helped him up, he warned, 'Don't do that again, you black bastard.'

His antagonist had inadvertently done Bennett a favour by providing that crude welcome to First Division football, because he knew that if he was to survive, he would have to find a way of dealing with this kind of abuse. Bennett was the first of a crop of talented black players, plucked from the local area and groomed within the club's youth, set up to be given a chance of wearing the famous Sky Blue. He wasn't about to let any of them down.

Bennett's dad had worked on the railways and after work one day was confronted by a pub regular, who'd heard Bennett senior's son had just signed for City. He'd insulted and ridiculed Bennett's father, incredulous that a black player could be good enough to play for the club. 'Your son's the sweeper,' he suggested. The exchange was nasty and, later, when his father related the story, it made Bennett angry. If any further motivation was needed to become a first-team player, this was it.

Dave Bennett had been brought up in Longsight, an ethnically diverse area near Moss Side and part of Manchester City's catchment area, and had grown up as a City fan. In Manchester at the time, there existed a great deal of racial tension, and Bennett and his friends had to take particular care to avoid the skinheads who roamed around parts of Manchester looking for likely targets. Being tough, like being polite or crossing the road, was something that, as a black kid, he had to learn in order to survive.

He was academically bright and managed to gain a place at Burnage Grammar School, and of course he played for the school team and became its stand-out performer. Playing as a striker, he was selected to play for Manchester boys' team and, upon leaving school, enrolled at college to improve his grades. While at college, Bennett played for open-age teams on Saturdays and Sundays, and as a fifteen-year-old did well enough to attract the attention of scouts. He first had a trial for Oldham Athletic but then got a chance to have a trial at City. Pitched in against City's youth side, he helped himself to a hat-trick in front of the watching City manager, Tony Book, and was offered apprentice forms the next day. However, it was discovered that Bennett was too young and had to wait a few months before he was able to sign as an apprentice.

He found that the coaches at City were brilliant, being encouraging and patient with both him and Roger Palmer, with whom he formed a striking duo. Bennett and Palmer attracted a great deal of attention, not only because the two black kids on the team played as central strikers – a novelty that no doubt in itself would have stunned some opposition defences and coaches – but also because between them they scored a lot of goals. Bennett was quick and wiry, Palmer also had pace and was brave, and they performed brilliantly as the main goal getters for a very talented City youth side.

Bennett and Palmer had an acute understanding of the fact that how they performed would have an impact on other black kids coming through the City youth system. Bennett's younger brother Gary was also on City's books, as well as Clive Wilson and Alex Williams, so they knew the challenges of carrying other black kids with them and breaking down a few barriers along the way.

Acutely aware of what black players supposedly could and couldn't do, Bennett played in the wind, the rain and the snow, scored a lot of goals, led City to the Central League title and gradually did well enough to break into the first team.

At the time Bennett broke into City's first team, there were very few black players in the First Division. Viv Anderson was still in the Second Division with Forest and Bennett was one of the few black players to play regularly in the top flight. As he became an established striker, Bennett had suggested that he and his dad go down to the pub, find the punter who had said Bennett was good enough only to sweep up, and have a word with him. Wisely, Bennett senior told him to forget it, but a few weeks later, the pub sceptic admitted to Bennett's father that his son could play.

However, in spite of his elevated status as a footballer, every so often the racist attitudes that existed in Manchester at the time reminded him that he was another local black kid. In the 1970s and 1980s, the nightlife in a town or city could be deeply segregated. On one hand, most clubs didn't play black music, or, where they did, they gravitated towards the more commercial end. Secondly, each town or city had clubs that didn't admit black people. The excuse would usually be some kind of violation of the dress code or the age policy, which, depending on the answer you gave or the ID you had, could be eighteen, twenty-one or twenty-five. You might also be told there was a private party, or that the club was full and you couldn't wait till enough people left, or that you wouldn't like it, or that you just couldn't come in. This would often happen even when black people were working on the door or in the DJ booth.

After a Manchester derby, Bennett and his teammate

Nicky Reid went to the new Britannia nightclub in Manchester. As they stood outside, Sammy McIlroy and Jimmy Nicholl, two of their opponents from the earlier derby game, were just leaving. They asked how the club was and when McIlroy and Nicholl said it was OK, they proceeded to go in. Both Reid and Bennett were well turned out, with suits and ties, but Bennett was denied entry and Reid was permitted to go inside.

A local journalist witnessed the event and asked Bennett for a comment, which he declined to give. Nevertheless, a story about the incident appeared in the local paper on the eve of an important cup semi-final. He really didn't need the publicity. A few months later, Alex Williams chose the reception room attached to the club as the venue for his wedding, and later on in the evening they decided to go into the club. The same doormen who'd refused entry to Bennett now not only had to admit him due to the adverse publicity but also had to admit Williams, Wilson and others.

Bennett was also approached to play in Jimmy Hill's ill-fated tour of South Africa. He was offered a great deal of money to participate, but was urged not to go by his father, who proceeded to give him a lesson about apartheid and, in the process, save Bennett's legacy and standing as a pioneer amongst Manchester's black community.

CHAPTER 7

DRESSING DOWN IN THE DRESSING ROOM

*'When they announced the team, each player got a cheer …
every time they mentioned Canoville it was boo, especially
from the Shed End. Every time.'* – Paul Canoville

THE SUMMER OF 1984 had seen the domineering West
Indies humiliate England 5–0 in the famous 'Blackwash'
tour. The West Indies had set the tone early in the first Test.
England debutant and opener Andy Lloyd had just made ten
when his bat got nowhere near a short-pitched delivery from
Malcolm Marshall. It crashed into the helmet of the hapless
Lloyd, who was forced to retire from the innings and would
suffer from blurred vision for a week, never to return to
the England Test side. The pace and aggression of the West
Indies' bowling attack complemented the fearsome batting
of the West Indies opening and middle order. The tail proved
to be dogged and determined and the team as a whole were
ruthless in the field. England were beaten into submission,
from the opening session of the first Test to pretty much the
final session of the last. Football was Britain's national game,
but cricket was the game of the English establishment, which
the overwhelming majority of people of Caribbean heritage
felt alienated from and by. Dominating, rather than just

beating, England represented a way of asserting some pride in the face of hostility. The British Nationality Act had been introduced in 1981 and under its wide-ranging provisions, the automatic right of people born in the UK to acquire British citizenship was removed, as was the automatic right of women married to British citizens. Its introduction left nearly 21,000 people of Indian ancestry effectively stateless as British Overseas citizens, while white South Africans continued as citizens because of direct ancestry. No amount of official denials from government ministers could repudiate the singularly discriminatory nature of the Act.

With discrimination now enshrined in law, the new decade had not improved the fortunes of black communities. A 1982 survey found that 53 per cent of British Caribbeans and 51 per cent of British Asians said things had got worse for them over the previous five years. While the economic recession was the main reason for this, 41 per cent of Caribbeans and 49 per cent of Asians cited racism as a factor.

Disturbances of the kind that blighted British inner cities in the early and mid-1980s followed a pattern so familiar as to be almost predictable. A spate of over-zealous and heavy-handed policing would occur, which for the police and community alike would be considered as almost routine. For police, this would involve the deployment of additional officers and resources into a specific area, perhaps coupled with a specific initiative to target street crime or motoring offences. For communities and for individuals, whether black or white, young or old, anger and resentment brewed as mainly (though not exclusively) young black people would be stopped and searched on the way to work, school or while going about their daily business. So when a routine arrest, stop and search or motoring offence check occurred, it would provoke a response that took the police by surprise. This routine activity might include the gathering of a small group to protest, or resistance to an arrest. The police would respond with a display of force, which would add fuel to an already simmering fire. What couldn't be predicted in these circumstances was the date, location or time, but inevitably and inexorably, all hell was guaranteed to break loose. Such was the pattern that saw Handsworth and nearby Lozells explode in September 1985. A routine check for a motoring offence, followed by a routine attempted arrest, followed by the deployment of more officers, resulted in a pitched battle at a Lozells café between local youth and police. Eleven people had been injured in the café disturbances and, like a dam that had been unplugged, there was no turning back. When, inevitably, the looters moved in, sensing a quick pay day, all bets were off. The horrific violence that ensued left shops burned and led to the death of two brothers who, seeking to protect their livelihood, stayed in the post office they owned and died of smoke inhalation in their burning building.

When the dust settled, ex-West Midlands Police Chief Constable Geoffrey Dear identified five factors – massive social deprivation, inadequate housing, unsuccessful education, mass unemployment and racial discrimination – as the root causes, all of which were hugely significant factors, but he conveniently omitted the elephant-in-the-room issue of policing. James Hazell, brother of Bob, then signed to Reading, was one of those arrested and later found guilty of offences associated with the disturbances.

Two weeks later, armed police officers searching for one Michael Groce in connection with a firearms offence raided his mother's home in Brixton and shot and paralysed her.

Groce wasn't there. An angry crowd gathered at her home, marched to the local police station and demanded disciplinary action be taken against the officers involved. At this point, an opportunity to diffuse a fraught situation might have averted the inevitable, but a few skirmishes followed and then fifty officers in riot gear attempted to disperse the crowd. As sure as night follows day, pitched battles ensued, which were to continue over the next two days. The apology for the shooting of Cherry Groce came twenty-nine years later and three years after she had died.

A week later, on 5 October, a few miles north of Brixton on the Broadwater Farm Estate in Tottenham, in close proximity to White Hart Lane, four officers raided the home of Floyd Jarrett, who had been arrested over a car tax disc misdemeanour and then, seemingly randomly, charged and later acquitted on theft and assault charges. During the raid, Jarret's mother Cynthia collapsed and died from heart failure. At the subsequent inquest, Jarret's daughter claimed her mother had been pushed by a police officer.

A demonstration at the local police station took place the following day, with small skirmishes between police and local youths. Riot police attempted to clear the streets with baton charges, which was followed by pitched battles, scores of arrests and injuries, and extensive damage to property. Subsequently, an officer, Keith Blakelock, was murdered and three local residents were arrested, 'fitted-up', imprisoned and later acquitted on appeal for his murder.

From a policing perspective, the riots on 'the Farm' had been a disaster. The police had failed to act on intelligence, had conducted the shoddiest of investigations, had neglected to deploy officers appropriately, hadn't provided adequate protection for their officers or adequately secured a crime scene. A widow and mother's family had been left without loved ones or justice. A community was left stigmatised, many criminalised and families traumatised. It could all so easily have been avoided.

In the four years since the 1981 disturbances, little had changed. The factors that had been identified in Lord Scarman's inquiry into the causes of the 1981 disturbances were a mirror image of those that prevailed in 1985. There had been a temporary lull as a result of the 1981 events, as police, keen not to reignite tension and under scrutiny from local police committees and communities, ceased out-and-out hostilities. But, slowly and surely, familiar policing patterns had been re-established. Traditional police views of black communities as filled with aggressive, criminally inclined, drug-selling, volatile inhabitants, worthy only of heavy-handed methods of policing and control, had created a self-fulfilling prophecy. For black communities, however, policing was one of only a number of issues that impacted negatively. Unemployment, poor education and a general lack of confidence that the future could be better than that enjoyed by their struggling parents all added to the sense of frustration and alienation. The experience of family and friends who were well qualified but who were stuck in employment opportunities that were significantly below what should be expected, further eroded confidence.

Sport in general and football in particular had become one of the few areas where young black males could achieve success, but there was a problem. Many parents within black communities bemoaned how their children had been encouraged and supported to succeed at sport, often at the expense of their academic studies. The stereotypes that abounded about black athletic prowess proved hard to shake off

– and remain so to this day. The all-black 1984 Olympic 100 metre final reaffirmed these stereotypes, based as they are on 'common-sense' understanding and observations, but feeding into widely held notions that are part of everyday discourse and ideas about race.

The prevailing notion of black players as fast, skilful, athletic and strong, but lacking the cerebral qualities necessary to play in central midfield, where dictating the play and taking creative responsibility is crucial, made it inevitable that these positions would be dominated by white players. These ideas had stunted the progress of a succession of black players. Players like Paul Davis, who refused to fit the mould, were forced to challenge these assumptions more times than they cared to remember. Davis wasn't quick or brawny, but he had a brain par excellence. In a career for the Gunners that spanned the late 1970s to the mid-1990s he was very often the silk in an Arsenal side that was chock-full of steel.

Davis was born in Dulwich in south London to Jamaican parents who arrived in the area in the mid-1950s. His parents left two older brothers and an older sister with relatives in Jamaica, a not uncommon occurrence amongst those migrating from the Caribbean and elsewhere. Eventually, Davis grew up in a household with his mother and younger sister. Eschewing local sides Crystal Palace, Fulham and Chelsea, he had been seduced by Arsenal's double winning side of 1971 and grew up with the team firmly fixed in his affections. In school, he excelled at sport and even at the age of nine was singled out for his drive and commitment. He captained the school at football, cricket and the little-known skittleball. His mother wanted Davis to go into commerce or banking, but as far as he was concerned his future lay in football; he did his school work, but never really applied himself to it fully. He represented south London boys, and was invited to train with Fulham, which he did. When an Arsenal scout invited him to train with them, he dropped Fulham like a hot potato and, ignoring his mother's concerns about how he was going to travel to north London, he began training with Arsenal twice a week.

As captain of his school team, Davis had also excelled at cricket. A left-handed opener or no. 3 batsman and a fast medium bowler, he'd had London-wide representative trials for football and cricket on the same day. He wisely chose football, further opening the generation gap between the cricket-loving first generation and the football-mad second generation of Caribbeans.

The process of selecting young players for professional contracts is far from an exact science. Every year, thousands of boys have their dreams shattered on the whim of a tiny number of individuals. Technical proficiency, combined with likeability, attitude, potential, physicality and a range of other intangible factors, not to mention a hunch, a feeling, are tallied up each year to select boys for a professional contract. In this case, five individuals held the fate of Paul Davis, the Arsenal midfielder for the next decade, in their hands. They were concerned about Davis's size. He was small and slight and they wondered if he had the strength to forge a career in the game. By a margin of three to two, Davis was offered an apprenticeship. By small margins are football careers made and lost.

Davis made his debut aged just seventeen and a half against bitter rivals Spurs. He played well, giving an assured performance in a 2–1 victory, but opportunities after that were few and far between. Part way through the following season, and frustrated at the lack of first-team opportunities, he went to see manager Terry Neill to tell him he wanted more games and playing time. First-team chances remained scarce, however, given that he had the experienced England internationals Brian Talbot and Graham Rix, and Arsenal's creative fulcrum Liam Brady ahead of him in the pecking order. Brady's transfer to Italian giants Juventus gave Davis his chance and he was to remain a regular member of the side.

He took time to win over the fans – after all, filling Brady's boots was always likely to be a thankless task, but slowly he won them over and they began to value his qualities. Although strength wasn't his forte, he wasn't afraid to 'put his foot in', as it's known in football parlance, and as an elegant, creative midfielder, his calming presence became quietly appreciated by fans and management alike. The Arsenal side of the 1980s was respected rather than admired. The foundation of the side, particularly under George Graham, was defensive solidity, hard work and strong running rather than attacking prowess. During this period, they became famous for their ability to win 1–0. They would get an early goal and grind out a result, or somehow conjure a late goal after a solid but unspectacular, somewhat vapid performance. In that side, Davis stood out. Whereas his teammates often appeared to treat the ball with contempt, Davis treated it with respect, if not outright love. Where his teammates were happy to be rid of it, Davis would demand it. He wanted to dictate the play and was a composed, reassuring presence in a team full of abrasive characters who would aggressively contest every refereeing decision and take any opportunity to make the game tough, physical and attritional.

In that side, Davis appeared to be something of an out-sider. He was quiet, except when demanding the ball, and both his short and long passing were exceptional, all carried out by that sweet left foot. In a team that scurried, hurried and harried, he always seemed to be playing in slow motion. It's unlikely the side could have been so successful without his presence. He was radically different from the stereotypi-cal image of black players, given his lack of pace, which was more than compensated for by his speed of thought. He was one of the few black players to be given the responsibility of being the creative focus for their side. Of his generation, only Luton's Ricky Hill played a similar role in a top-flight side. Others like Vince Hilaire, who had all the qualities to play there, were frustrated by managers who couldn't see beyond their blackness, pigeon-holing them into narrow, suffocating roles.

As Davis established himself as a first-team regular, one of his first challenges was to work out how to negotiate the tricky political environment of the first-team dressing room. In dressing rooms, it is usually the senior professionals who dictate the prevailing culture. Working out your place within it can be a tricky task. In Davis's case he'd been an Arsenal apprentice. This might have afforded him some knowledge of the club, its traditions and its expectations, but it couldn't provide him with all the tools necessary to manage his inte-gration into the team.

Firstly, his apprenticeship status could confer on him a degree of contempt from senior pros. Only months before he became a first-team regular, he had been cleaning their boots and sweeping up their changing room. Apprentices were often treated with a casual, dismissive attitude in keeping with their status and their tender years. Secondly, Arsenal hadn't had a black player in the side since Brendon Batson, almost a decade earlier, and Davis was the first black player to be an Arsenal regular. Very few of the first-team squad had shared a dressing room, a coach seat or a hotel room with a black person.

As the only black player on the team bus, Davis felt isolated. It wasn't that he was deliberately made to feel unwelcome – he wasn't – but, as with many black players, he found cultural differences between him and his teammates were exposed during dressing room chat. A discussion about rock music, for example, would be outside of Davis's frame of reference. As he couldn't contribute to discussions of that kind, soon he wouldn't be invited into conversations on anything and then there would be the tricky issue of dressing room banter and racist jokes.

Within British culture and beyond, when young men from any walk of life get together, be it in a workplace or social situation, banter and having a laugh are critical. It isn't that women don't do this also, it's just that for men it's the number one priority and the essential part of their bonding process. Ridiculing each other and possessing a self-deprecating attitude are essential components of male group identity, so an inability to laugh at yourself, or a tendency to take yourself too seriously, can lead to varying levels of ostracism from the group as a whole. As such, racist behaviour and abuse can often be masked by this kind of banter.

For black players, dealing with racism in the dressing room was an ongoing war and like all wars, real or metaphorical, it's impossible to fight every battle every time and in the same way. Players who adopted this approach would eventually be sapped of all energy and be left horribly isolated. They would be forced to seek another strategy, be moved on, be starved of playing opportunities or, in a few cases, would quit the game.

Choosing not to fight any battles at all would very rarely prove to be effective either, as invariably it would invite increasing levels of racist jokes, banter and behaviour that would often tip the scales into a world of racist bullying. The impact of this, like all bullying, would be to systematically drain the player of self-confidence, which would eventually impact on their game.

Therefore, most players had to decide which battles to fight, when to fight them and how to fight, but this also was no easy task. Sometimes it would depend on the dressing room itself. Two or three bullies in a dressing room, especially if they were senior pros, along with a manager who would not or could not provide support for a player, could make for a decidedly unhappy existence. If a player was isolated within the dressing room, it could be a thankless task to withstand the bullying. Complaining would invariably lead to accusations of a lack of mental toughness. At other times, an uneasy dressing room truce could be reached, whereby the holder of racist attitudes would tacitly agree not to express their ideas in a black player's presence – only for wholesale dressing room changes or a transfer to another club to start the whole sorry process again.

Therefore, fighting a war in the dressing room was often a constant process of negotiation and accommodation. Players had to negotiate truces with out-and-out racists; ignorance had to be accommodated depending on upbringing, education, seniority or other factors. Just when you thought you were winning, the rules of engagement would change, requiring you to respond in new ways, and it all had to be done in the name of the team, the squad, the club and the game.

In some cases, the need to compromise your dignity and self-respect for the good of team was a one-way street. As George Berry observed,

> When you're on the pitch and you're a team, you expect your teammates to rally round, but because they had that ignorance about them, because it was acceptable, so when an opposition player said 'eh, you fucking nigger' … you wanted to damage somebody, but you found your teammates were laughing, because they thought it was funny. So you felt isolated.

Davis often had to deal with jokes that were very close to the knuckle and make a judgement as to when and how he would challenge racism. When it was close or it crossed the line, he'd politely but firmly tell his teammate that the joke wasn't appreciated. He would always find the right time to confront their behaviour. Something inside him wanted to challenge: perhaps it was a by-product of the inner confidence and steely drive he'd displayed as a nine-year-old. On one occasion, he'd confronted two senior pros about a remark they had made, to which they responded with the time-honoured suggestion that Davis had 'a chip on his shoulder' – the default position of many when challenged to moderate their racist behaviour – but he'd earned their respect and after that he never had too many problems from teammates. He was later joined in the first-team set-up by Chris Whyte and Raphael Meade, two other black apprentices who progressed through the ranks at Arsenal at the same time as him. Their presence removed much of the sense of isolation that he felt in the dressing room and paved the way for a number of black players to join the club. This would have an impact way beyond the Arsenal dressing room.

On the international front, before the 1980s, support for the England national team on away trips was small. Supporting England was something of an anachronism for English football fans, the preserve of a small number of cranks and eccentrics. Club loyalties were the only show in town. Scotland had much more fervent support for its national side, bringing hordes of supporters south of the border for the bi-annual pilgrimage to Wembley to support their team in the Home Internationals. During the 1970s, as English clubs began to take away support to foreign fields, there were sporadic outbreaks of hooliganism involving fans of English clubs. Often, foreign police forces were far more benign than their British counterparts and were taken by surprise by the behaviour of fans. Serious outbreaks of violence involving fans of Leeds, Tottenham and Manchester United took place during European competitions. As the 1980s began and foreign travel became ever more affordable, groups of fans, who were starved of European football, began to attach themselves to the England side. England hadn't participated in a tournament since the 1970 World Cup and so when the team qualified for the Euro 1980 competition in a new expanded format involving eight teams, it enabled a new generation of England fans to attend the tournament, held in Italy. During a first-round game between England and eventual runners-up Belgium, there was serious crowd violence in which tear gas was used and the game was held up for several minutes. Meanwhile, the demise of the far right as an electoral force stripped them of their need to maintain an air of respectability and so, opportunistically as ever, a contingent of far-right football fans hitched themselves to the national side.

Their involvement in support for England first came to prominence during an England international against France in Paris in 1984, where there was considerable crowd trouble. The game was also notable as the match in which South African-born Brian Stein won his one and only cap. The event was followed later in the year by a tour of South America, in which National Front members travelled on the official team plane and racially abused John Barnes and Mark Chamberlain.

Before the events of 1984, hints of far-right influence amongst the England support had surfaced at an England U-21 international in Denmark in September 1982, when Cyrille Regis, Chris Whyte, Paul Davis and John Barnes were subjected to monkey noises every time they touched the ball.

The increasing number of black players winning international honours reflected the growing number coming into the game. What few discussions there were in media circles on racist abuse advanced the somewhat naïve theory that the novelty of black players into a historically white game had led to the abuse, and that a combination of time and an increase in the numbers of black players would provide the cure. The abuse, however, continued unabated. At Upton Park, Paul Davis was greeted with monkey noises, coins being thrown, bananas and spitting. He also remembered Everton, Roker Park, Sunderland and Anfield as places where a hostile reception was to be expected as standard and black players had to steel themselves in preparation for the abuse they knew was coming. Each player's method of dealing with this would be different. For Davis, absolute concentration and focus on what he needed to do on the pitch characterised his approach. 'Just get on with the job', he would implore himself. To do anything else would be unprofessional. On bad days, when the team was performing poorly and they were being soundly beaten, when thoughts would turn more towards a desire for the game to end rather than to your own futile performance, it would be harder.

Other players reacted differently. On a visit to Goodison Park, Davis's teammate Gus Caesar faced a torrent of abuse as he went through his warm-up routine in preparation for a substitute appearance. As monkey chants, spitting and abuse rained down on him, he waved, blew kisses and slowly and provocatively went through his routine, right in front of the baying, snarling crowd. In solidarity, Arsenal fans chanted 'Caesar, Caesar, Caesar'. From his position in front of the mob, he waved in appreciation of his fans' support and continued to smile and blow kisses to the chanting Everton fans. They were apoplectic with rage.

• • •

Bobby Robson had been appointed England manager after the side had crashed out of the 1982 World Cup. In September of that year, silky smooth midfielder Ricky Hill of Luton Town became the first black player to make his debut for England in the Robson era. Later that year, in December, another landmark was reached when Watford's Luther Blissett was given his debut against Luxembourg. In scoring a hat-trick, he became the first black player to score for England. In the same game, Stoke City's Mark Chamberlain was given his first cap as a substitute and also scored in the 9–0 demolition of a hapless Luxembourg. John Barnes received the first of seventy-nine caps in May 1983, in a now defunct Home International tournament game against Northern Ireland. The following month, Danny Thomas, Coventry's classy right-back, was given his international debut, and

Luton striker Brian Stein got his debut in a 2–0 defeat to France in Paris.

The increased number of black players began to cause some contradictory behaviour on the terraces. Where teams had no black players, levels of racism on the terraces increased whenever a black player appeared for the opposition. Where black players became team regulars and were therefore subjected to a level of idolisation that came with playing for their team, two broad responses developed. At some, racism began to disappear, while at others, black players on opposing teams continued to be abused despite the fact that the fans had black players in their side. Where the latter occurred, black players on the home side seemed to be afforded some sort of 'honorary white' status, which allowed them to be accepted almost in spite of their blackness. Millwall fans had always practised this racist double standard. Trevor Lee and Phil Walker were lauded while opposition black players were abused. Later, when John Fashanu was leading the line at the Den, the same pattern would play itself out. Racist abuse meted out to opposition black players; hero worship for their own black players. At these clubs, in the eyes of those supporters, wearing the shirt rendered black players as somehow transcending their blackness. This status was neither black nor white, but afforded those black players with some of the 'privileges' of being white. These 'privileges' were, firstly, adoration for wearing the shirt and, secondly and most importantly, freedom from racist abuse. However, a misplaced pass, a mistake or a poor performance would see this status removed and they could instantly be reduced to the subhuman level of the black players on the opposition team. At West Ham, Bobby Barnes was honoured in a similar way. The Upton Park faithful nicknamed him

'Superwog', a kind of 'new and improved' or 'gold standard' black. Opposition black players were just the normal, ordinary, inferior species.

At times, this type of racism could be the most disturbing, as Brian Woolnough recalled in his book *Black Magic*:

> The only time it really got to Hill and his coloured team-mate Brian Stein was when the Luton crowd used to hoot and make jungle noises at black players on opposing teams. 'We used to sit in the dressing room afterwards and shake our heads in disbelief,' he says. 'That was difficult to stomach. We were their heroes and yet they were trying to crucify young kids on the same pitch.'

However, at Chelsea, this honorary status wasn't bestowed upon Paul Canoville. He was treated with outright hostility by his own fans. Chelsea's racist following was well known around the country, and within the club it was feared to the point where it affected team selection. At the start of the 1982/83 season, manager John Neal said, 'I can't just throw the coloured kids in.'

Despite growing up in west London, as a child, Canoville had supported the Leeds United side of Giles, Clarke, Bremner and especially Peter Lorimer, who was famous for his 70 mph shot. Amongst some bizarre 1970s football fashions, one item that has been held in almost universal admiration was the set of sock garters with team numbers on them that was worn by Leeds in the early 1970s. Canoville had begged his mother to get some and, after weeks of him haranguing her, she got him a pair. He proudly modelled them at the first opportunity at an impromptu football game, gaining the envy and admiration of his friends, and swiftly had them stolen.

Like many Caribbean parents, Mrs Canoville was uninterested in football, and wanted her son to be a policeman or a solicitor, but all Paul was interested in was football. He eventually signed for non-league Hillingdon Borough at the age of sixteen, where the youth team manager, Colin Barnes, was extremely patient and supportive. Canoville was an erratic trainer, frequently missing sessions for no apparent reason. Barnes took a fair amount of stick from other players and their parents as they complained about Canoville's preferential treatment. However, Barnes's faith was rewarded, as Canoville soon progressed to the first team. Before his first-team debut for Borough, he was taken by the first-team manager, Alan Patterson, to Spurs legend Steve Perryman's sports shop. Canoville owned a pair of cheap Winfield boots, which were Woolworths' own brand. They were horrible and plastic and unbecoming of a semi-professional footballer. He was invited to select a nice pair of kangaroo leather Patrick boots costing £75. Quite a sum in 1978.

He progressed well and began to make a name for himself. After trials at West Brom, Wimbledon and Southampton, Chelsea invited him for a week's trial, and then another week, after which he signed in November 1981. He was nineteen.

He couldn't believe his new life as a professional footballer. Playing in the Football Combination, the reserve team league for southern teams, he was enjoying life. A physio would give a pre-match rub to anyone who wanted one, he had his kit and boots laid out and he was doing well, scoring goals and getting Man of the Match awards aplenty. After three months or so, he was told he had been selected as substitute for the first team, away at Crystal Palace. He was going to make his debut. Beside himself with excitement, he told friends and family to come down to Selhurst Park to cheer him on. Travelling on the team coach to the game, it was only the second time he'd ever been on a coach, and this one had tables, table lamps and toilets.

The game was tight and goalless; Canoville was itching to get on: 'I was looking at the right-back, thinking, if I get on, I'm roasting him.' In the Palace side that night was one Vince Hilaire. In the second half, Chelsea manager John Neal instructed Canoville to warm up, as he was going on. This was it, the moment he'd dreamed of for as long as he could remember, the moment he'd acted out in scores of games in the street and in the park. As he went through his routine, he heard it, the sickening abuse and monkey chants. 'OK, this is how it goes on at Selhurst Park,' he tried to tell himself. He began to get increasingly upset, turned round to look at who the protagonists were and, in a state of utter disbelief, realised it was his own supporters. 'I was completely gobsmacked. I had to look again, is that Chelsea? ... And it was Chelsea fans. I was lost, didn't move from the side, just wanted to get off, when I got the ball, I gave the ball straight back, I just wanted the whistle to blow.'

That night he didn't remember getting home, so affected was he by his experience. His debut had been one to remember, but for all the wrong reasons. He'd dreamed of getting on and making an impact on the game, scoring the winner and milking the adulation of his teammates and the supporters, but it had been the stuff of nightmares.

The pattern had been set and it was to continue in that vein. Over the next few weeks he began to get more time and get more starts, but the treatment of the nineteen-year-old continued. Every time he touched the ball, he was booed and abused by Chelsea fans. When the team was announced

just prior to the start of a game, tradition dictated that each
member of the starting XI would be cheered when their
name was announced. Canoville's name was always booed.
In the match programme, each player had their kit sponsored by local companies or individuals. Canoville never
had his kit sponsored, and when he scored against arch
rivals Fulham, the Chelsea fans said his goal didn't count.
He received razor blades in the post as well as death threats
and hate mail. He took to waiting two or three hours after
a game before he left for home, pulling his cap over his
head to avoid being recognised. He also took the Tube to
and from games and was once handed an NF leaflet on
match day by a Chelsea fan, who hadn't recognised him as
he emerged from Fulham Broadway Tube on his way to the
ground to play.

Furthermore, he was deeply isolated in the dressing room.
For a long time nobody ever really spoke to him, except for
the pre-game call to arms: 'Come on, Canners, do it today,
come on.' He had no one to speak to and was forced to carry
this on his own. The club did nothing by way of a response,
possibly too scared to take on the racists or too indifferent
to the welfare of one of their valuable assets.

His first season was daunting, but he'd done reasonably
well. The following season, Chelsea had signed Pat Nevin
and Kerry Dixon and, on the pitch, things started falling into
place. The worst away grounds to visit were Upton Park and
Millwall. He once played at Millwall in a cup game and in
the line-up for Millwall was John Fashanu. As well as the
usual racist abuse, they suffered intimidation and threats of
violence. In the away dug-out, Canoville sat in such a way
as to keep one eye on the hostile crowd, for fear someone
would get over the fence and attack him. On leaving the

ground, a group of Millwall fans had chased some of the Chelsea players, who had to flee to the comfort of their transport. On another occasion, they had played Millwall in a reserve game and amongst the sparse crowd on the terraces were three Millwall supporters with pillow cases on their heads. Stewards, and indeed any other officials from the club, failed to challenge them or ask them to remove their headgear. Canoville was incensed. He was flying erratically into tackles, such was his anger. The referee had to tell him to calm down or he would be sent off. He was eventually substituted, in order to protect opposition players from serious injury.

Towards the end of the season, and with Chelsea chasing promotion, they visited Selhurst Park again to take on Crystal Palace. The abuse was as bad as the previous season but the result this time was different. Once again, Canoville had come on as substitute to be greeted by the now familiar though no less sickening abuse. Ironically, the black Palace players had not been abused as badly as Canoville by the Chelsea crowds. Canoville set up a late winner, which Nevin scored in a 1–0 victory for Chelsea. The game had been broadcast on TV and, as Nevin had scored the winner, the programme was keen to interview him about his goal and the game itself. However, Nevin didn't want to talk about the game. Post-match interviews usually consist of hackneyed sound bites and stock clichés. In this one interview, though, Nevin used the airtime to express his disgust at the actions of the fans and the racist booing of Canoville.

A significant minority of Chelsea fans had conducted an orchestrated campaign to drive Canoville away from the club. While the abuse of black opposition players was routine at Stamford Bridge, they saved their most ardent, most passionate and fervent abuse for their own player. Many had far-right affiliations and sympathies and there were regular chants of 'Sieg Heil' and Nazi salutes on display within the Chelsea support, which increased every time Canoville was in possession or came on as substitute. Black players at the time could not have expected to speak out against racism, given that this would have left them open to accusations of a lack of mental fortitude. Nevin's intervention, freed as he was from such baggage, was nonetheless a brave stand. The subject of racism was never spoken about and rarely discussed, certainly not publicly, and the issue was very rarely acknowledged in media circles during the mid-1980s. As Paul Davis pointed out, there were no forums, no Kick It Out campaigns and no networks in which black players could get advice, so they had to go it alone. The campaign to drive Canoville out of the club was sustained and went unopposed until Nevin made a stand; it is to Canoville's credit and strength of character that he continued to play. There were many times when he considered whether it was all worth it and, ultimately, what was to keep him going was his love of the game.

One of football's unwritten rules is that criticism of fans by players, chairmen or managers is taboo. Nevin's bravery in breaking one of football's reverential taboos, and doing so in such an unapologetic manner, marked the first time any player, black or white, had made such a public stand against racism. A stand that should have been made by the clubs' hierarchy had instead been made by one of its star performers. Nevin's speech hadn't been contrived or pre-meditated and he hadn't spoken to Canoville or any other member of the team.

The club was now shamed into taking some kind of action. Anti-racist statements and notices threatening to impose bans on supporters for racist abuse began to appear in match-day programmes, although these threats were never carried out. In the hospitality and post-game players' lounges, some fans began to express a degree of shame for the behaviour of the Chelsea support and let it be known to Canoville that not all Chelsea fans were like the ones who abused him. While Nevin's stand was welcome in that Chelsea were finally forced to admit they had a problem at their ground, Canoville still felt a deep sense of isolation in the dressing room.

His friends, including his childhood pal the comedian Geoff Schumann, had explained how he'd made a lot of black people stronger, but although this gave him a degree of comfort, he was a footballer and not a politician and he still had to go it alone. It would be two and a half years before other black players, like Keith Jones and Keith Dublin, came into the first team. In that time, he would also have to challenge racist banter in the dressing room. He found that players from London, who had gone to school and grown up with other black people, had a practical, concrete understanding of racist behaviour and its taboo nature and impact. Commentators from today who recall racism within the game in the 1970s and '80s often give the impression that racism was acceptable as well as accepted, but this was far from the case. Other players in the dressing room who were from outside London and other large urban centres, or who, unlike Nevin, did not find racism loathsome, had to be challenged. Racist behaviour would often be carried out under the auspices of banter.

Promotion brought the club and Canoville bigger stages to play on. One of the highlights was playing at Anfield. He got to touch the famous 'This is Anfield' sign, and was amazed at the great atmosphere; although he found it intimidating, the ground was free from racism.

He also recalled a game at Arsenal. He'd not long moved to Hackney and many of his friends were Arsenal fans. With several of them in the crowd at Highbury, and up against England right-back Viv Anderson, Canoville played well. Tracking Anderson's forays forward and causing him all manner of problems when he got the ball, it was a great personal performance.

However, things were beginning to change off the pitch. John Neal had retired, citing ill health, and John Hollins had been appointed as manager and had brought along Ernie Walley as his no. 2. Walley had been in charge for six games at Crystal Palace and had brought Jerry Murphy with him. While Murphy had a fantastic left foot, he didn't track back and didn't beat anybody: in short, he wasn't as good as Canoville. As a favourite of the new management team, however, Murphy was ahead of Canoville in the pecking order.

Canoville considered Walley a poor coach who masked his inadequacies by acting as some kind of drill sergeant. His attitude alienated the players, and results began to suffer. For Canoville, there was also a stalemate over a new contract, and a combination of this and a serious incident involving racist abuse from a teammate would usher in the end of Canoville's career at Chelsea.

At the start of the 1986/87 season, the team had gone to Wales for pre-season training and on the last night a 9 p.m. curfew had been imposed by the overbearing Walley. Canoville hadn't gone out, preferring to stay in the hotel and play cards with some of the younger players. Outside the room, they suddenly heard a commotion: Ernie Walley was severely reprimanding three individuals who had broken the curfew. Giggling as they listened from their room, they heard Walley laying into the three in his usual hectoring style. Lecture over, Walley left and, still laughing, Canoville opened the door to their room, stepped into the corridor and said to them, 'Bwoy, you get a right tellin' off innit.'

One of the three latecomers, who would later be known for making racist remarks, said to Canoville, 'What you laughing for, you black cunt? Shut up.' Canoville was amazed.

> And I'm looking at him … 'No disrespect, I know you're drunk so I know you don't know what you're saying.'
>
> 'Shut up, you black bastard.'
>
> I'm already vexed, pissed off with the club, and you're now talking to me like that. I said, 'Look mate, do it again and I'll knock you out.'
>
> He said, 'Yeah, you black cunt, come here.'
>
> That was it … so, bam, I hit him … drop him … he was knocked out.

In those circumstances, given a night to reflect on the incident and assess the situation, the sensible strategy from Canoville's teammate would have been to apologise for the drunken outburst. Pride may dictate that an apology is a step too far, in which case quietly pretending the incident never happened and hoping that it will never be spoken of again is the usual strategy adopted in these circumstances. However, Canoville's teammate had other ideas.

> When I done that he come back again in the morning … We're making our way back to London … Jonah [Keith Jones], says, 'Canners, man, you ain't going to believe this, but [teammate] coming…'

'I'll knock him out again.'

'He's got a golf club.'

'You what!'

The rumours were true. While Canoville was eating break-fast, his racist teammate, brandishing a golf club, attacked him in the canteen. Canoville had been ready for him, so fortunately he managed to escape with only a glancing blow to his shoulder, while at the same time landing a few telling blows of his own. It was Walley who pulled Canoville away from his attacker.

To keep the two apart, Canoville was driven back to London by the physio, while his attacker was allowed to travel back on the team coach. Even then, his attacker was keen to continue the dispute. He carried a brick in his bag, which he planned to attack Canoville with when they made their scheduled stop. As it turned out, Canoville didn't stop at the scheduled service station, so another confrontation was avoided, but the next day he was told not to report to the ground. He realised he would need to look for another club.

He had an offer from Brentford but eventually signed for Reading, who were newly promoted to the Second Division. A bad injury at Sunderland was followed by a year of reha-bilitation. He never recovered fully and was forced to retire at the age of twenty-six.

Canoville's career at Chelsea had been blighted by racism from start to finish. Chelsea went on to have the first black manager since Tony Collins, who managed Rochdale in the 1960s, in Ruud Gullit, who also became the first black man-ager to win a major domestic trophy. That Gullit's accept-ance into the role was achieved with little apparent hostility is due in no small part to the trials and tribulations Canoville went through. He now works with young people in schools and has made peace with Chelsea, working on their corporate side as a match-day host.

Canoville's story highlights the casual acceptance of racism in the game at the time, but it was never seen as one of football's major problems throughout the 1980s. The game itself, however, had been in a particularly dark period for some time. Attendance at games was at an all-time low; the game's image was even lower. 1985 proved to be a watershed year in English football. In March, at an FA Cup tie between Millwall and Luton Town at Kenilworth Road, thousands of pounds' worth of damage was done and thirty-one arrests were made as Millwall fans invaded the pitch and mounted battles against police. In May, a fire ripped through Bradford City's dilapidated, antiquated wooden stadium, killing fifty-six fans, and, on the same day, a teenage fan was killed after fighting between Leeds United and Birmingham City fans. On 29 May, thirty-nine Juventus fans died when a wall collapsed during skirmishes between Liverpool and Juventus fans in the Heysel Stadium in Brussels. It led to an indefinite ban on English clubs competing in Europe.

Racism was seen as a by-product of hooliganism and far-right activity in the game. This meant that any attempt to solve the problem at this stage was very narrowly focused, concerned only with terrace abuse. While ending terrace abuse was an important issue, this approach meant that the issue of racism was reduced to no more than tackling racist chanting, and then only as part of a broader crackdown on hooliganism. However, two issues had raised the wider consciousness of football fans: the impact of the Heysel Stadium disaster and the government's proposal to introduce ID cards. The banning of English teams from European competition, supported by the government, as a result of Heysel meant that sanctions were imposed not only on supporters with a record of hooligan behaviour on foreign shores, but also on groups of supporters whose record in attending matches in Europe had been exemplary. The ID card proposal required football supporters to carry an ID card to attend football matches and would have an impact on casual attendance at football matches as well as civil liberties implications. Together, these two events would spawn a new fan culture, one that would have anti-racism as one of its core objectives. It would kick-start the campaign to tackle racism in the game.

CHAPTER 8

THE CROWD GO BANANAS

'You look at the grace and the poise and when John Barnes was on blob he was absolutely fantastic.' – Viv Anderson

JUST OFF LODGE Lane, one of the main thoroughfares in Toxteth, is Ken's Barber Shop. Owned by Kenny Drysdale, the shop, like many in black communities, is where men go to chat, gossip, exchange ideas and find out what's going on.

In Kenny's shop, on the wall and taking pride of place, are two photographs of him cutting the hair of John Barnes. The images were taken on the day that Barnes officially opened the shop, not long after he signed for Liverpool. Drysdale, like most barbers, is required not only to be skilled in the wide variety of hairstyles for black men, but also to be a news agency, confidant, relationship advisor, consumer expert and political analyst. Within black communities, haircuts are tribal. A certain hairstyle identifies the wearer with a certain style, music, fashion or political outlook and throughout the years the hairstyles of footballers have reflected the changing patterns and fashions of black communities.

Within black communities, footballers have held a unique position as far as hair is concerned. For the most part, they were freed from the restrictions placed on hairstyles by workplaces and schools and, much like musicians or college students, have been largely free to have any haircut they like. In addition, their 'down time' and relative wealth afforded them the time and money to spend on their hair.

Observation of any fan forum or blog about terrible football haircuts will inevitably bring mention of George Berry. In the 1970s, wearing an Afro signified the new black pride imported from the US and copied from American cop shows, bands featured on *Top of the Pops*, and other limited opportunities to gain a glimpse into black US culture. The older generation often disliked the Afro. It was viewed as unruly and rebellious, but nonetheless it was popular amongst younger members of the community.

Eventually, the Afro went out of fashion and, in fact, became something of a source of embarrassment. The bubble perm, which was popularised by Kevin Keegan and far too many '70s footballers, was a white version of the Afro. A twist on the bubble perm with added 'wet look' became extremely popular in the early part of the decade. Called the 'Jheri curl', the style found perhaps its finest exponent in Luton's Ricky Hill, but others also sported the look. It was perfect for footballers. The style signified 'aspiration' and could be seen in any club that specialised in soul and dance music. Their hair was expensive to maintain, requiring regular attention. Hill sported one well beyond its sell-by date and must have spent a small fortune in maintaining it.

There were other variations on the style. Dave Bennett, in his Coventry days, wore a combination of a Jheri curl and a mullet. Such was the monstrosity of the mullet, it seemed difficult to top, but Bennett managed it well. As bad as it was, the mullet also had a strange impact on black hairstyles. The late David Rocastle wore a variation of Bennett's style. It had less of a 'wet look' about it, but did have a distinct sheen.

In many ways the opposite of the Jheri curl was the short-cropped hair with a parting. Before the popularity of elaborate lines and patterns, a simple, but distinct parting on one side was cut into the hair. Cropped hair with a parting was for self-styled bad boys. This trend could be seen at many a blues gathering, and its followers hated the Jheri curl crowd. Jheri curl wearers were flash, high maintenance and slept in hairnets to stop their hair drying out.

As the 1980s progressed, a style not seen for some two decades made a return. Popular in the 1950s as worn by a young Pelé at the 1958 World Cup, it was known as the 'Table Top', but the '80s version, which was called a 'Fade', was extremely popular. Les Ferdinand had a version, as did Des Walker – so much better than the woeful Jheri curl he sported early in his career. The style returned in the 2010s, as illustrated by Danny Welbeck.

At the start of the 1990s, the 'Funky Dread' became popular. This was a uniquely British invention, rather than one imported from the US. It was a cross between a Fade and dreadlocks: the sides were cut short with dreads on top. Where the traditional dreadlock was highly political, the Funky Dread said black and proud, but was less politically charged. Jason Lee of Nottingham Forest wore a version of this style and was ridiculed mercilessly for it; to some extent, it defined his career.

Over the course of the 1990s, the tribal nature of haircuts, whereby your style reflected music, fashion etc., gradually diminished. But it didn't completely end. Dreadlocks made an appearance some twenty years after they first appeared in Britain's black communities. The style had been too political for mainstream tastes in the 1970s. It was a hairstyle worn almost exclusively by Rastafarians. Its appearance in the 1990s was still political, but its religious or spiritual significance was no longer a part of its character. Richie Moran and Ricky Otto, both of Birmingham City, wore their hair this way.

Other styles weren't tribal, followed no particular association with any movement and were nothing more than a law unto themselves. Iffy Onuora, in a chance holiday meeting with a cousin of Paul Ince, was informed that the then West Ham midfielder did little with his hair except to wet it and pat it down. Ince later sported a low-maintenance crop and was clearly a man who placed the maintenance of his hair extremely low on his list of priorities. In contrast, Jamie Lawrence cared a great deal about his hair. Sporting a succession of bizarre colours on his closely cropped hair, there was no way Lawrence could have been part of a tribe, given that he would have found it difficult to recruit disciples to his cause. It's easy to forget that Lawrence wore Funky Dreads early in his career, but he is best remembered for his bleached blond, bright red, green and purple hair.

Lawrence's bleached blond affair was also seen on the heads of others. Jermain Defoe briefly deviated from his no. 1 crop to sport a blond one, and then there was David James. James's hairstyles were legendary. He had the bleached blond crop à la Defoe and Lawrence, but there was so much more to his repertoire. He had cornrows and bleached cornrows, an Afro and a bleached blond Afro, and he also had a kind of Clark Kent effort. Rio Ferdinand, along with his brother Anton, has had almost as many styles as David James and as the 2000s and 2010s progressed, many styles were recycled and reinvented, Welbeck being a case in point. Raheem

Sterling, for example, sported a similar style to Tony Daley's Jehri Fade, but with a dancehall twist.

Although he spent most of his career with a low-maintenance short crop, Barnes did sport a Jehri curl when he scored his wonder goal for England, but thankfully the style had disappeared by the time he signed for Liverpool. Barnes had been staying at a Liverpool city centre hotel when he was contacted by Charlie Sealey, a local DJ, who invited him to attend functions and social events in and around Toxteth. Sealey's approach to Barnes developed links between him and the black community that remain strong to this day. Prior to Barnes signing, Anfield was renowned as amongst the least welcome places for black footballers. Paul Davis remembered both Anfield and Goodison Park, the home of their neighbours Everton, as being hostile places to play football.

The two clubs are located less than a mile from each other and have no obvious geographical affiliation from which to draw support. However, south Liverpool, where Toxteth is located, has a tendency towards support for Liverpool. Like the rest of the city, Toxteth is a footballing hotbed, with a number of successful and entertaining sides, but very few of the city's black population had ever made it through to the professional ranks, especially compared to the likes of Manchester or Nottingham.

Cliff Marshall had rejected overtures from Liverpool and Manchester United to sign for his boyhood club, Everton. He made his debut in January 1975 and went on to make only eight further appearances for the club before becoming disillusioned with the club's stifling, safety-first approach under then manager Billy Bingham, and drifted away to spend time playing in the USA. Boyhood Liverpool fan Howard Gayle became the first black player to play for Liverpool when he made his debut in 1981. He made only a handful of first-team appearances before he moved on.

In the intervening years, however, both clubs seemed uninterested in seeking out talent from within the black community. This seeming reluctance, and the racist abuse served out to any black player who played for opposing clubs, caused a schism between the club and the predominantly Liverpool-supporting black population.

Barnes arrived at Liverpool at the beginning of the 1987/88 season. Everton had just won the league, and newly appointed manager Kenny Dalglish set about rebuilding the Liverpool side. They had tried to sign Barnes the previous February, but Graham Taylor refused to sanction the move and told Barnes he couldn't transfer until the end of the season. Barnes informed Liverpool of the situation and while the club was happy to get their man at the end of the season, Liverpool fans interpreted his failure to sign for the club as a snub and he was racially abused by Liverpool fans in one of his final games for Watford.

A hole in the Kop end meant that Liverpool's first four games were away from home and Barnes's new club had started the season well, with their new signing as the stand-out performer. An air of expectancy filled Anfield in the run-up to his home debut. Liverpool won and Barnes scored, and if there was any residual hostility to his signing, by the end of his Anfield baptism it had disappeared.

The impact that Barnes's arrival on Merseyside had on Everton fans set in motion a period of fifteen years or so in which the club was associated with racism and indeed was regularly nominated as the most racist in the Premier

League. The racists took pride in the fact that they were a white team, although whatever benefits this 'whiteness' had brought the team were difficult to identify as the team lurched from one mediocre season to another. As Barnes's arrival was supplemented by that of Mark Walters, David James, Michael Thomas and Phil Babb, the racists relished the dignity or purity of the 'all-white' yet sub-par Everton side. As terrace racism subsided even at places like Elland Road, Upton Park and Stamford Bridge, it increased at Goodison Park. Attitudes in the game were changing and a sizeable chunk of Everton's support steadfastly clung to the 1970s and '80s models of match attendance and support.

Barnes's upbringing in a military family meant that any complaints about racist abuse would have been given short shrift. He was always unmoved by the racist abuse he received, which was just as well because he got a lot of it. Barnes had a thorough footballing and sporting pedigree. He was named John Charles after the legendary Leeds, Juventus and Wales forward. His father had played for the Jamaican national side and had also been captain. After his playing days were over, Barnes senior coached the national side. He also played rugby at Sandhurst, where he trained as an army officer and became the military academy's boxing champion. Barnes's sister represented Jamaica at swimming and squash. Football was the dominant sport in Jamaica – unlike other Caribbean islands such Barbados or Antigua, where cricket was more popular – and Barnes played organised football from the age of six. At twelve, his promise attracted the attention of scouts from US universities and he was offered a football scholarship by Washington State University. His father was posted to the UK for four years, so the thirteen-year-old Barnes had planned to stay in the UK and return to

Jamaica at seventeen with a view to taking up the scholarship offer.

Barnes attended a rugby-playing school but played
football for Stowe boys' club from the ages of thirteen to
sixteen. The club, based in Harlesden in west London, was
a predominantly black team with only two white players.
Barnes used to attend matches at QPR, where he saw Derek
Richardson and remembered Vince Hilaire. He never considered the impact of Regis, Cunningham and others, as his
experience in Jamaica and his predominantly black team in
London meant that, unlike other black kids who'd grown up
in Britain, he wasn't looking for black sporting role models
and wasn't aware of racism in football. His first experience
of racism in football came when Stowe boys, as winners of
an all-London five-a-side competition, were invited to and
won the national five-a-side competition in Bradford. He'd
never been outside London and was taken aback when his
all-black team played an all-white team from Newcastle:
'There were all these lads going, "You black cunt, you black
bastard" in these funny accents.'

Playing local league football for Sudbury Court, he was spotted at age seventeen and invited to sign for Watford. With
his family due to return to Jamaica as planned, Barnes was
offered a professional contract to play football. The family
decided that they would return to Jamaica, but John would
stay in England, leave school and pursue a football career.

At Watford, Luther Blissett was already an established
player. Charlie Palmer, who would go on to acquire legendary status at Notts County, was an apprentice at Watford at
the time. David Johnson and Worrell Sterling were a year
younger than Barnes.

With the exception of the trip to Bradford for the national five-a-side tournament, Barnes had never come across racism while playing grassroots football, but as soon as he became a professional he heard it in training from his own team-mates, even towards Luther Blissett. As Graham Taylor put it, 'Some of the things said at football clubs during training would make the Race Relations Board call for an inquiry. It is all in-the-heat-of-the-moment stuff, more often than not good-humoured abuse. In the street, that is different. It is cold and calculated.'

Barnes signed as a first-year professional thus avoiding an apprenticeship. In his first match, a reserve game, he scored after thirty seconds. He followed this up with a youth game. In the first game of Watford's season, an away game against Newcastle, Blissett was sent off for kicking an opponent after suffering a racist taunt. His subsequent suspension earned Barnes a place in the squad, where he made his debut with fifteen minutes of the game remaining. He did well and earned himself a start against Chelsea, after which he became a regular in the side after only three games as a professional footballer.

His performances led to a call-up to the England U-21 side and, later, the full England squad. On a tour of South America, he scored the famous wonder goal against Brazil, officially recognised as the sixth-greatest England goal of all time. As he picked up the ball on the left-hand side he had no particular idea as to what he wanted to do. He beat one man, looked to pass, with nothing on, he beat another and got to the box looking for a shot on goal. Tony Woodcock got in his path, so he dragged the ball away and then carried on going and eventually rounded the keeper to leave himself with a tap-in. The NF claimed it didn't count.

NF members had travelled on the tour with the official

England party, along with FA officials and journalists. They aimed racist taunts at Barnes and Mark Chamberlain, the father of future England international Alex Oxlade-Chamberlain. Fellow players, FA officials and journalists did nothing to challenge the racists, too embarrassed to do anything. As Barnes said of the journalists, 'Some of those people who are the first to write about and condemn racism were on that plane at the time and did nothing.'

After his first season at Liverpool, Barnes had won the league and the team were runners-up in the FA Cup to Wimbledon, where John Fashanu and the Crazy Gang, supplemented by a cameo from Laurie Cunningham, who came on as sub, outwitted the Liverpool side. Barnes won the PFA Player of the Year and the Football Writers' Player of the Year, Thierry Henry being the only other black player to win the two awards in the same season.

Therefore, for the black community in Liverpool, what Barnes possessed that Marshall and Gayle didn't was genuine superstardom. Like Regis and Batson before him, he was prepared to build a relationship between himself and the community. Whether it was attendance at community events, award ceremonies for football tournaments or end-of-season prizes, he was generous with his time, not only within Toxteth and black community events but also in other areas of the city. In a community with few positive male role models and years of terrace racism that had caused a fracture between the club and the community, Barnes had not only gone a long way to healing that relationship but had also re-invigorated grassroots football within the community.

As for his England career, it rarely hit the heights of that brilliant night at the Maracana, the spiritual home of Brazilian football. Barnes could have won over 100 caps, but was a victim of the 'control-freak' attitude of English football. At Liverpool, he was given licence to drift from the left-hand side and take up more central areas as the play and the game dictated. For England, under a succession of managers, he was forced to stay out wide, hug the touchline and track back. Barnes cites Glenn Hoddle and Chris Waddle as two other England players who were similarly stifled on England duty and, while this is true, it was Barnes whose England performances came under the most intense criticism, the implication being that his Jamaican birth impacted upon his commitment to the national cause. Barnes was racially abused by England fans on more than one occasion when playing for the national side.

Barnes broke down barriers for both club and country and was a trailblazer for his side. His impact on the black community in Liverpool and beyond was palpable, as Liverpool attracted black supporters from well beyond Merseyside's borders. After playing for Liverpool, he would go on to play for Newcastle and Charlton and he became the first black manager in Scottish football when he managed Celtic.

CHAPTER 9

BLACK ACROSS THE BORDER

THE LATE 1980s and early 1990s began to see a radical change in the experiences of black footballers. In England, only a minority of clubs had no black professionals regularly turning out for the team. This gave the racists something of a dilemma. How could they racially abuse a black player on the opposing team when they had black players in their own side? The signing and integration into the team of a black player was often the catalyst for the end of terrace racism at most clubs.

The situation in Scotland was somewhat different. While football south of the border began slowly to come round to the idea that black footballers were here to stay, questions of racism had never really been as big an issue in the Scottish game. Scotland had had its share of both home-grown and foreign black footballers, but had been more concerned with issues of religious sectarianism. Historically, Dundee United, Hibs and, of course, Celtic had been formed by Irish Catholic communities, and while sectarianism had somewhat diminished over the course of the twentieth century in both Dundee and Edinburgh, in Glasgow it remained strong and virulent.

Graeme Souness had been appointed as player manager of Rangers in April 1986 and set about trying to reclaim the club's ascendancy over its great rivals. Capitalising on the banning of English clubs in Europe after the Heysel Stadium disaster, Souness had bought a number of England international footballers and sold them the lure of European football. The mighty Rangers hadn't won the league since 1978, while, during that period, Celtic had won it four times and the upstarts of Aberdeen and Dundee United had won it three times between them, but by the end of his first season in charge, Souness had brought the championship back to Ibrox. The signing of English players certainly caused debate in Scottish football. Scotland's best players had a tradition of moving south to England, as Souness himself had done, and here he was reversing the trend. Rangers were back on top, with a new manager, new (English) players and once again ready to take their place at the head of Scottish football. As for Celtic, they had been taken by surprise by the new money that had come into Rangers and found themselves unable to compete financially. They had been wrong-footed by the boldness of Souness's signings and his exploitation of the ban on English clubs playing in European competition. They had not only lost the league but had also been defeated by Rangers in the League Cup. Rangers had all the bragging rights; Celtic carried renewed resentment. A history of sectarianism, arch rivalry, new money and a changing of the guard. Their fierce antagonism had intensified and, if it was possible, had become even more embittered. Into this combustible environment stepped Mark Everton Walters, a 23-year-old black kid from Birmingham.

Walters's parents had arrived in Birmingham in the late 1950s and had settled in Handsworth, where he was born. His heroes were Pelé and Cyrille Regis, whom he regularly saw round the streets and restaurants in and around

Handsworth along with the two other Three Degrees. Fellow Handsworth resident Bob Hazell was another of Walters's heroes. At his school, Handsworth Primary, he played his first organised football. He went on to play for his secondary school, Holte High School, and later played Sunday league for Dunlop Terriers, a team considered as a nursery team for Aston Villa and whose manager was a scout for the club. Bob Hazell himself had played for the Terriers in previous years, as had other players like Brendan Ormsby, who would later go on to play for Villa.

It was through this connection that Walters came to the attention of the club and began to train regularly with them. As a twelve-year-old, he had attended a game at Villa where Regis had been racially abused by Villa fans and by the Holte End in particular, which had singled him out for especially vicious treatment.

Walters was an outstanding schoolboy footballer, playing for Aston boys, Birmingham boys, West Midlands boys and an England schoolboys side that included future Rangers teammate Trevor Steven. His talent was such that, while still at school, he played in an FA Youth Cup tie for Villa at Millwall against players aged eighteen. He was to suffer racist abuse for the first time as a player when he was spat at by Millwall fans as he emerged from the tunnel at the start of the game. He was fifteen years old.

Playing in and around Birmingham with a group of other talented young black footballers, he would regularly discuss with his friends the frequency with which they would suffer racism and how they might respond to it. Seeking to debunk stereotypes about the inability of black players to play in the cold, Walters made a conscious decision to always wear short-sleeved shirts when he played, a policy he practised throughout his long career. However, he and the other black boys with whom he played football considered racism an integral part of the game, both at grassroots level and in the professional set-up, as through televised coverage of football they regularly saw and heard the abuse of black players. They had several conversations as to whether they had the capacity to put up with the abuse that came with being a black footballer and a few of his contemporaries who had the talent to make a successful career in the game decided they were not prepared to play in those circumstances. For Walters, he had decided that the dream of playing professional football was too irresistible to allow racism to impede his progression into the professional ranks and upon leaving school he signed Youth Training Scheme (YTS) forms.

He made his debut as a seventeen-year-old in April 1982 against Leeds United, weeks before the greatest night in the history of the club. A three-month injury lay-off had delayed his progress into the first team for his debut and he therefore hadn't played enough time to feature in the squad that was to contest the final of the European Cup in Rotterdam.

League title-winning Villa manager Ron Saunders had resigned over a contractual dispute with the side in the quarter-finals of the European Cup. Saunders's assistant Tony Barton was appointed as manager, but the senior players ruled over the dressing room and effectively picked the side. Older players on the periphery of the squad got to go to Rotterdam while younger guys like Walters stayed at home as Villa won the trophy with a scrappy goal against the mighty Bayern Munich. The greatest moment in Villa's history was the first big disappointment of Walters's career, as he missed out on European glory.

During the following season, the older pros demanded

improved terms on their contracts, but chairman Doug Ellis wasn't prepared to pay them any more money, so the team began to break up. Too many young players came into the side and, just six years after winning the European Cup, Villa were relegated.

During this period, Walters had emerged as the side's brightest talent and was regularly watched by his brother, who attended his games, but Walters was never keen on allowing his mother to attend, as he sought to protect her from the racism directed at him and other black players.

Villa weren't buying quality players and the club lacked ambition, so when they were relegated he decided to leave his boyhood club. Everton had just won the league title and had agreed a fee and personal terms with Walters and he was set to sign. Rangers made a last-minute offer, however, and invited him up to Glasgow for talks. Walters hadn't realised just how big Rangers were. Seeing the size of the stadium, impressed with the club's ambition and seduced by the prospect of once again playing in Europe, he signed for Rangers and became the first black player of the modern era to play in the Scottish top flight since Gil Heron, the father of poet and musician Gil Scott Heron, had played for Celtic.

Walters's shock signing from Aston Villa to Rangers on New Year's Eve 1987 was met with unprecedented levels of racism within the Scottish game. He made his debut a few days later, on 2 January 1988, and could hardly have chosen a more hostile baptism. In the incendiary atmosphere of an Old Firm derby at Parkhead, Walters was subjected to staggering behaviour. Hundreds of bananas were showered on him, and Celtic fans dressed in monkey suits rained down verbal abuse. While he could have anticipated a hostile reception from Celtic supporters, the behaviour of Rangers fans was bad enough for the club to take the unprecedented step of banning some season ticket holders for racially abusing their own player.

To their credit, Celtic immediately condemned the actions of their own supporters. Match reports in the Scottish press, meanwhile, barely acknowledged the incidents, and the Scottish FA's silence on the matter was deafening.

Two weeks later, at Tynecastle, the home of Hearts, the racist abuse gained momentum and Walters was struck with a banana. Hearts chairman Wallace Mercer condemned the banana throwing. Rangers operations executive Alistair Hood demanded the Scottish Football Association act. SFA president David Will finally commented, stating that all possible action would be taken to stamp out racism and expressing the hope that 'sensible supporters will let the minority know they shouldn't be so stupid in the future'. The Scottish football authorities had never with any seriousness attempted to tackle the thorny subject of sectarianism. Prior to Souness, Rangers had stuck rigidly to its policy of never signing a Catholic. Sectarian chanting and clear discriminatory practices were accepted, seemingly as normal practice, within the Scottish game generally and amongst the Old Firm particularly. Even when sectarianism had manifested itself as violence on the terraces, which occasionally spilled onto the pitch, the usual fines and protestations from the authorities followed, but no real attempt was made to tackle the cancerous sectarianism that characterised the relationship between the country's two biggest clubs.

The Scottish media, both press and television, with few exceptions, adopted the same attitude as the SFA. There was never a concerted attempt on their part to challenge these deep-rooted sectarian attitudes.

No wonder, therefore, that the authorities were so dilatory

in their response to racism. They could hardly take club and fans to task over racism when they'd repeatedly done so little about sectarianism. In Scotland's biggest city, home to its two biggest clubs, there would be an expectation that its derby would be of a particularly intense nature. Adding the combustible material of sectarianism made the poisonous atmosphere generated at Old Firm games the most intense in European football.

BBC Scotland reporter Archie Macpherson subsequently said of Walters's debut game:

> On reflection, I should have been more vocal about it ... I wrongly saw the banana-throwing as in essence puerile; an insipid form of the Celtic's support's capacity for a wind-up, at which they are the best in the business. If more had been made of Walters's treatment at Celtic Park, he might not have had to put up with so much at Tynecastle.
> – *The Scotsman*, 30 December 2007

Macpherson's comments are illuminating on two points. Firstly, he acknowledges the behaviour as infinitely more sinister than the usual winding-up of an opposing player and, secondly, he understands the power of inaction of those with the means to do something about it. The fact that Walters's treatment passed without action or comment created an environment in which fans felt they could act with impunity. After the game at Tynecastle, Macpherson stated in his report on BBC Scotland, while holding a banana to the camera, that he'd felt 'ashamed to be Scottish'.

Walters's introduction to the Scottish game brought into sharp focus the critical role of the authorities in responding to racism in the game. The lack of leadership and inertia on the part of the SFA, as illustrated by the abuse suffered by Mark Walters, remains largely intact today.

Notwithstanding the attitudes of a section of the Rangers support, Walters was warmly welcomed within the club and settled well. Leaving home for the first time enabled him to grow up a little and the success of the club gave him a winning mentality. He was not particularly well regarded by the Scottish press, but generally he didn't read the papers.

Eighteen months after Walters's debut, Paul Elliott was signed by Celtic from Italian side Pisa. Walters and Elliott were close friends. Elliott had been signed by Villa and when Elliott had moved from London to Birmingham, Walters had taken him under his wing, shown him around Birmingham and developed a firm friendship with the Londoner. Elliott proved to be a success in Scotland, winning the Scottish Player of the Year Award as well as trophies and other honours with Celtic.

Walters went on to triumph at Rangers, winning three Scottish titles and two League Cups, before moving with Souness to Liverpool in June 1991. He won his only England cap in a 1–0 England victory over New Zealand in Auckland after an outstanding season with Rangers.

The impact of Walters and Elliott forced Scottish football to confront the issue of racism, something they had hitherto had little experience of. Like their English counterparts, the response of the Scottish FA was to do virtually nothing. In the next few years they would get an opportunity to take a firm stand and demonstrate strong leadership in combatting racism in the Scottish game. It would be interesting to see how they would respond.

CHAPTER 10

PUSHING ON WITH THE PREMIER LEAGUE

'I do think that Thatcher going in '92 was the Ancien Regime just disappearing off and ... a bit of a younger-thinking society coming in ... It was almost a generational change as well ... It was almost like National Front, racism ... and don't forget things like Heysel ... It seems these things belong to the '80s, we're children of the '90s now and that was the past and this is a new time now.' – Iffy Onuora

DAVE BENNETT WAS out for revenge. The experience the last time was going to stand him in good stead and he was determined to prepare and prepare well. They were under-dogs, but a cup final was a cup final – anything can happen – and a few of the lads who'd denied him a winner's medal last time out were still in the Spurs side. They wouldn't deny him a medal this time if he had anything to do with it.

Bennett was elected to the Coventry City Hall of Fame in 2005, one of only thirty former players to be recognised with such an honour. He played over 170 games for the Sky Blues, but if there's one game that most contributed to that Hall of Fame election over all others, it would be the one that he played on a sunny May afternoon, when Coventry won their only major honour to date. The 1987 FA Cup final was one of the best in living memory. Underdogs Coventry City had three black players in their side: Dave Bennett, who had played in the 1981 final for Manchester City, ironically against Spurs; Cyrille Regis, playing in his first and only cup final; and journeyman midfielder Lloyd McGrath, all of whom were to play roles in the key moments of the game. Tottenham had taken an early lead after only two minutes, when Allen headed in a cross from Waddle. Spurs were ahead for only six minutes before a deep cross from the left was flicked on. In the Tottenham goal, Clemence hesitated, and Bennett nipped in, took the ball past Clemence and from a tight angle turned the ball into the net to equalise for the Sky Blues. At 1–1, Regis had a goal disallowed for a seemingly innocuous infringement and just before half-time Spurs went ahead thanks to an own goal by Coventry captain – and former schoolboy opponent of Calvin Plummer – Brian Kilcline. Just past the hour, Bennett provided a peach of a cross for Keith Houchen to head a stunning equaliser, and in extra time a cross from the right by Lloyd McGrath was deflected by Spurs captain Mabbutt over his own keeper. Coventry had won, and Bennett became the first black player to be named Man of the Match in an FA Cup final. That win, coupled with his fine form, earned Cyrille Regis the last of his five England caps a few months later, in October of 1987, when he came on as substitute in an 8–0 win for England against Turkey.

Bennett's historic contribution to the 1987 final, along with the appearance of Regis, McGrath and Spurs' Chris Hughton, signalled the start of a new trend that would figure consistently in all subsequent finals. The first all-Merseyside cup final in 1986 had resulted in a 3–1 victory for Liverpool. It would be the last FA Cup final not to feature a black player. The same year brought a similar development in political representation.

By the time of the disturbances in 1985, the issue of political representation of black people as elected officials at local and national level was firmly on the agenda. Black communities had overwhelmingly given their political support to the Labour Party and, across the country, small numbers of black men and women had been elected to public office at local council level. Combatting the issue of the underrepresentation of black people as MPs, in order to turn this support for Labour into black political representation, was not a priority amongst the majority of overwhelmingly working-class minority ethnic communities and had been promoted by only a small group of councillors and other activists. The general election of 1987 resulted in the Conservatives winning a third consecutive term of office. However, Diane Abbott, Paul Boateng, Bernie Grant and Keith Vaz were elected as Labour MPs, so becoming the first minority ethnic MPs to win parliamentary seats since before the First World War. Their election raised the visibility of people of colour within mainstream institutions and cemented the emergence of a still small but burgeoning black middle class. Representation was also increasing in those areas where working-class people were organised into trade unions. In 1991, Bill Morris became the first black leader of a trade union when he was elected as General Secretary of the Transport and General Workers' Union, the country's largest. His historic election signalled the significant distance the TGWU and the black community had travelled since Tilbury dockers and union members had gone on strike in support of Powell in the days after his 'Rivers of Blood' speech in April 1968.

• • •

While Dave Bennett and his teammates were celebrating their historic achievement with the traditional winners' lap of honour, their smiles and celebrations briefly deflected attention from the fact that the game in England was in crisis. The 1980s represented the English game's nadir: crowd safety issues, illustrated by disasters at Bradford, Heysel and Hillsborough; hooliganism; increasing ticket prices; ticket allocations; and racist chanting and abuse were all blighting the game. By 1985, the Conservative government had responded by supporting UEFA's ban on English clubs in European competition, thus denying Coventry the opportunity to participate in the following season's UEFA Cup Winners' Cup competition, and had revealed plans to introduce ID cards for football fans.

In the wake of the Heysel disaster in 1985, the Football Supporters' Association (FSA) was launched to provide a voice for supporters and to campaign for the interests of ordinary fans. They provided opposition to the government's ID card scheme, demanded supporters be treated with dignity and respect, and really came of age in the aftermath of the Hillsborough disaster, when they stood up for and articulated the concerns of victims, as *The Sun* and other media outlets sought to blame fans for the disaster. When the challenge from the FSA to the official National Federation of Football Supporters' Clubs (NFFSC) came, it caught the Federation off guard. The development of independent supporters' groups proved to be the catalyst for a desire for a greater voice for fans to articulate their issues and concerns, and what emerged from this was the development of fanzines.

In tandem with the earliest development of football clubs, there had been the parallel development of organised supporters' groups. These groups played a key role in the early establishment of clubs, particularly in raising funds in order to finance key developments and infrastructural changes. These included: land purchase for grounds; building of stands; purchase of players; payment of players' wages, particularly during the off-season; stewarding; toilet facilities; turnstiles; bars; refreshments; and a host of other necessities to ensure the smooth running and day-to-day operation of the club. When football clubs were banned from organising their own lotteries by FA regulations, supporters' groups obliged by organising their own schemes to bolster clubs' income. Some of these schemes were so successful they were able to pay for quite significant developments. For example, Southend United supporters' clubs had, by 1953, raised enough money to purchase a new ground. Other supporters' groups raised money for floodlights and club premises and provided subsidies for the unemployed and old-age pensioners. The extent to which organised supporters' groups raised revenue to contribute to the material running and well-being of football clubs would, in many cases, have warranted an invitation to join the board of directors, had they been contributed by individuals or a consortium. However, with very few exceptions, no such privilege was extended to representatives of fan groups for their efforts, even when their contribution had been extensive.

By the late 1960s and early '70s, the role of supporters' groups in raising money diminished as clubs became more professional in raising revenue. The appointment of commercial directors and other, similar, roles coincided with the development of football as a TV spectacle. Therefore,

outside of the amateur game, the role of official supporters' clubs was gradually reduced to that of organising social
activities and arranging travel to away games.

As a vehicle for voicing the concerns of ordinary fans,
supporters' clubs and the NFFSC, to which they subscribed,
were meaningless. Any attempts to raise issues of concern to
fans were quickly suppressed in favour of maintaining good
relations with the clubs and football authorities. Legitimate
issues such as ticket prices and facilities for fans were, by
and large, dismissed by clubs and the FA alike. Each year
the Federation would remain virtually silent as the issue of
allocation of cup final tickets would be raised by ordinary
fans, only to be summarily dismissed with the same disdain
as in the previous year. By the 1980s, the Federation that
represented supporters' clubs was almost exclusively made
up of grey-suited, middle-aged, middle-class men, mirroring
the FA structures themselves, both at county and national
level, and was a self-serving clique, officially sanctioned
by the FA and Football League, with little relevance to the
needs of ordinary fans. Its cosy relationship with football's
hierarchy was summed up by its motto, 'To help and not to
hinder'; its philosophy was illustrated by the fact that the
Federation had never provided any opposition to the instal-
lation of perimeter fences at football grounds and had done
little to oppose racist behaviour amongst fans.

The participants from the FSA were by a long way a
younger and more radical breed of football fans, and
alongside the FSA came the development of football fanzines. They were keen to provide a voice that went largely
unheard amongst supporters and were opposed to two
prevailing notions of supporters that existed within the
game at this time. Firstly, they were opposed to the official

supporters' clubs that were characterised by those within the NFFSC. These were often closely monitored, sanctioned and controlled by the board of directors themselves and were usually conservative in outlook and membership. From the outset, the new fanzines sought to provide an anti-establishment voice, which often turned out to be highly critical of the board of directors, highly critical of poor team performance, and irreverent towards players and management staff, and which provided entertaining, witty and often caustic observations about the current state of the club and its main rivals.

Although each fanzine highlighted different issues depending on what was going on at their respective clubs, they also covered topics such as ticket prices, lack of investment, away travel arrangements, policing and stewarding, fashion and music. They also provided fans with a distinct, authentic terrace perspective and, while some were opposed to football violence, others adopted a somewhat indifferent view of hooligan behaviour.

Whatever their perspective, however, the second prevailing notion of football fans that fanzines sought to challenge was the idea that fans were all racist, neo-Nazi hooligans. The fanzine movement sought to distance itself from racism, provided a forum to discuss the impact of racist abuse and behaviour, and tried to put pressure on clubs to take action against it.

Every black footballer of this era recognised Elland Road, the home of Leeds United, as a singularly distasteful place to have a game of football. As well as the racist abuse inside the ground that greeted black players, by 1987, the area around the ground was littered with far-right groups openly selling racist and fascist material.

This was the point at which a group of fans, sick of the poisonous atmosphere at the ground, came together under the auspices of Leeds Trades Council and formed Leeds United Against Racism and Fascism (LUARAF) specifically to combat racism and the activities of the far right. When police were told that the group was to peacefully leaflet the ground with anti-racist material, they were hostile. Shamefully, through press statements, the police let it be known that they feared political violence and portrayed the anti-racists as troublemakers. Far-right groups had been allowed to harass and intimidate black supporters and players with impunity for well over a decade and now, when anti-racists tried to organise against the neo-Nazis, the police opposed their actions. The leafleting campaign outside the ground was encouraging: tentative at first, but once it was clear LUARAF weren't outsiders, the support grew. They initially produced anti-racist leaflets and stickers, but this soon became a fanzine entitled *Marching Altogether*, which had anti-racism as its founding principle and which regularly lampooned, castigated and otherwise ridiculed the behaviour of racists and the far right. Despite LUARAF informing them of its actions, the club claimed not to know who had produced the anti-racist material and threatened to sue the campaigners for unauthorised use of the club badge on their leaflets. Far-right groups had appropriated the club logo for years and placed it on all manner of racist literature and had never been threatened with legal action.

Club officials were eventually persuaded to meet LUARAF, but only after considerable pressure from the council, who owned the ground, having bailed the club out some years before when it had amassed a mountain of debt. The club denied there were any problems and demanded proof.

LUARAF, in conjunction with the local trades council and Anti-Fascist Action, produced it in bucketloads. In March 1988, they published their report 'Terror on the Terraces'.

The evidence contained in the report was gleaned entirely from previous media reports, so no new evidence was uncovered and all of it had been readily available to the club had they sought it. It included findings from the Popplewell Inquiry into rioting at the Birmingham City *v.* Leeds match in May 1985, where a teenage boy had died. The report had identified racist behaviour and fascist organisations as key elements of the disturbances, including large groups of Leeds hooligans parading in Nazi armbands. The evidence also included details of racist attacks, the use of match days as opportunities for the far right to meet and organise, and details of an undercover investigation by the *Yorkshire Evening Post* into Leeds National Front, whereby journalists had made contact with the group at Elland Road. There were also details of racist chanting, sales of fascist material, and fascist recruitment on match days. If the challenge by the club's directors to find evidence was designed to deflect criticism from their lack of action, it backfired spectacularly.

The report attracted widespread media coverage, including a *Daily Mirror* headline on 29 March 1988 that read: 'Fascist, racist and violent – club branded a breeding ground for the NF thugs'. The club had thrown down the gauntlet to LUARAF and had had their bluff called by the report. The negative media criticism of the club, which they would have been anxious to avoid, left them with no option other than to act. They produced anti-racist statements signed by the manager Billy Bremner and all the players, and distributed them to fans.

The local Labour council – who, due to their ownership of the ground, had local councillors on the board – had also, like the club, denied knowledge of any problems. They now suddenly remembered that they were on the board not as fans but as elected officials who should oppose racist abuse and represent the best interests of the club, and began to suggest that racists should be banned from the ground and other council facilities. Finally, a new police commander replaced his previous, highly critical, colleague, which led to a much healthier police attitude.

Slowly, due to persistent activism, continued pressure from the council and an eventual change of management at the club, the atmosphere at Elland Road started to improve. Regular statements from the club's senior management condemning racist chanting and regular adverts against racist behaviour appeared in the programme.

It was at this stage that the club took its anti-racist work in a new and altogether more proactive direction, one that would begin to build bridges and heal the rift that the club had effectively engineered between itself and local black and Asian communities. Howard Wilkinson was appointed manager in October 1988 and represented a new and defining break from Leeds' greatest ever manager, Don Revie, who had transformed the club in the 1960s and '70s from a provincial outfit in a city where Rugby League and cricket were the dominant sports into European powerhouses. Leeds's four previous managers, Allan Clarke, Eddie Gray, Billy Bremner and Norman Hunter, had all played in that successful Leeds side and were steeped in Revie-era culture and folklore. The team and, by extension, the club had famously developed a siege mentality during that period. This team had fostered a fearsome reputation on the pitch as a skilful but distinctly tough and combative side. During Revie's tenure, a strong bond between the team and its fans had also developed. As the only club in a large city, it had drawn support not only from within Leeds, but also from other parts of West Yorkshire, and had extended this support into significant parts of North Yorkshire, therefore giving it a large fan base. This siege mentality and bond between team and supporters had been perfectly illustrated in a league game between Leeds and West Brom at The Hawthorns in 1982. In serious crowd disturbances, forty-six Leeds fans had been arrested, fencing at the ground had been ripped apart and a pitch invasion had eventually been quelled by baton-wielding police. When asked about the behaviour of Leeds fans, manager Allan Clarke stated that he hadn't seen the pitch invasion and that he was concentrating on team matters. He reiterated that Leeds support was the best in the country, said he was uninterested in second-hand reports of violence, and wouldn't be drawn on suggestions that he should condemn the behaviour of the fans. That mentality had continued throughout the period when Revie's four protégés had managed the side, and if there was little chance managers were going to criticise the fans for violence, criticism of any type of fan misbehaviour was off limits.

Howard Wilkinson's appointment therefore represented a clean break with the past as he set about rebuilding the side. Off the field, Ces Podd had been appointed as the club's community development officer and he set about the task of forging links between the club and local black and Asian communities. Leeds had had the legendary South African Albert Johanneson as its first black player in the 1960s, and Johanneson had formed an integral part of Revie's first successful side. He had become the first black player to appear

in an FA Cup final, in 1965, and his participation and ongoing legacy had attracted interest in the club from within the
black community. Podd had friends from Chapeltown who
wanted desperately to go to Elland Road to watch Leeds
play, but because of far-right activity in particular and the
racist atmosphere in general, the ground was patently unsafe
for supporters from black and Asian communities to attend,
so that notion was completely out of the question. Seeking to
build upon the legacy of Albert Johanneson, Podd could have
taken on a similar role at Bradford City, but the opportunity
to make a difference in his home town and amongst his own
and other communities was an opportunity too good to miss.

The new hierarchy knew that the club desperately needed
to shake off its racist and violent image. Terrace racism at
English grounds was becoming increasingly polarised. It was
largely absent at clubs that had black players, and could be extremely vicious at the increasing minority of clubs that didn't.
In addition, a new generation of footballers were coming into
the game who'd grown up in and around black communities
and had forged friendships and working relationships with
their black peers in schools and through football. At Wimbledon, a team containing Eric Young, Terry Phelan, John
Fashanu and the substitute Laurie Cunningham had won
the 1988 FA Cup final. Vinnie Jones, a member of that side
and a close friend of Fashanu, epitomised the new breed of
footballer who was beginning to enter the game. Jones had
pointedly remarked at Wimbledon that racism wasn't something that should be dealt with solely by black players. As
role models and team members, white players had to take
a stand and demonstrate that racism was unacceptable. The
response to racist abuse on the pitch by opponents was often
organised by Jones and other white players like Dennis Wise.

It ensured that the issue was a team matter as far as Wimbledon were concerned. If you were going to abuse one of their black players, you had to deal with the Crazy Gang as a whole. That was the Wimbledon way, so when Jones signed for Leeds in 1989, he was informed that the club wanted to tackle racism in and around the club and that he would be an asset in assisting the club to achieve that aim.

Podd was surprised to be appointed to the role of community development officer. There were a number of former Leeds players who were out of work and could easily have been appointed and there were other potential candidates who had much stronger ties to the club than he did, but the club clearly appointed him to bring a fresh new perspective to its work and viewed him as someone who could build bridges between the club and black and Asian communities. He was given licence to develop the role as he saw fit.

He introduced a programme of activity to ensure the club was seen as welcoming. Each week they would go into schools and deliver coaching sessions and conduct anti-racist work. Wilkinson was highly supportive, as was club captain Gordon Strachan, who would ensure that any request for a player to conduct community work was met. If he couldn't get a player to attend, Strachan would attend himself. Chris Whyte, a former teammate of Paul Davis at Arsenal, was a massive supporter of the work and Vinnie Jones was a brilliant advocate for the programme. Jones proved to be highly popular with children and young people and would enthusiastically slide tackle children and generally throw himself around as they played games of football during coaching sessions.

However, Podd was keen to ensure that his community work was more than mere photo opportunities and PR bluster. Coaches working on community programmes would bring groups of children to the ground on match days, show them the changing rooms and other parts of the stadium and take them to the game. The work was also linked closely with the Youth Development Centre under the leadership of Paul Hart. Podd and Hart would work together to identify and develop promising players, and Podd was responsible for coaching the under-16s, where he worked with a generation of talented players including Aaron Lennon, Jonathan Woodgate and Harpal Singh, the latter of whom would become one of the first Asian players to play professional football.

The campaign begun by a group of ordinary fans had succeeded in shaming the club into action. To its credit, the club developed a more proactive approach and through Podd's leadership built strong links with local black and Asian communities. While there were sporadic outbreaks of overt racist abuse over the next two and a half decades, by 1991, the far right had given up and had ceased to organise and have a presence in and around the stadium. It had taken only four years for a small group of right-minded fans to see off the fascists, who'd had the run of Elland Road for over a decade, and, in so doing, they had proved what strides could be made with will, determination and good organisation. Other fan initiatives were launched in the wake of the Leeds United campaign, such as Leicester City's *When You're Smiling*, a fanzine that also had anti-racism as its founding principle.

A stand had been made. Along with providing a vehicle through which fans could air their views on a whole range of issues, the new fans' movement had sought to challenge the popular perceptions of fans as right-wing, racist hooligans. Here was evidence that anti-racist campaigns could be

launched and, most importantly, could be effective. Confidence, as everyone in football knows, can take those with
modest resources further than they imagined.

Finally, the government took action. ID scheme proposals,
which had been put forward under the Thatcher-led government, had been shelved in the wake of the Hillsborough disaster. The scheme had aimed to issue football fans with an ID
card in order to attend games. The impact of the proposals
would be to infringe upon the civil liberties of football fans
and prevent the attendance at games of casual supporters.
Thatcher's government had also actively supported UEFA's
decision to ban English clubs from Europe, and amongst the
vast majority of new supporters' groups and fanzines the
government was viewed as being decidedly anti-football. So
when the Conservatives ditched Thatcher in the wake of opposition to the poll tax, the new John Major-led government
sought to place some clear blue water between itself and
the previous administration. It deliberately sought to play up
the new Prime Minister's footballing credentials and Major
and David Mellor, Cabinet minister and Treasury Secretary,
made much of the fact that they were long-standing Chelsea fans. In 1991, the government introduced the Football
Offences Act, making it unlawful for spectators to throw
missiles, to get onto the pitch or – inserted as something of
an afterthought – to participate in racist chanting. However,
under the terms of the Act, it was only an offence if mass
chanting took place. Significantly, individual acts of racist
abuse were not unlawful and the practicalities of arresting
hundreds or thousands of people all engaged in racist chanting were never addressed. In terms of a sanction against
racist abuse, it was of little use, but, nonetheless, the legislation was important in representing a shift in government

discourse on racism in football. Whereas racist abuse had previously barely featured as a government issue, a degree of lip service was now being paid.

• • •

Meanwhile, historic events were taking place on the pitch. The 1987/88 season would prove to be a personal triumph for John Barnes. In his first season after a big-money move to Liverpool from Watford, his new side had won the title at a canter. As we have seen, he'd also finished as that season's PFA Player of the Year and the Football Writers' Footballer of the Year, thus becoming not only the first black player to win either award but also the first black player to win both in the same season. Barnes's club, Liverpool, were narrowly denied a historic 'double double' when Wimbledon won that year's FA Cup final.

In the previous March, England had played Holland in a pre-Euro 1988 friendly at Wembley. BBC commentator John Motson had described as 'good-natured barracking' the racist abuse meted out to then European Footballer of the Year and world's most expensive player Ruud Gullit every time he was in possession of the ball. The Euro 1988 championships saw perhaps the most serious disturbances of any football tournament, with running battles between England and opposing fans. Once again, there was significant evidence of far-right involvement in the disorder. England was to lose all three games in the group stage and Gullit was to captain the Dutch to victory at the tournament.

In the wake of England's disastrous campaign at Euro 1988, it was clear that changes were necessary. Paul Davis had received a call-up to the squad and was set to win his first cap in October of 1988. In a game against Southampton, he'd received particularly close attention from Southampton midfielder Glenn Cockerill. Cockerill had committed a series of fouls and late challenges on Davis, who had asked the referee for more protection, but no action had been taken against Cockerill. When Cockerill stamped on him, the normally mild-mannered Davis exacted revenge. Davis had been an excellent all-round sportsman in his youth, and his response demonstrated that had he taken up boxing, there's a good chance he would have been a decent pugilist. Davis floored Cockerill with an impeccable left hook and in the process broke Cockerill's jaw. The incident wasn't seen by the referee or the other officials, but was captured by TV cameras and Davis was charged by the FA. He was advised by Arsenal officials not to say anything in the lead-up to his FA hearing and rumours circulated in the media that Cockerill had racially abused him. This hadn't been the case, but Davis's silence on the matter exacerbated the situation. Had his punch been seen by the referee and he had been sent off in the game, he would have received a far more lenient sanction. A new ITV deal to show football matches meant that the broadcaster was keen to show off their new product and had displayed Davis's punch several times and in super-slow motion. The subsequent media hype around the incident had contrived to significantly raise the profile of Davis's action, and meant that the FA was under considerable pressure to make an example of him. He was served with a nine-match ban – at that time, the longest in the history of English football – and he received a £3,000 fine, a substantial amount for a footballer in 1988. Davis was removed from the England squad and lost the opportunity to represent his country. He would never gain an England cap.

Meanwhile at Davis's club, under the management of George Graham, opportunities for black footballing talent continued to reap benefits, both on and off the field. Arsenal's youth system continued to produce some outstanding black footballing talent. David Rocastle, Michael Thomas and Kevin Campbell had emerged from the system to supplement Davis as regular members of the first-team squad and had all been called up to the England under-21 set-up. In the most dramatic end to a league campaign in the competition's history, for the second season in succession Liverpool missed out on winning the double. After beating city rivals Everton in a dramatic FA Cup final, they lost out on the league to Arsenal in that pulsating night at Anfield. Moments before Michael Thomas's dramatic winner, John Barnes had an opportunity to whack the ball into the Kop, where no doubt it would have taken an age to be returned. Liverpool would have had a chance to regroup and regain their shape and would no doubt have seen out the final few seconds to claim the title and add to their FA Cup triumph. Barnes had cut in menacingly from the right wing and was seeking to get a shot on goal or make a chance for a teammate to slot the goal that would have left Arsenal two short and, in so doing, kill off their title challenge. Given the same circumstances again, Barnes would probably still have taken the same option as he did in those dying seconds, except that he would no doubt doubly ensure that he'd have beaten Richardson, who stole the ball from him. In the event, Richardson returned it to keeper John Lukic, who was able to quickly throw the ball out to Dixon, who'd pumped it forward to Smith, who'd turned the ball on to Thomas. A poke forward, a lucky ricochet, a quick shuffle of the feet, a toe poke and that forward roll and swallow-like dive in iconic celebration heralded Arsenal's first title in eighteen years.

The Hillsborough disaster represented the end of the 1980s in more ways than one. The game had received several warnings, but a combination of complacency and contempt had meant that those warnings had gone unheeded. The crush at the Leppings Lane end of the ground, resulting in the death of ninety-six Liverpool fans at the 1989 FA Cup semi-final, came after previous crushes in semi-final games at the ground, where tragedy had been avoided by the grace of God. What should have been a loud, wailing alarm bell to the authorities was instead treated as an opportunity for a collective lie-in, as the health, safety and well-being of fans were treated with thinly veiled contempt. The Popplewell Inquiry in the wake of the fire at Bradford City should have been the catalyst for wholesale improvements to football grounds, but by focusing solely on the specific and unique circumstances of the fire at Valley Parade, an opportunity to prioritise the well-being of supporters in general was missed by those with responsibility for leading the game. The Taylor Report into the causes of the Hillsborough disaster focused on two areas. The interim report into the causes of the disaster on the day concluded that police incompetency led to the deaths of the ninety-six. While this was broadly welcomed in so far as it absolved Liverpool supporters of blame for the disaster in the face of unprecedented media hostility from *The Sun* newspaper particularly, and other media outlets in general, it failed to hold other agencies to account, including the FA as organisers of the competition and selectors of Hillsborough as the venue for the game without adequate checks in place to ensure its suitability.

It was, however, the final report by Taylor that was to

have the biggest impact on the game in England and, by extension, on the fortunes of black footballers. The immediate
impact of Taylor was to remove perimeter fencing at football grounds, but its recommendation to bring in all-seater
stadiums to clubs in the top two tiers of English football
would have the impact of ushering in the Premier League,
the explosion of money within the game, the development
of football as a global game with a global presence and the
recruitment to the UK of footballers from all four corners of
the globe. All of this was to have a profound effect on the
game and on the experiences of black footballers.

• • •

As Lord Justice Taylor was preparing his report into Hillsborough, on 15 July, just outside Madrid, a car driven by
Laurie Cunningham crashed, tragically killing the West
Brom and Real Madrid legend. He was just thirty-three years
old. Although he was entering the twilight of his career and
his electric change of pace no longer allowed him to glide
effortlessly past defenders, he still had much to offer. He
could have done a decent job for another season or two, but,
more importantly, the game sorely missed the opportunity
to honour one of its pioneers, to capture his experiences, to
get his perspective on the abuse he suffered and the ongoing campaign for equality, to hear about his time with West
Brom, England and Real Madrid and to understand how the
most mild-mannered and gentle of men managed to become
a member of the Crazy Gang.

• • •

In July 1990, UEFA had announced that English clubs were to be readmitted to European competition after the five-year ban in the wake of the Heysel disaster. Liverpool were forced to serve an additional year of the ban due to their fans' involvement at Heysel. The lifting of the ban was dependent, however, upon the good behaviour of English fans at Italia '90. During that year, John Barnes had once again won the Football Writers' Association's Footballer of the Year Award, the second occasion he had been honoured in this way, but undoubtedly his greatest achievement that season had been to pen and deliver the rap on the greatest football song ever, as 'World in Motion' provided the soundtrack to England's campaign at that year's World Cup.

As well as Barnes, Des Walker and Paul Parker were also selected for the squad. Barnes played in the group games and in the second round and quarter-final against Cameroon, but missed the epic semi-final against West Germany. Parker played in all but the opening group game and had provided the cross that led to Lineker's equaliser against the Germans. Walker was to play in all England's games, earning rave reviews in the process. His performances earned him a move to Serie A, to play under Sven-Göran Eriksson at Sampdoria. His time at Sampdoria somewhat derailed his career. At Forest he had played as a central defender in a back four and was required to do nothing but defend, needing only a rudimentary approach to distributing the ball. At Sampdoria, he was required to play on the left-hand side of a back three or at left-back. Here, his positional sense went awry and his poor distribution was horribly exposed. In addition, injury had dulled his greatest asset, his pace, and he was never quite the same imperious force he'd been in his first spell at Forest.

After a year he returned to England to join Sheffield Wednesday, with whom he stayed for eight seasons.

Besides Arsenal, other clubs were beginning to include significant numbers of black players as regular members of the team. For the 1990 FA Cup final between Crystal Palace and Manchester United, Palace fielded a record five black players in the side that lost to United after a replay. Mark Bright, Andy Gray, John Salako and Richard Shaw had started the game for Palace. The semi-fit Ian Wright had come off the bench to score twice for Palace, making him the first black player to score twice in a cup final since Mike Trebilcock of Everton had achieved that feat in the 1966 final against Sheffield Wednesday. The side had been promoted to the First Division via the play-offs in 1989 and their meteoric rise had been spearheaded by the Wright and Bright strike force. The side, including its black players, had performed brilliantly in the Second Division, where Wright and Bright in particular garnered a great deal of attention. They had continued to perform brilliantly again when they were promoted. They had reached a cup final and finished third in the First Division, the highest position in the club's history. Therefore, club chairman Ron Noades should have been well placed to adequately assess the contribution of black players in his side. In an interview in a 1991 TV documentary, *Great Britain United*, Noades had suggested that black players had great skill and were great athletes but couldn't read the game: they could only play with the ball in front of them and needed tough white players to get them through the winter. He added that 'the black players at this club lend the side a lot of skill and flair, but you also need white players in there to balance things up and give the team some brains and some common sense'.

His opinions reflected the ideas that had confronted black players since the mid-1970s. The side would never have been so successful unless every player had performed brilliantly, from sunny Saturdays at Brighton in August to wild and wet January nights in Carlisle and Sunderland. Noades's remarks did his players, both black and white, a great disservice. Soon after his comments, his side began to break up. Wright was transferred to Arsenal and Bright went to Sheffield Wednesday.

In August, the Premier League was launched at the start of the 1992/93 season. Although the league was launched amid razzmatazz and US-style marketing, at least outwardly, little had changed from its previous incarnation – but it wasn't to last. It was soon to create a system of haves and have-nots within the professional game as the new broadcasting money turned the English top division into a global brand and began to attract players from across the world. Chapeltown-born Brian Deane scored the first ever Premier League goal for Sheffield United, in a 2–1 win over Manchester United.

Many sides now fielded a significant number of home-grown black players and as the development of a squad, rather than a team, began to increase in importance in the Premier League era, more black players got the opportunity to play in the top flight. Aston Villa under manager Ron Atkinson regularly fielded as many as seven black players: Ugo Ehiogu, Tony Daley, Earl Barrett, Cyrille Regis, Paul McGrath, Dwight Yorke and Dalian Atkinson appeared frequently and were supplemented occasionally by Brian Small and Martin Carruthers. At Wimbledon, Roger Joseph, Terry Phelan, Robbie Earle, Carlton Fairweather, Steve Anthrobus, Andy Clarke and John Fashanu were all members of the first-team squad. At Crystal Palace, Ian Wright, Mark

Bright, Eric Young, Bobby Bowry, Richard Shaw, Dean Gordon, Paul Mortimer, Stan Collymore, John Salako and Andy Gray were members of the 1991/92 squad. The sense of isolation that the earlier generation of black players faced was beginning to disappear as more and more sides featured black players on a regular basis. Some teams, like Everton and Blackburn, provided pockets of resistance to the multicultural new league, but by and large the numbers of black players in the leagues and at clubs began to change dressing room dynamics and engendered a new confidence amongst black players.

Michael Johnson began his career just prior to the Premier League era and had paid close attention to the mood and confidence of black players in the game. As more black players entered the game from home and abroad, and racist abuse from the terraces began to wane, it also began to diminish on the pitch. The culture of the game was changing. Whereas in previous years opponents would employ racist abuse as a legitimate part of trying to intimidate and rile an opponent in order to gain a psychological advantage, this strategy was becoming increasingly anachronistic. White players were growing up in multiracial teams throughout their formative years, within club youth structures and at grassroots level, and were less likely to resort to racist abuse. Additionally, the generation of black players entering the game were of a more confident and assertive breed altogether and were having an impact in the dressing room and on the pitch.

In previous eras, the culture within the dressing room had been set by the senior professionals. This often meant that they formed cliques that would protect their own interests and they would have the ear of the manager and chairman. At many clubs, for a young player to raise an issue with the manager or chairman, they would often have to do so via the senior players. Besides this, the pay structure often reflected the seniority of the players. As more money flowed into the game, most of it went on players' wages and, as players' agents became more prevalent, the old pay structure's link to seniority could no longer be maintained. As young men with large amounts of disposable income entered dressing rooms, the old cliques began to break down into something more fluid. The old divide between senior players and their younger counterparts began to break down. Friendship groups in dressing rooms could now be based on age, overseas status, language, music and other factors. Furthermore, players were more likely to move freely between dressing room groups, which reflected the more open and looser arrangements. Therefore, as Michael Johnson stated, 'There was an area of the dressing room where black players would gather together. It was a cultural thing ... you had an understanding you could talk ... and one of them's got cream ... or hair products.'

As the confidence increased in using cocoa butter and body creams after washing, which, in previous eras, would very likely have been met with a disapproving, overly masculine reaction from senior players, now they would be freely shared around the dressing room. In addition to the use of skin and hair products, other forms of black cultural expression began to be asserted. In many dressing rooms, younger black players introduced and dictated music policy. With support from younger white players, the older players, managers and coaches who objected soon realised that this was a battle they were going to lose. Slowly but surely, the 'ghetto blaster' and, later, oversized headphones became ubiquitous dressing room accompaniments. With

the confidence that came with a more democratic atmosphere in the dressing room, it was inevitable that this would
translate onto the pitch. English football grounds began to
witness the widespread use of greetings and hand gestures
that were popular within black communities. The grip,
the touch and the high five were now being used amongst
players as greetings before kick-off and in the aftermath of
games that had produced a good result, as well as at strategic points in matches. They also appeared during goal
celebrations, which were becoming increasingly elaborate
and choreographed. Amongst black footballers, the bogle
began to make an appearance on English football pitches.
Bogling was a style of dance taken directly from dancehall
culture and was employed by a number of black players to
celebrate goals.

While the introduction of overt expressions of black culture had occurred in part because of increased numbers of
black players into dressing rooms, wider changes in society and within youth culture were also having an impact.
Dance music culture was having a huge impact on the way
in which groups of young people were interacting with
each other. The tribalism of youth sub-cultures was beginning to blur. Where there had previously been varied groups
such as mods, punks, goths, casuals and other tribes, who
would socialise separately, many young people within these
groups now began to embrace dance culture. Within towns
and cities, young people began to attend raves and clubs
to dance. Whereas previously black kids and white kids,
middle-class kids and working-class kids may have developed their own unique sub-cultures and may have expected
to have limited opportunities for social interaction, dance
culture broke down these barriers. Adding to this new

openness was the impact of the dance drug ecstasy, whose effects dovetailed perfectly with the new open culture of the movement. Amongst this generation, racism simply became unfashionable, something that belonged to a bygone age. Furthermore, groups of men who had regularly participated in hooligan and racist behaviour at football matches began to cease hostilities, albeit temporarily, as dance culture took hold, and many left their fighting and racist days behind them for ever. The government introduced the Criminal Justice Bill, which had wide-reaching implications for the rights of UK citizens. The Bill made changes to the right of silence, gave greater rights to police to take and maintain body samples, and broadened powers of 'stop and search'. It also sought to specifically criminalise young people who wanted to do nothing more than have a good time and dance. The impact was that young people who were otherwise hard-working, well-meaning and harmless could be subject to arrest and imprisonment for dancing in a club, field or empty warehouse, and they immediately made the parallels with the experiences of those black young people who were at risk of being criminalised by discriminatory policing and application of the law.

While of course all young people weren't necessarily involved in dance culture, the idea that racism was something from a bygone age affected much broader groups of young people, including footballers, so that young white people, particularly in large towns and cities, were far more familiar and comfortable with black culture due to wide social interaction. These wider societal changes were reflected in the relationships and culture of the dressing room. This new, more open, environment provided the conditions that would enable football to embrace change.

• • •

Michael Johnson was born in Nottingham to Jamaican parents, who raised him in a strict religious environment. His family were friends with the Anderson family and Johnson had met Viv on a few occasions when he was he was a child. Johnson had been spotted playing for Nottingham boys' team and was invited to sign schoolboy forms for Notts County. His mother took some convincing and he was only allowed to train with County on the condition that he maintained a commitment to education and school work. Upon leaving school in 1989, he signed YTS forms and, while still a trainee, made his first-team debut in 1989 at the age of seventeen. At County, at the time, a trainee was selected to travel with the first team on away trips. They would run errands and get anything that was needed for first-team players. This might include obtaining liniment, tape, studs and laces and also taking orders and collecting the fish and chips after the game. He'd been asked take his boots with him, which he found strange, but had been told he would run out on the pitch during the warm-up in order to experience the atmosphere. During the trip he was summoned to the front of the coach. Feeling apprehensive and racking his brains to think of what he might have done wrong, he was asked by manager Neil Warnock if he was ready to play.

His debut could hardly have been more auspicious. County were away at Arsenal and the young Johnson was tasked with marking none other than Ian Wright. Wright was one of Johnson's heroes. Two years previously, Johnson had been collecting Panini stickers of Ian Wright and here he was up against him, trying to prevent one of the hottest properties in English football from continuing his rich vein of form.

During the game, Johnson's centre-back partner suffered a serious injury, which necessitated a team re-shuffle. With a centre-back pairing of a seventeen-year-old debutant and a forward acting as a makeshift centre-half on the County side, Arsenal ran out comfortable 2–0 winners. Johnson had done well against Wright, however, and had kept him reasonably quiet, though, in a moment of class, Wright had twisted him inside and out to score Arsenal's second.

After the game, Wright had sought out the still star-struck Johnson to give him some sage advice. He told him he was going to be a good young player and suggested he be more patient in his defending. Specifically, he should refrain from trying to nick the ball in front of his marker and stop getting into wrestling situations with his opponents. It was good advice that Johnson was to heed for the rest of his career.

Johnson made a few more appearances that season, in which County were relegated. He became a first-team regular the following season, in which County struggled but avoided a second successive relegation. However, the following season, they succumbed to relegation. At the start of season 1995/96, he received a call from Birmingham City manager Barry Fry, who told him they needed a centre-half and had been watching him. Ever the wheeler-dealer, Fry said he was certain he could get the twenty-year-old Johnson cheap in a tribunal. The Blues had a massive fan base and had just been promoted to the Championship. The club were also on the up and the atmosphere at County was subdued. Johnson jumped at the chance and was to play for Birmingham for the next nine years. During his time at City, they achieved promotion under Steve Bruce and got to a League Cup final under Trevor Francis, which they lost to Liverpool. He still maintains close links with Birmingham.

Johnson's reaction to the racist abuse he received differed to that of previous generations of black footballers. At a game at Millwall, he'd gone to retrieve the ball after it had gone out of play and had heard someone from the crowd shout the 'N' word at him. Looking round to see who had made the remark, he realised it had come from a young boy, who was with his father or grandfather. Both were laughing. Like previous generations of black footballers, he was advised that scoring or winning was the best answer to the racists, but for Johnson this wasn't a solution as the thought process of the racist wouldn't be challenged and the attention would be turned to the next black player.

When, in 1990, former Cabinet minister Norman Tebbit suggested that the 'cricket test' would be a good barometer of ethnic minorities' Britishness, within black communities, the discussion confirmed for a second – and, by this time, increasingly third – generation of black people that they were in a no-win situation. Mainstream politicians and media continually questioned the patriotism of black people while simultaneously informing them that to be black and British was incompatible. Because Tebbit's test sought to deny black people the opportunity to celebrate their heritage and also respect that of their parents, black people rejected Tebbit's narrow, myopic vision of identity and actively set out to fail his test.

Former England striker and TV pundit Jimmy Greaves had picked up Tebbit's central theme when he wrote an article in which he questioned John Barnes's commitment to England, due to his Jamaican birth. At Liverpool, the team were set up to get the most out of their brightest star. Barnes would receive the ball on twenty or thirty occasions per game and was given licence to roam across the front line. For England, Barnes's talents were horribly wasted as he would receive the ball only six or seven times per game and was required to stick rigidly to England's left side. He rarely produced a performance for England to rival those of his club. As a pundit and ex-England international, Greaves could have provided a degree of insight and analysis into the differences in performance between the John Barnes of Liverpool and that of England. Instead he seemed to play to the gallery and ingratiate the decidedly right-wing element of the England fan base by invoking Tebbit's sentiments. In this atmosphere and in an insipid England performance against a weak San Marino side, Barnes was specifically singled out for booing and was racially abused by a section of England fans in a World Cup qualifier in February 1993.

The incident demonstrated that more needed to be done. Buoyed by the success of grassroots campaigns at Leeds and elsewhere, the Commission for Racial Equality (CRE) and the Professional Footballers' Association launched the 'Let's Kick Racism Out of Football' campaign at the beginning of season 1993/94. The players' organisation had taken a leading role in the initiative, and Garth Crooks and Brendon Batson as leading members had played an important role in highlighting issues of racism and putting the organisation at the forefront of the campaign for equality.

By 1997, the FA, the Premier League and the Football Foundation were funding the campaign and had ninety-one of the ninety-two professional clubs sign the Kick It Out charter. The exception was York City: its chairman, Douglas Craig, a former Conservative councillor, had decided that there was no need for such an initiative at Bootham

Crescent and was a vociferous opponent of the 'Kick Racism Out of Football' initiative. Craig's objections reflected the anti-equality backlash that was a feature of all progressive campaigns to promote equality. It was not until April 2001 that the club agreed to sign up.

The launch of the campaign had come weeks after an important milestone had been achieved. On a June evening in Boston on a tour of the USA, Paul Ince became the first black player to captain the England side when he led his team to play against the host nation. Some eighteen months later, Ince was to be a bit-part player in an event that was to change the landscape of anti-racism in the English game forever. It involved a mercurial Frenchman and was to be played out not at Manchester United's self-styled 'Theatre of Dreams' but at Selhurst Park, the south London home of Crystal Palace.

CHAPTER 11

MAKING A STAND

'Have fans got a responsibility? They wouldn't behave like that at work or in the street. Fans can't go round going, "OK, I can do exactly what I want because I'm in a football ground." That started changing.' – Iffy Onuora

WE WILL NEVER know how many footballers were lost to the game in the days before the authorities moved to impose sanctions for racist behaviour in the game, when issues of racism were scrutinised in far less detail than they are today. Amongst those who were lost, there may have been someone who was able to earn a decent living or someone else who could have developed into a superstar or perhaps become a British Mourinho or Guardiola. The case of Richie Moran is a case in point. It is unlikely Moran would have developed into a superstar but he could have been a club legend and might have earned a decent living from the game had it treated him with more dignity. Moran is an intelligent thinker, speaks several languages and is a passionate analyst of the game. He might have made an excellent manager but left the game because he was no longer prepared to put up with the racist attitudes of coaches and managers he worked with, and walked away before his professional career really got into its stride.

Moran was born in London in 1963 to Nigerian parents and adopted by Irish parents who named him Richard and whose surname he adopted. He never knew his biological father and was in contact with his biological mother until the age of fifteen. Inspired, like so many others of his generation, by the 1970 Brazil side and by West Ham's Clyde Best, he wrote a letter to his school PE teacher asking to be part of the school football team. As a child, he'd gone to watch his local side, Millwall, and was excited at the prospect of going to see his team play for the first time. Listening to the racist abuse received by an opposition black player, he decided that Millwall was no longer his side.

Moving from multiracial south-east London to predominantly white Gosport in Hampshire to live with his adoptive parents, he was only one of two black kids in his school. He moved back to London at age ten to live with his biological mother and had trials for a representative London schoolboys' side. When, two years later, his biological mother became too ill to care for him, he moved back to Hampshire to live with the Morans and played school and local Sunday league football in and around Gosport. Playing him as a winger or up front, his PE teacher had warned him to be careful as he wouldn't like the cold. Upon leaving school, he found a job as a care worker, then discovered women and alcohol and so stopped playing altogether for four years until, at the age of twenty, he was invited to play for his work football team. From there he caught the attention of local non-league and semi-professional outfit Gosport Borough. His pace and goal-scoring prowess translated well at Borough, where he began to get attention from league clubs. He was offered a trial at Leeds United, but the weekend before he was due to go on trial, he received a kick in the kidneys during a game, was coughing up blood and so couldn't attend the trial. His chance at the big time appeared to have been dashed with one kick.

However, a pre-season game against Aston Villa earned him enough attention to get him an opportunity to play professional football. Borough were playing Villa in a pre-season game and for non-league teams, these matches are like cup finals. It's an opportunity for the semi-pros to put one over on their more illustrious counterparts and, perhaps, to play well enough to gain the attention of someone who'll be able to offer them an opportunity to play higher up the league ladder. For top-flight outfits like Villa, the games are designed to provide them with an opportunity to gain some match fitness against a side who aren't expected to provide stiff competition. The players are keen to get through the game without injury and generally want an easy ride before the serious business of the start of the league campaign begins. Therefore, the result and performance is of little importance for the big-name team. For the non-league club, the result and performance is everything.

Moran ran the Villa centre-back pairing ragged. Up against Derek Mountfield, an experienced defender who'd won a league title and Cup Winners' Cup with Everton in 1985, and Martin Keown, an England international, he earned the award for Man of the Match. Keown, perhaps annoyed that he was forced to work harder than he'd intended, or just wanting to put Moran in his place, taunted him by telling him that he probably earned more in a week than Moran earned in a year and asking him how many England caps he had.

After this, Moran's reputation began to grow and after another pre-season game against Leyton Orient, he was approached by an agent and offered a chance to play professional football. Giving up a chance to study for a qualification as a social worker, and at the age of twenty-six, Moran signed for Fujita Kogyo in Japan.

Fujita were managed by Alan Gillett, who had been assistant to Dave Bassett when Bassett had been manager of Wimbledon and Sheffield United. Japanese football teams are traditionally sponsored by large corporations and, upon moving to Japan, Moran lived in a team dormitory. Some players were full-time professionals and others worked part-time for the company. He found the change in culture fascinating and managed to learn Japanese in only three months. He did, however, find racism widespread, endemic and crude, often being asked by teammates how it was he was able to speak their language given that he was black and therefore must be stupid. A statement by the then Prime Minister of Japan, explaining the reason for Japan's economic dominance over the USA as being the intellectual and moral inferiority of blacks and Hispanics, further illustrated the kind of endemic racism that was prevalent within parts of Japanese society.

He found the standard of Japanese football better than he expected; in fact, very high. Due to his experience in non-league football, he was frustrated to pick up a lot of yellow cards for challenges that in Britain would have been regarded as innocuous, but in Japan were considered overly robust. In addition to the Japanese players, the team included midfielder Ian Griffiths, a Liverpudlian whom he got on well with, a Frenchman and some Argentinians. As Moran spoke Spanish, he could speak with the Argentinians, and he also spoke a little French so could converse with his French teammate.

His relationship with some of his Japanese teammates got steadily worse, however, and he would often come in to find his kit had been thrown in the bin. He clashed with Gillett, who, as a disciple of Bassett, favoured a direct, long-ball approach, rather than Moran's preference, a more considered, possession-based passing style. Besides this, the side were struggling in the league and were eventually relegated. After a season in the Japanese top flight, the club didn't want to keep him and Moran didn't want to stay, so he packed his bags and returned to England.

Upon his return home, he wrote a letter to all the clubs in the league, detailing his experience in non-league and Japanese professional football, and received an invitation to spend a few weeks at Leeds United on trial. At the time, Leeds had just won promotion to the First Division and he trained with a Leeds side that included Gary Speed, Vinnie Jones and Gordon Strachan. Gary McAllister had just been signed and Moran stayed at David Batty's house during his time there. He considered them the nicest bunch of players he'd ever met.

At the end of his trial, Leeds weren't prepared to offer him a contract, explaining they had players who could do a better job, so, undeterred, he then went for a trial at Norwich City, after which he moved on to Birmingham City, then of the Third Division. At his trial, Birmingham were impressed with his all-round game and particularly with his pace. Moran could run 100 metres in around ten seconds, which was very quick even for a decent club sprinter, and after a week or so of his trial he was offered a full-time contract.

So, at the age of twenty-seven, Moran made his football league debut in the Blues' first home game of the season against Leyton Orient, coming on as substitute in the seventy-seventh minute and scoring in the eighty-eighth to seal a 3–1 victory for Birmingham. He'd made an auspicious start to his football league career.

During his time on trial at various clubs, Moran had

spoken to a number of black players and had conducted his own unofficial research into the grounds where he was likely to suffer the most racist abuse, in preparation for his career as a professional footballer. From his discussions, and in keeping with the experiences of earlier generations of black players, the same few clubs were consistently cited. These were Leeds, Newcastle, Chelsea, Millwall, West Ham and Portsmouth, and all had a fearsome reputation as the most unwelcoming places for a black player to play football.

Moran had anticipated that he would suffer racist abuse from opposing supporters, but the first time he was forced to confront racism as a professional footballer in England came from an unlikely source. A few weeks after making his debut for Birmingham, he was sent off for dissent after swearing at the referee in a heated reserve team game against Halifax Town. As he made his way to the dressing room he was followed by two members of the opposition coaching staff, who were abusing him, calling him a 'black bastard' and a 'black cunt'. Cornered by the pair in the dressing room, he punched one of them on the chin, decking him in the process.

On his return to Birmingham, he was hauled up by the club; evidently, someone from Halifax had complained. Moran told the manager and his assistant exactly what had happened. Expecting support and a degree of sympathy, he was stunned at their reaction.

They were uninterested in the alleged abuse and informed him that he had to take it. They ordered him to write a letter of apology. Moran informed them that if the vilifier had followed him into the dressing room and told him he was a 'crap player' then he would be entitled to his opinion; however, he wasn't entitled to abuse him based on the colour of his skin, and he would not write the letter of apology. He also told the pair that if they were to abuse him in a similar way, he would mete out the same treatment to them. The club was outraged at Moran's refusal and the PFA was contacted to check whether there were any grounds to have Moran sacked.

Within football, clubs often employ a siege mentality, which can be positive when it fosters support, bonding and a team ethos, but, negatively, it can mean that clubs will defend the indefensible. Moran had been followed into the dressing room and cornered by two opposition coaches. In the circumstances, Moran found himself in, he felt he was entitled to expect support from his manager. Instead, in the event, he was fined two weeks' wages and ordered to train with the youth team. He truly felt that his manager had displayed no respect for him as a human being.

Meanwhile, Moran's team, Birmingham City, had made a good start to the season and there was a degree of optimism that the team could win promotion, but results soon fell away and, before long, optimism around the club waned and the side was slipping down the table. In February 1991, the management team at the club were replaced.

Moran had been playing well and was scoring prolifically for the reserves. At the time, the first team were playing poorly and in particular were struggling in front of goal. Moran had expressed his frustration at his lack of first-team opportunities and this hadn't been received warmly by the new manager, Lou Macari, who had a reputation as a disciplinarian. The Macari training methods were also a source of disquiet amongst some of the players. Macari had gained a degree of success in his managerial career by making his sides extremely fit. However, his teams were functional rather than attractive and as his sides climbed up the leagues, opposition teams were able to match Macari's sides for fitness and also outplay them. Macari had played for Celtic under the legendary Jock Stein and for Manchester United under managers like Tommy Docherty, who liked to play a passing game rather than the long-ball style that Macari favoured. Displaying deep mistrust in the ability and skills of footballers outside the top flight, he prioritised running in his training methods and the players rarely trained with a football. Amongst the squad he had some skilful players, like Dougie Bell, a Scottish midfielder, who was probably the most talented player at the club but was rarely given a chance in the first team.

One day, Moran was called into the manager's office by Macari and his assistant Chic Bates and asked why he had dreadlocks. Surprised to find this was the reason for being summoned, he stated his hairstyle was 'part of my African heritage', at which Macari and Bates laughed at him. Moran informed Macari that he had insulted him and Macari responded by telling him he had to cut his hair as it wasn't appropriate for a professional footballer. Moran's adoptive father had been a keen fan of Macari's former team, Celtic, and Moran had followed their fortunes closely since childhood. He reminded Macari of the terrible haircut the latter had sported during his playing days in the 1970s. He also told Macari that his suggestion that he cut his hair would be like asking Macari to take elocution lessons to rid himself of his Glaswegian accent. Macari threw him out of his office and he never played for the Blues again.

Moran had also clashed with both Mackay and Macari over playing styles. Macari's direct approach was at odds with Moran's previous experience in non-league football. Moran was allowed to drift anywhere across the front line and generally express himself, and in his first game for Birmingham he had beaten a defender with a trick and had been admonished severely by Bobby Ferguson at half-time. In addition, Ferguson's criticisms slowly chipped away at Moran's confidence, consistently being told he wasn't any good and facing disbelief that he was a professional footballer.

Marked out as a troublemaker, he was loaned out to Torquay United. He'd been there for a few days and was participating in a training session. At the end of the session, the players were told that there would be a five-a-side game, and, according to Moran, they were told that the 'whites' would play on one side and the 'coons' would play on the other side. This led to Moran turning his back on football.

> I said, 'I beg your pardon', and I was told, 'You're a nigger, you're a spade, off you go over there.' I said, 'I'm not being funny but do you know what my name is? My name's Richie Moran, if you want to speak to me, you'll call me the same respect [sic] you would to any other human being. If you call me anything racially derogatory, I'm actually going to tear your head off, right here, right now, in front of everybody,' and it was at that stage I thought, 'I actually don't want to play this game anymore' – not because I couldn't take it, but because I didn't have to.

Two black players, Paul Hall and Darren Moore, who were young trainees at Torquay at the time and would later go on to play in the Premier League with Portsmouth and win

international honours with Jamaica, both offered support
for Moran, but were young players at the beginning of their
careers and expressing their support explicitly might have
impacted upon their careers.

Throughout his time at Birmingham, Moran got on well
with the most of his fellow professionals. However, he did
fall out with one player who had head-butted a nineteen-
year-old reserve team goalkeeper at a Christmas party,
breaking his nose in the process. Moran liked Birmingham,
then as now an ethnically diverse city, and got on well
with the club's supporters, even though one Birmingham
City fanzine voted Moran as their worst ever player – a
harsh judgement given some of the awful players who have
pulled on the blue jersey. It was the treatment and attitude
of managers and coaches, those who wielded power and
influence and who had petty egos and backward attitudes –
and the culture within the game that found their behaviour
acceptable – that caused him to stop playing professional
football.

Unlike the majority of professional footballers, Moran
was never signed to a club on schoolboy terms, never progressed through the youth system as an apprentice or trainee
and never learned as a young professional the art of understanding and negotiating the politics of the dressing room,
the training pitch and the racist attitudes of coaches and
fellow professionals. Players who came through the non-
league route, such as Cyrille Regis, Ian Wright or Les Ferdinand, also tended to come into the professional game at a
young age and had time to gain something of an education
in dealing with racist attitudes. Moran himself had suffered
abuse while playing non-league football. At Waterlooville,
an opposition player had given him a torrent of racist abuse

during a match. After the game, Moran went into the opposition changing room, grabbed him by the throat and invited
him to come outside and repeat the abuse to his face. Even
the other opposition players told Moran that their teammate
deserved a smack. Therefore, he was never schooled from a
very early age in football's culture, where building a career
as a black professional footballer came at a price to personal
dignity. His maturity, along with the fact that he did well
academically, gave Moran an entirely different perspective
on what he was prepared to accept in his place of work and
provided him with other options outside professional football.

Briefly, Moran drifted back into non-league football
before becoming, amongst other things, a travel writer and
an active campaigner for anti-racism in football. He was
invited by a police officer to be a guest speaker at an event
during the 1999/2000 season at Watford Football Club, attended by a former England manager who would provide
Moran with an insight into the attitudes of senior FA officials towards black players.

> Graham Taylor come up to me ... and said, 'Look, I'm going
> to tell you something ... I'm never going to admit it, I will be
> sued for libel.' He said, 'When I was manager of England I
> was called in by two members of the FA, who I won't name...'
> I volunteered two names. He said, 'I'm not prepared to say,
> but I was told in no uncertain terms not to pick too many
> black players for the national side.'

Moran's revelation reveals that the FA's primary concern
was to preserve a predominantly white image of the England team, an image that they themselves had constructed

and took great steps to preserve. Taylor was appointed England manager immediately after the World Cup of 1990 and lost his job three years later, as England failed to qualify for the 1994 World Cup. There is no question of Taylor having acted on those instructions, but the episode raises some important questions as to how many other England managers were given the same instructions and therefore felt pressurised to limit the numbers of black players selected to play for the national side. During his playing career, Paul Davis had wondered whether some kind of unofficial quota system was in operation, but had never considered it beyond mere speculation. It would raise the question of how many black players had had their chances of playing for England restricted and what impact this might have had on England's fortunes.

The inner-city disturbances that had occurred in the early part of the 1980s, and the Scarman Report that came in their wake, had highlighted the issue of the policing of black communities as a major cause of the disorder. Alongside this, the issue of racial discrimination in employment was also highlighted as one of the underlying causes of the resentment felt by black communities. Whereas previous disturbances in Nottingham and Notting Hill in the 1950s and at the Notting Hill Carnival in 1976 had been carried out by black people who were overwhelmingly born outside the UK, the significance of the disturbances in the early and mid-1980s was that the anger and resentment came from young black people who had been born in the UK. Issues of language, integration, education and familiarity did not readily apply to the same degree as in previous disturbances and therefore the issue of racial discrimination as an explanation for unequal patterns of employment and unemployment could not be so readily dismissed. As a result, many progressive local councils, particularly those in large urban areas with significant proportions of black and Asian communities, began to actively develop equality policies in line with the provisions of the Race Relations Act, which had been introduced in 1976. The legislation outlawed racial discrimination in employment and in the provision of goods and services and required councils and other public bodies to monitor these provisions. With public bodies actively embracing equality policies and also under increased scrutiny by black community organisations, a proportion of people from minority ethnic communities began to gain employment opportunities within organisations that had hitherto been denied them, and a smaller number were appointed to middle and senior management positions. These developments ushered in a new, albeit small, black middle class, employed almost exclusively within the public sector. However, these developments would not be allowed to go unchecked and, as is usual, there developed a backlash against providing opportunities for equality of employment for racial minorities. The most inflammatory opposition was led by the tabloid press, but their counterparts in some broadsheets were hardly more restrained in their dismissal of equality policies as an example of the wastefulness of so-called loony left local councils. The discourse around the implementation of equality policies illustrated the thinly veiled contempt in which issues of racism and discrimination were held, and while it was true that Labour-controlled councils adopted equality policies and strategies with most enthusiasm, most councils, irrespective of their political outlook, began to embrace equality policies to some degree by the end of the 1980s.

The development and implementation of these policies produced something of a contradictory assessment of their worth on the part of black people. While, collectively, black activists campaigned for the adoption of more comprehensive policies, the backlash against equality campaigns, led by the media and supported by large numbers of Conservative and some Labour politicians, had impacted on the willingness of black individuals to participate in anti-racist campaigns. Before deciding whether to give active support to such campaigns, a number of key considerations had to be made. Will I be the only person to support or 'front' the campaign? Shouldn't white employees be involved? Is the campaign tokenistic? Is my involvement reduced to promotion of the campaign rather than shaping the nature of the campaign itself? Will I be perceived as being militant? Will supporting the campaign be seen as legitimising my employer? Will I leave myself isolated? Will my white colleagues ostracise me? Will there be some kind of backlash? These were the kinds of questions that many black people in the workplace would ask themselves when considering involving themselves in anti-racist campaigns, and, inevitably, within the highly conservative, slow-changing environment of football there was a great deal of unwillingness on the part of black footballers to participate in the early campaigns against racism. Overseas players, both black and white, had no such cultural baggage to influence their decision. To them it was an anti-racist campaign; they were against racism, so they took part, often with a great deal of enthusiasm. Shaka Hislop of Newcastle United and Lucas Radebe of Leeds United were pioneers in their support for the early development of anti-racist campaigns. It took some time before home-grown black players began to embrace these movements with the same degree of whole-heartedness. However, as 1995 began, one event saw black players become more vocal and active in their support for anti-racist initiatives.

With a history of falling out with the authorities and coaches in his native France, Eric Cantona was widely considered a gifted, maverick talent who had been the catalyst for the resurgence of his club. His disciplinary record had been poor and he was regarded as a player who could easily be provoked. After a series of niggly challenges from Richard Shaw, he lashed out at and was shown a red card.

His 'kung-fu' kick on Matthew Simmons after being subjected to anti-French abuse by the Crystal Palace supporter at a hostile Selhurst Park in January 1995 earned Cantona a lengthy ban. In the immediate aftermath of the game, attention had focused upon Cantona's unprecedented and seemingly unprovoked attack on a spectator. As information began to emerge that Cantona had been subject to provocation, the tide began to turn and the incident finally made the authorities wake up. Cantona's response to Simmons's xenophobic rant highlighted, in a small way, the kind of treatment black players had been forced to endure for years.

For many black footballers, there was secret admiration for Cantona's action. Most had experienced his frustration and anger, but had been rendered impotent by their inability to respond with anything other than the 'head-down-get-on-with-the-game' approach. Most black footballers had, at one time or other, wanted to take the type of action that Cantona did. Some had even come close and, in one or two cases, like that of George Berry, had even strayed into the kind of territory that Cantona's abuser had provoked, but Cantona's action was one that had been played out on an altogether bigger stage.

Simmons had initially been portrayed as a victim, but as news of his actions became more widely known, sympathy for him began to erode.

Everyone initially talked about Cantona, what a disgrace he was to football ... and by the time the court case came round, I always remember this guy, was it Matthew Simmons ... his court statement became the stuff of legend ... he alleged he marched down the steps and said something like, 'Oi, Cantona, that's off for an early bath, you Frenchman', or something like that and you know, you could almost picture the court convulsed, saying, 'Are you serious, is this your defence?'
– Iffy Onuora

As it turned out, Simmons had a previous conviction for a racist attack on a Sri Lankan-born petrol station worker and had National Front sympathies. As this information became known, the issue of terrace racism, and fan behaviour more generally, came into sharp focus. The idea that supporters were entitled to behave as they wished with impunity, as some sort of right by virtue of paying an admission fee, began to be challenged.

Cantona had inadvertently done black players a favour. Although the object of abuse had been his nationality, it highlighted the experiences of black footballers, who'd regularly been forced to endure this kind of behaviour and much worse. As Bobby Barnes remarked, 'We'd have been banned for life and the FA would probably have pressed for a heavy prison sentence. Cantona did us a favour by highlighting the issue ... Because he was French, because he played for Manchester United and because he was Eric Cantona, he got away relatively unscathed.'

In February, the month after Cantona's Selhurst Park kick, the issue of far-right influence and terrace hooliganism came to the forefront again during a friendly international between the Republic of Ireland and England at Lansdowne Road in

Dublin. The match was abandoned after twenty-three minutes due to crowd trouble on the part of England fans, with the far right, and specifically the neo-Nazi organisation Combat 18, implicated in the violence. Reports from British intelligence had indicated that Combat 18 were intent on causing violence and had passed information to the Irish authorities that went largely ignored. With questions being asked about the lack of action on racism on the part of the authorities, and suggestions that England's hosting of Euro 1996 was in jeopardy, the FA felt compelled to do more. So, too, did the clubs. A more proactive approach to the issue of racism was adopted by a number of clubs, while the FA, the Premier League, the PFA and the Football Foundation all agreed to join forces in funding the new and rebranded Kick It Out campaign.

The impact of all this on black British footballers was palpable, as more were prepared to take a stand and become involved in anti-racist initiatives. This increased confidence in undertaking anti-racist work was only the most obvious outcome for black footballers. With few exceptions, black footballers had previously been unwilling to take this kind of stand against racism for fear that it might have an impact on their careers. Such a stand would, in general, have been unlikely to be viewed with any degree of sympathy. Their commitment and mentality would have been called into question amid reminders of how lucky they were to play professional football. Other talented footballers had taken the decision not to pursue a career in the game, reckoning that the racism and abuse they would be required to suffer was too much of a burden on their self-respect or state of mind.

As it transpired, England's hosting of Euro 1996 was never under serious threat. The England squad, now featuring Paul Ince, then of Inter Milan, Les Ferdinand of Newcastle United and Sol Campbell of Tottenham, were the host nation of a major football tournament for the first time since the World Cup of 1966. Both Holland and France featured more black players within their squads than England, although of the three, Ince was the only one to feature regularly in the side, playing in four out of England's five games. The flag of St George replaced the Union Jack as the flag of choice for England fans, and its presence at the tournament seemed to be divorced from its previous far-right associations. England were finally knocked out of the tournament at the semi-final stage by eventual winners Germany, but with the tournament on home soil and the nasty, vindictive, overly patriotic siege mentality of England's support largely absent, serious disturbances didn't materialise, although there was a ripple of violence and anti-German sentiment after England's elimination, fuelled in no small part by anti-German jingoism by a large section of the tabloid press.

• • •

John Barnes, his pace dulled by injury but his football brain still intact, had successfully reinvented himself as a central midfielder. No longer able to play as an out-and-out winger, his relocation to a central midfield role had given his career new purpose. He had been made captain of Liverpool and, as an old head in a youthful but talented side, he was able to dictate the tempo of the play, keep the ball moving and be available to take possession. As a winger, his pace and dribbling ability had caught the eye, but his passing range had gone somewhat unappreciated. Now, with his ability to glide past defenders at will no longer available to him, his range of passing took centre stage and in April, at the back end of the

1995/96 season, he was able to demonstrate how successfully he had made the transition. In an epic game at Anfield,
Liverpool had raced into an early lead against title-chasing
Newcastle, so keeping alive their own slim chances of winning the Premier League title. Newcastle themselves bounced
back to take a 2–1 lead after only fourteen minutes and that
remained the score at the end of the first half. After half-
time, Liverpool drew level, which was to last for only two
minutes, after which United took a 3–2 lead. Stan Collymore
got yet another for Liverpool on seventy minutes and, as the
game became stretched, it ebbed and flowed from one end to
another as each side looked for the goal that would maintain
their bid for the title. With the game deep in stoppage time,
Liverpool launched one last frenetic attack. A series of quick
passes, with Barnes in the thick of things, brought Liverpool
to the edge of the Newcastle box. As the ball pinged around
the area, it fell to Barnes. Amid the mayhem, and surrounded
by Newcastle players, he seemed to have all the time in the
world as he picked out Collymore, unmarked and in acres
of space, who ruthlessly dispatched the ball into the net to
end Newcastle's hopes of the title and keep Liverpool's slim
chances of glory alive.

Barnes's journey from winger to midfield creator had been a
long one from the days when black footballers were considered
unfit for the responsibility of playing as a team's creative hub.
In later years, players like Tom Huddlestone would carry on
the baton first picked up by the likes of Barnes and Arsenal's
Paul Davis. This playmaker position required an appreciation of time and space, distance and angles, technical ability,
vision and ability to read the game. This blend of technical
and cerebral qualities was successfully negotiated by Barnes
towards the end of his career and, after his time at Anfield

ended, he went on to perform reasonably well with Newcastle and Charlton. With the quality he had, his high profile and undoubted ability to analyse the game, surely a career in management at a big club awaited him. He would get his chance.

• • •

Three months into 1997 – ironically, the European Union's Year Against Racism – Wales striker Nathan Blake vowed never to play for Wales again while manager Bobby Gould was in charge. The incident in question took place as Wales prepared for their World Cup qualifier against Belgium in March 1997. Initially, Blake's withdrawal from the squad was passed off as 'sickness or diarrhoea', but as news of the circumstances surrounding his withdrawal became public, Gould stated in a radio interview:

> The situation was that I was selecting teams for a five-a-side, I told some players to put on yellow bibs, some to put on green and said, 'Nathan, you stay with the blacks' ... For that I apologise but never in my life have I been taken to task over racism.

Blake had stated that Gould had once racially insulted him during his time as a youth player and also brought up details of a team talk that Gould had given the previous October, in a home game in which Wales had been beaten 3–1 by Holland. Blake alleged that Dutch striker Pierre van Hooijdonk had been described as a 'black bastard' by Gould. In response, Gould stated:

> I refute Nathan's allegations. It hurts very much. If I am guilty, I will stand up and be counted. With this one, no way.

Let me take you back to the beginning. Let people judge. Van Hooijdonk had scored two first-half goals against us and I said at half-time: 'Who is picking up that black so-and-so?' That is not in dispute. But it was said in football talk, the way I would if the bloke was big, fat or hairy.

Gould had managed the Crazy Gang during his period as manager of Wimbledon and used this experience to illustrate the somewhat hackneyed defence of his record in managing black players.

I am not a racist, never have and never will be. The very thought abhors me. I have signed or managed players like Eric Young, Keith Curle, Phil Babb, Cyrille Regis, Terry Phelan, John Williams, Mickey Bennett, Carlton Fairweather, John Fashanu, Lloyd McGrath, Roger Joseph and Peter Ndlovu. I would like you to ask everyone if I had ever said a racist remark. Go on, ask them. I even tried to sign Nathan once when I was manager of Coventry. I had agreed £3 million with Blackburn for Peter Ndlovu and offered £300,000 to Cardiff for Nathan but the deal fell through. Does that sound like a racist manager? I would still pick him if his form warrants it and I hope he will turn up. But the whole affair is cutting into me.

While admitting he wasn't fully aware of the circumstances surrounding the incident, Ken Tucker, chairman of the Association of Wales committee, was quick to rush to Gould's defence and stated, 'I do know Bobby Gould very well and would not have thought there was any question of racism in his behaviour ... He is just not that type of man and I am very surprised at this allegation.' In his knee-jerk response,

Tucker's comments echoed the lack of understanding and poor leadership in keeping with the game's hierarchy in England and Scotland.

In the aftermath of the incident, Blake revealed he'd received an anonymous package at his club, Blackburn Rovers:

> Inside were some nuts and also some abusive writing, also a picture of Jill Dando [the murdered television presenter] with a picture of a gun with a bullet going towards her head. Underneath was written: 'You're next.' The club captain wanted me to take it to the police. But you tend to chuck these things away and move on. That was just one of numerous things that happened to me in my career. The racial element – I don't think people quite understand the nerve that touches because of the history involved. I had made various complaints and pulled out of squads. It had been well publicised and that's when I received the parcel.

Blake was to resume his international career after Gould resigned following Wales's failure to qualify for the 1998 World Cup. His stand would have been difficult to imagine even a few years previously and would have been the stuff of fantasy when Regis, Batson, Crooks, Anderson et al. were in their prime. Blake's action was significant in another way, too. Anti-racist campaigns had focused on terrace behaviour and the activities of the far right. Blake's withdrawal from the national squad shifted the agenda in another direction. There had always been an unwritten rule that what happened in the dressing room stayed in the dressing room. By exposing the hitherto unseen world of the dressing room and training pitch, Blake had broken one of football's taboos and in doing so shifted the focus of anti-racism towards some of the ingrained attitudes that existed amongst those within the game's leadership.

After Blake had taken his stance, James Hussaney was to win a case at an industrial tribunal for race discrimination, the first involving an English club. Hussaney was a trainee at Chester City, and in January 1997, prior to a reserve team game against Oldham Athletic, he had put the wrong size studs into his manager Kevin Ratcliffe's boots, to which Ratcliffe, former captain of both Everton and Wales, responded by calling him a 'black cunt'. Hussaney made a formal complaint to the club. The club chairman, Mark Guterman, told Hussaney and his mother not to take the matter any further, warning that 'no other club would touch [him] with a barge pole'. In the spring of 1997, Hussaney was informed he would not be receiving a professional contract. Ratcliffe stated that 'he had neither the technical ability nor mental strength to be kept on', so confirming Guterman's statement that he would be leaving the club. Despite this, the tribunal found that Hussaney's dismissal was on purely footballing grounds, but did find Ratcliffe was guilty of racist abuse and awarded Hussaney £2,500 in compensation.

This could have been the catalyst for the FA to actively demonstrate its new-found commitment to anti-racism by holding some form of inquiry or investigation, in keeping with its zero-tolerance policy towards racism. It stated it would hold an inquiry but never did and instead left Chester to deal with the issue as an internal matter. Ratcliffe was to remain manager until 1999.

In February 1998, Aston Villa's Stan Collymore claimed that former teammate Steve Harkness had racially abused him.

I was being wound up all game and was getting racial abuse

... Harkness called me a coon. There were also other things
said that were even worse. It was racial abuse of the worst
kind and totally out of order ... It hurt me very much indeed
and I am still considering whether to make an official complaint. I went out of my way to tell the black players at Liverpool what had happened. Harkness has to live with them
as well as himself.

Collymore had informed the referee at the time Harkness
was alleged to have made the remark. Despite making noises
about holding an inquiry, the FA never took action, leaving
Collymore frustrated and Harkness, who denied the remark,
without an opportunity to put forward his own case.

The FA's duplicitous, two-pronged strategy of ignoring
racism when specific allegations were made but publicly
advocating zero tolerance was perfectly illustrated when,
barely a month after the Collymore–Harkness incident, they
enthusiastically supported the first report from the newly
elected Labour government's 'Football Task Force', which
released 'Eliminating Racism from Football' in March 1998.
The taskforce included key stakeholders within football
and wider sport and government. The FA, Premier League,
Football League, PFA, League Managers Association, Premier and Football League Match officials, the FSA, Sport
England, Commission for Racial Equality and a variety of
other bodies and individuals formed the 'taskforce'. The
report was the most far-reaching and ambitious report into
racism in European sport. It asked a number of key questions on topics such as Asian participation in playing and
spectating; the diminishing number of black spectators; lack
of black and Asian administrators, coaches and referees;
and lack of representation on the FA council. The report

advocated that the FA should introduce guidelines to make racist abuse a red-card offence. It also recommended that the Football Offences Act be amended to make individual racist abuse by spectators a criminal offence, and it made a number of recommendations about tackling racism in grassroots football and in supporting anti-racist campaigns. Overall, the report acknowledged that the game had serious problems at all levels and in 2001 the law was amended to make racist chanting or abuse by one individual a criminal offence.

Terrace abuse of the kind that was common in the 1970s and '80s was becoming rarer, slowly being replaced by other forms of racism. The kind of chanting that had occurred for the full ninety minutes and been accompanied by banana throwing was disappearing from the English game. Racist chanting at black players could still be heard but was undertaken by smaller sections of fans. It was often directed at footballers who were of Asian, north African or other heritage as the league became more ethnically varied. Chanting directed at opposing fans in order to denigrate their town or region was also common. In February 1998, Leeds fans taunted their Leicester City counterparts with chants of 'Town full of Pakis' and Coventry's Moroccan international midfielder Youssef Chippo was racially abused by Newcastle United fans in October 1999.

The increasingly cosmopolitan and diverse nature of the Premier League meant that teams without black players were very much the exception. Everton had signed Nigerian Daniel Amokachi from Belgian Club Brugge in 1994, making him the first black player to play for the club since Cliff Marshall in 1976. In the intervening years, racist chanting had been witnessed on a regular basis at Goodison Park and had been elevated since the arrival of Barnes at Liverpool. As the side's fortunes on the pitch deteriorated, their reputation as a racist club increased and they began to gain national notoriety for the behaviour of their fans and their seeming reluctance to sign black players. Everton's most successful manager, Howard Kendall, had returned for a second spell in 1990 and under his management, the club went through the strange practice of expressing interest in seemingly every available black player, yet in each case refusing to pay what the club deemed to be too high a transfer fee. Kendall finally resigned in December 1993, after agreeing a fee with Manchester United for Dion Dublin only for a board member to block the deal at the eleventh hour. This apparent refusal to sign a black player, along with a vocal minority of racist support, gave the club a reputation as being amongst the most racist clubs in British football.

Ian Wright and Les Ferdinand appeared to reserve their most impressive goal-scoring performances for games against Everton, Ferdinand in particular, ending his career with more goals against Everton than any other side. Wright scored a number of spectacular and important goals against Everton and had done so since his Palace days, when he'd scored two in a 4–1 win in the Zenith Data Systems Trophy at Wembley, a competition played during English clubs' enforced hiatus from European competition. He'd achieved his first Arsenal hat-trick when he scored all Arsenal's goals in a 4–2 win against Everton at Highbury, and regularly found the net against them throughout his career. In 2000, a University of Leicester research survey found that of all clubs in the English and Scottish leagues, Everton was the club at which fans had witnessed most racist abuse. It further cemented their reputation.

Outside the top division, racist abuse in the form of terrace chanting was taking longer to die out of the game. There was still a sizeable proportion of black British players, but the kind of multinational feature of Premier League teams was absent. In addition, media focus on issues of racism outside of the Premier League was such that events often went unreported even by local and regional newspapers. For black players like Huddersfield's Iffy Onuora, the smaller crowds in sometimes cavernous stadiums often meant that individual taunts could be heard from supporters, who would abuse the 13 stone, 6 foot 3 athlete from the safety of the terraces. 'I've heard it from fans, of course, I've had it shouted to me from people stood a few metres away and I'm thinking, if me or you were a bit closer, it would be a very different situation.'

The worst abuse he received was in a first-round FA Cup tie at Darlington. From his first touch of the ball, monkey noises provided the soundtrack to the game. To compound the situation, Onuora had won a disputed penalty, which only seemed to further inflame the racists. He was substituted after around seventy minutes of the game and his manager was later quoted in press reports as saying that he'd substituted Onuora to protect him from further abuse. The following Monday, he arrived at training to find he'd received a handwritten letter from a Darlington fan who'd taken it upon themselves to state how appalled they were at the treatment Onuora had received and to apologise on behalf of decent Darlington fans. Tellingly, there had been no official apology from the club itself.

• • •

Of the black British players who played professional football since the 1970s, the majority were of Caribbean heritage. There were also significant numbers of black footballers of Nigerian heritage who made their way into the professional ranks. While the majority of those of West Indian heritage were, overwhelmingly, working-class, those of Nigerian heritage came from a far wider social spectrum. Many first-generation Nigerians had arrived in the UK to work in transport and in factories and public services like health, in the same way as their Caribbean counterparts. Others were seafarers who had settled in the UK; others had arrived in the UK as students and had settled; others, like John Fashanu's barrister father, had come to work in the UK as professionals; and others still, like John Chiedozie's family, had fled Nigeria during the 1967–70 Biafran War.

Whereas the first generation of West Indians were, by and large, cricket fans, that was never the case with Nigerians. Although Nigeria had produced its fair share of boxing and athletics fans, those enthusiasms paled in comparison to the country's love of football. John Fashanu, Gabby Agbonlahor, Ugo Ehiogu and John Salako are footballers of Nigerian heritage who won full England caps. Justin Fashanu, Remi Moses, Shola Ameobi and Nedum Onuoha were amongst others of Nigerian heritage who have won England U-21 caps. Whereas black people from the Caribbean settled almost exclusively in England and Wales, Nigerian patterns of settlement in the UK were far broader, with a sizeable number venturing north of the border to make Scotland their home. Unlike in England and Wales, therefore, the majority of the black community in Scotland is of African heritage, including Scottish internationals Chris Iwelumo and Ikechi Anya, who are both of Nigerian heritage.

Iffy Onuora was a journeyman striker who spent his career playing outside the top flight. He was born in Glasgow and grew up in Liverpool, playing representative football. He'd attended Bradford University, gaining a degree in economics. He was also selected to play for British Universities, where he was spotted by Dai Jones, who coached the side and had links with Huddersfield Town. Onuora had had trials at Chesterfield and Chester City, but impressed former Republic of Ireland and then Huddersfield manager Eoin Hand when he was invited to pre-season training.

Onuora's pace and athleticism persuaded Hand to give him a professional contract, but to be on the safe side, he offered him a one-year contract worth around £100 a week. The day after Onuora signed professionally, he played his first game in a pre-season friendly against Grimsby and came off the bench to score a 25-yard screamer, winning the game for Huddersfield. The only other black player at the club was Huddersfield-born winger Junior Bent, causing a journalist to remark to Hand at a pre-season press conference that the team contained two black players; one was iffy and the other one bent.

In stereotypical fashion, Hand played Onuora on the wing, rather than as a central striker, where he had played at university. Onuora moved to Mansfield in 1994, where he made twenty-eight appearances in two injury-hit seasons. He signed for Gillingham, was converted back into a striker and formed a deadly partnership with Ade Akinbiyi. The two terrorised opposition defences. They were both quick, powerful and strong in the air, and Onuora in particular could, in football parlance, put himself about.

The partnership broke up when Akinbiyi, also of Nigerian heritage, left for a big-money move to Bristol City, after which he went to Wolves and Leicester. In March 1998, Onuora signed for Swindon Town, then embroiled in a relegation battle in the First Division. He teamed up with George Ndah, south London-born and fellow Nigerian, whom he knew from a brief loan spell that Ndah had spent at Gillingham. Onuora was thrust straight into the side, where his debut began ominously as opponents QPR took an early lead through Nigel Quashie, later to become the first black player to play for Scotland since Andrew Watson in the nineteenth century. Ndah then won a penalty after tempting a Rangers defender into a clumsy challenge in the box, which was tucked away by Mark Walters. With the scores at 1–1, Town had their keeper sent off and had to re-shuffle, which involved their centre-half pulling on the keeper's jersey.

When a team is reduced to ten men, it often has the effect of galvanising them, particularly when the sending-off has been a harsh one and the team feel a collective sense of injustice. From a tactical perspective, their options are relatively straightforward and they usually reorganise to prioritise defensive solidity and sacrifice attacking intent. For the opposition team, the psychological impact of knowing that your opponents will defend for their lives can play cruel tricks on a side's mentality. A situation like this often requires tactical adjustments to provide more width or to maximise possession in order to break down a stubborn defence. The burden of expectation often nullifies any numerical advantage and leaves the side devoid of ideas, which increases the longer the game goes on without a breakthrough. With Swindon needing to play for seventy minutes with ten men and desperately needing to get something out of the game, a corner on the stroke of half-time provided a rare opportunity to throw men forward. After a short corner routine, Walters put the ball in the box; Onuora just got ahead of his marker to get on the end of the cross with a diving header. The

Rangers keeper, unable to move, could only watch as the ball sailed past him to bulge the top corner of the net and give Town the lead. Ndah was the first to congratulate the recently prostrate Onuora, as he disappeared under a sea of red shirts. Shell-shocked after throwing away a lead against a struggling side that had a man sent off, Rangers' second-half onslaught never materialised and Swindon stayed in relative comfort for the remainder of the game.

The following season ended with Town finishing just below mid-table and Onuora finishing as top scorer with twenty goals, a decent return for a side that had previously finished just three points off the relegation places. It was about this time that Onuora was linked with a call-up for the Scottish national side. Under Craig Brown, Scotland played with a succession of diminutive strikers, such as Eoin Jess, Billy Dodds and Mo Johnston, and even used midfielders Neil McCann and Don Hutchison in the striker's role. At the time, Scotland were playing with one up front with a player completely unsuitable for the role. They were desperate for a target man who could hold the ball up and Onuora fitted the bill perfectly. He was in good goal-scoring form in a league one removed from the Premiership and could provide an option that Scotland didn't have. Brown had been made aware of Onuora's form and eligibility and was questioned about a possible call-up by the Scottish press. Speculation mounted as to whether Onuora would be the first black player to represent Scotland in the modern era. However, Onuora was consistently overlooked, as were the claims of young Hibs winger Kevin Harper. Brown had stuck rigidly to the same set of players who had qualified for Euro '96, but desperately needed to refresh the ageing squad with new blood. Brown's conservatism militated against the claims of Onuora and Harper and it wasn't until the appointment of Berti Vogts that the honour of becoming the first black player to receive a Scotland cap in over 100 years went eventually to Nigel Quashie in 2004.

• • •

Professional footballers were responding positively to football's anti-racist initiatives. The instances of players racially abusing their fellow professionals were becoming increasingly rare. The results of a PFA survey published in April 2000 showed that 58 per cent of footballers had witnessed racist behaviour and that 90 per cent thought that initiatives such as Kick It Out had reduced racist incidents. However, although the attitude of players was changing, amongst those who were responsible for running the game, attitudes seemed entrenched. In December 2001, former referee Gurnam Singh won a landmark employment tribunal case against the Football League, who had overlooked him for promotion to the Premier League because of his Asian background. The tribunal found that he had been passed over for promotion despite finishing top, in favour of two other referees who had lower scores than him, and that in 1995, the FA Director of Refereeing, Ken Ridden, had commented about Singh that 'we don't want people like him in the Premier League'. Singh was removed from the league list of referees in 1999, the highest-ranking referee ever to be sacked.

CHAPTER 12

YOU CAN'T SAY THAT
ANY MORE

ON 3 MAY 1998, Justin Fashanu was found dead in a lock-up garage in east London. Fashanu had been one of the most promising strikers in England when playing for Norwich City in the early 1980s and became England's first £1 million black footballer when he was sold to Nottingham Forest in 1981. He was by no means the first big-money striker to be labelled a flop, and a combination of the psychological weight of the fee, plus poor management of him, led to an unhappy time at Forest. Fashanu came out at a time when the government employed openly hostile discourse and discriminatory legislation against homosexuality. The language used by tabloid newspapers was often designed to incite outright hostility. Unlike other footballers who came out at a time of their own choosing, so enabling them to manage their announcement and choose whether they wanted to inform friends, family and colleagues, Fashanu was denied the right to choose when and whether to go public. With his sexuality about to be exposed by the tabloid press, Fashanu negotiated a five-figure deal with *The Sun* to come out, and in the process he told lurid and questionable tales of sexual encounters with MPs and soap stars, lying about many of his exploits in return for cash. Subjected to homophobic chanting, he was also vilified by *The Voice*, the newspaper targeted at Britain's black community, who described his sexuality as an affront to the black community. He was also ill equipped to manage his public relations affairs. He seemed embroiled in a pattern of self-destructive behaviour: the by-product of being openly gay in the hyper-masculine world of football, as well as being an evangelical Christian, and therefore belonging to a group whose attitude to sexuality was distinctly Old Testament. Not only did Fashanu become the first openly gay footballer, he remains the only openly gay, high-profile black British male in the game. While his status as a victim was cemented after the coroner's verdict of suicide at the age of thirty-seven, it is easy to forget how talented a player he was. His brother John went on to win full England caps and had a very good career, but Justin was technically a far more gifted footballer than his brother and, with the right handling, at the right club and in the right age, could have gone on to have the kind of career that would have greatly eclipsed his brother's substantial achievements.

• • •

On 22 April 1993 at around 10.30 in the evening on a main road in Eltham in south-east London, an event that was to last for no more than ten to fifteen seconds was to have a profound impact on British society – so much so that few areas of public life, including football, would escape its impact. Eighteen-year-old Stephen Lawrence received two stab wounds to a depth of about 5 inches on both sides of the front of his body to his chest and arm, with both wounds severing axillary arteries. In spite of the partial collapse of his right lung, which had been inflicted by one of the stab wounds, he managed to stumble 130 or so yards up the road before collapsing and bleeding to death.

The BNP had located its headquarters in Welling in 1987, close to where Stephen Lawrence was murdered. By 1993, Greenwich Council reported that there had been a 210 per cent increase in racist attacks, which had included four racist murders. Weeks before the murder of Stephen Lawrence, Gurdeep Bhangal was stabbed with a kitchen knife in Eltham by the same gang who'd attacked Lawrence. The knife went through his stomach and missed his spine by a centimetre. He survived. Twenty months earlier, in February 1991, fifteen-year-old Rolan Adams was set upon by a group of around fifteen white men who racially abused him and stabbed him to death. Only one of the group was convicted of his murder. In July 1992, Rohit Duggal was stabbed to death outside a kebab shop. A man with links to the gang who murdered Lawrence was convicted of his murder. According to local racism monitors, twelve families had fled the area and it was well known as a hotbed of racist activity.

The subsequent botched police investigation and failure to provide the Lawrence family with justice would likely have been the end of the matter, as far as the vast majority of the general public was concerned, had it not been for the determination and tenacity of the Lawrence family. The Macpherson Report was published in February 1999 and not only investigated the circumstances surrounding the murder but kicked off a wide ranging discussion into racism and race relations in the UK. It was in this context that a series of reports and recommendations into racism and football took place. The media, much of which had historically been hostile to anti-racist justice campaigns, reflected the mood of the political and social establishment in acknowledging that racism was a major feature of British society.

Macpherson's report had popularised the term 'institutional racism', a description of how, through structures and systems, organisations undertook racist practices unwittingly, rather than through a conscious decision to actively discriminate against racial minorities. A number of organisations fell over themselves to embrace the new terminology, providing them with an opportunity to characterise their discriminatory practice as accidental or unfortunate, rather than as a consequence of decisions taken by individuals. A perfect illustration of this came a few months after the publication of the report, when, in July 1999, Northern General Hospital in Sheffield accepted kidneys for transplantation from a donor who had insisted that the recipient should be white. When the news emerged, the hospital stated: 'Under no circumstances can we condone the acceptance of organs where there are conditions attached.' The institution appeared happy to take the blame for this rather than holding the individuals who had made the decision to account.

The report did have a galvanising effect in providing the confidence to tackle racism. Later that year, in October, staff at Ford's Dagenham plant held a strike ballot after both black and white workers walked out in protest at racist behaviour and bullying on the part of management. They also protested that only a small proportion of senior managerial posts went to non-whites in spite of an ethnically diverse workforce. The company had long been notorious for the degree to which racism was allowed to run unchecked within the plant. Far-right and racist literature had been openly on display at the plant during the 1970s and Brendon Batson had cited friends who worked at the plant as being constantly on the receiving end of racist abuse from middle and senior management. In 1996, Ford had invited five ethnic minority staff to pose for a brochure that aimed to show the racial diversity of the plant, where 45 per cent of the staff were non-white. When the brochures were published, the black faces were replaced with white faces. Citing the need to appeal to the eastern European market, Ford's were faced with a walkout from hundreds of workers, with an estimated £2.8 million worth of lost production as a result.

As Lord Macpherson was preparing his report and Parliament awaited its publication, the 'Eliminating Racism from Football' report was generally welcomed by the media as they caught the prevailing mood. For the first time a consensus was brewing in terms of media reporting of racism within football. Prior to Eric Cantona's watershed kung-fu kick, racist incidents and terrace abuse had gone largely unreported and had even been famously described by John Motson as 'good-natured barracking' when Holland's Ruud Gullit was on the receiving end of abuse by England fans in an international 'friendly' at Wembley in 1988.

Macpherson's report had gone much further than the issues surrounding the murder of Stephen Lawrence and the handling of the subsequent murder inquiry, and the issues he raised around the state of race relations in Britain were underlined when, in August 2000, Britain's record on race relations was harshly criticised by the United Nations. They condemned the number of non-whites who suffered police brutality and died in police custody; the disproportionately high incidences of black unemployment; underrepresentation of ethnic minorities in politics, the army and the police; and highlighted the large number of black children expelled from schools. The government would later sign up to a common EU plan to combat racism, but it pointedly opted out from an obligation to criminalise certain forms of racist behaviour. An amended Race Relations Act came into force in 2001, briefly providing some hope that issues of racism and discrimination in public life would be systematically challenged and that comprehensive plans to achieve equality would be made. Where the introduction of the new Act should have acted as the start of an onslaught against racism and discrimination, instead it became the point at which the politicians seemed to congratulate themselves on a job well done and went about their business, much the same as usual.

Meanwhile, a resurgent Leeds United made a bold statement of intent when, in November 2000, they broke the British transfer record and the world record fee for a defender when they signed Rio Ferdinand from West Ham United for £18 million. The sale of Ferdinand, who had come through the Hammers youth system and was one of a crop of talented youngsters, naturally caused concern amongst West Ham's fans about the future direction of the club. Their concerns would prove to be well placed as the club struggled over the next few seasons and sold an entire generation of its youth system.

• • •

Despite the increased willingness to embrace and celebrate football's diversity, the issue of attendance of black supporters at matches continued to receive very little attention. A 2001 fan survey found that of all the clubs in the Premier League, Arsenal had the highest proportion of black supporters of any top-flight team. It is common to find at football grounds across the country that there are more black

people on the pitch than there are in the stands. Cyrille Regis
has suggested that the lack of black supporters in attendance
at football matches is due to cultural differences. Attending
football matches as part of a Saturday afternoon ritual was
something that people from black communities didn't do
in the way that was ingrained within many white working-
class communities. This lack of attendance at matches even
extended towards the football-mad older generation of Nigerians and other Africans. For those of Caribbean heritage,
a preference for cricket also militated against widespread
attendance at football matches, particularly where the cost
of attendance added an additional impediment to active
support. Amongst later generations of black supporters, the
widespread incidence of racist abuse, along with far-right
influence at grounds, made attendance at games a threatening experience. Clubs in London and the West Midlands,
Manchester City amongst others, were located in areas with
large, ethnically diverse communities, but generally failed to
attract a significant proportion of these fans to games.

For Arsenal, their position as the side with the highest
proportion of black fans in the country began with a crop
of young apprentices who came through the Arsenal youth
system. Paul Davis was the first of the crop to play in the first
team and was later joined by Raphael Meade, Gus Caesar
and Chris Whyte. Meade, Caesar and Whyte all moved on,
but it was only when Davis was joined by David Rocastle,
Michael Thomas, Kevin Campbell and then later by the signings of Viv Anderson and Ian Wright that the incidence of
four or five black players in the side gave a message to the
local black community that Highbury was a safe place to
go. Furthermore, Arsenal began to attract black fans from
other parts of London, a process that gathered pace upon

Wright's arrival at the club. The era also coincided with a period of success for the club under George Graham and then later under Arsène Wenger's stewardship. Other clubs have at times played black footballers in their side, but have rarely played a number of local black players, and certainly not for a sustained period of time. In the Premier League era, black footballers from overseas have provided important role models for Arsenal's black supporters to identify with. Players such as Thierry Henry, Patrick Vieira, Nicolas Anelka, Lauren, Kanu, Eboué and Touré have been joined by black British players like Cole, Campbell, Walcott, Oxlade Chamberlain, Welbeck and others to maintain high numbers of black players, with the result that the club have attracted support not only from its north London hinterland but from outside of London too.

One of Arsenal's legends, Ian Wright, retired at the end of the 1999/2000 season after a four-month spell with Burnley, in which his four goals from fifteen games helped them win promotion from Division Two. It brought to an end a playing career that had elevated Wright to the status of cult hero not only, as you'd expect, from fans of Arsenal and Crystal Palace, but also amongst a generation of black football fans who were drawn to his ability and goal-scoring feats. They were also drawn to his attitude and persona, and to his rags-to-riches story as a late developer who had been signed from the amateur ranks at the age of twenty-one and who at Palace had formed a legendary strike partnership with Mark Bright, their goals helping to fire Palace into the top flight. A dramatic cameo in the 1990 FA Cup final against Manchester United, where a semi-fit Wright's two goals forced extra time and a replay, sealed his legendary status as an all-time Palace great. Over six seasons at Palace, Wright became their record post-war goal scorer and third on the Palace all-time scoring list. In 2005, he was named by Palace fans as their player of the century.

Wright's style of play contained an 'edge' that endeared him to Arsenal fans and made him a figure of hate amongst opposing fans. This side to his game could probably be best characterised as somewhat spiteful and was best illustrated by the altogether nasty two-footed challenge Wright inflicted on Manchester United keeper Peter Schmeichel in February 1997, which was widely interpreted as revenge for an allegation that Schmeichel had called Wright a 'fucking black bastard' after the two had collided the previous November in a typically feisty encounter. Wright had refused to press for action against Schmeichel and in spite of lip-reading evidence suggesting the contrary, police claimed there had been insufficient evidence to press charges.

Arsenal had paid a club record fee of £2.5 million in September 1991 for Wright and he quickly set about becoming an Arsenal legend by ending his first season as top scorer in the English First Division. He was Arsenal's top scorer for six seasons in a row, breaking Arsenal's post-war goal-scoring record with a hat-trick against Bolton in September 1997, and helped Arsenal to achieve the double later that season. Wright also won thirty-three England caps.

On 31 March 2001, David Rocastle, one of the crop of players who had helped to catch the imagination of London's black communities, passed away. Rocastle, who had won two league championships and a League Cup with the Gunners, died of cancer. He had played fourteen times for England and later played for Leeds United, Manchester City, Chelsea, Norwich City and Hull City, with a stint in Malaysian football. His illness had forced his retirement in

1999 and he was just thirty-three years of age at the time of his death.

On 9 November 2001, an unsung black football hero retired from playing league football at the age of forty-two. Grimsby-born Tony Ford made 931 league appearances, not only the highest number of appearances of any black footballer in the English league, but also the appearance record for any outfield player. He was also the first outfield player to play over 1,000 first-team games. Ford had made his debut for Grimsby Town as a sixteen-year-old in 1975 and had gone on to win two caps for the England B team. He received an MBE in 2000.

Like Ford, a number of his generation of black footballers had retired and were considering alternative careers, and for the first time the issues around the lack of opportunities for coaching and management were being voiced. Ford himself had played for far longer than could reasonably have been envisaged, but since the mid-1990s, there had been a steady stream of black players retiring from the game to become the first generation of coaches and managers. The 2001/02 season proved to be something of a seminal year for black managers. The tiny trickle of black managers in the game became a relative flood with the appointment of three in the space of six months. In November 2001, Carlton Palmer took over at Stockport County after replacing the sacked Andy Kilner; in December, former Coventry, West Brom, Aston Villa and Sheffield Wednesday striker Garry Thompson became manager of Bristol Rovers for the second time; and in May 2002, Keith Alexander was appointed as caretaker manager at Lincoln City.

One of the most surprising managerial appointments in Scottish football history took place in June 1999 when John

Barnes was appointed as manager of Celtic. Barnes was brought to the club by the newly appointed Director of Football, his former Liverpool manager Kenny Dalglish. Preferring someone with previous affiliation to the club, the Celtic board were sceptical of an outsider, but Dalglish got his way.

Celtic had appointed non-Scottish managers before, but Barnes was the first Englishman, and he had no managerial experience. Grave doubts were expressed by press, players and other managers in interviews and commentaries. Rangers had assembled a fine squad on good salaries. Celtic's players, on far less money than their Ibrox counterparts, were demanding new and improved terms at the time of Barnes's arrival.

At the beginning of the 1999/2000 season, Celtic started well, winning eleven of their first twelve matches. The problem was, however, that Rangers had a perfect record. Going into the first Old Firm derby at Ibrox, Celtic were four points behind their rivals. Preparation for the Sunday game had not gone well. Talismanic striker Henrik Larsson had suffered a horrendous fracture to his leg in a freak accident during a European tie in Lyon. In spite of conceding an early goal, Celtic were 2–1 up as half-time approached, but in stoppage time, captain Paul Lambert committed a reckless challenge, conceded a penalty, broke his jaw and lost three teeth into the bargain.

From the resulting penalty, Rangers equalised and eventually ran out 4–2 winners to go seven points clear. Celtic managed to stay in touch with the leaders throughout winter and into the New Year. Ideally needing a win against a rampant Rangers, they achieved a 1–1 draw against their arch-rivals in January, which saw Barnes awarded the Manager of the Month award.

Drawn at home in the Scottish Cup against lowly Inverness Caledonian Thistle, a club that had only been formed in 1994, Celtic found themselves a goal down at half-time after a turgid, dispirited performance. In dispute with the club over a new contract, striker Mark Viduka was singled out by Barnes's assistant Eric Black during the half-time interval for an insipid performance. A row ensued and Viduka refused to go out for the second half – as serious a breach of discipline as is possible. Ian Wright was instructed to warm up to replace Viduka, and the team emerged from the dressing room clearly affected by the events at half-time. They managed to fashion themselves an equaliser before Caley Thistle took control of the game and deservedly ran out 3–1 winners, providing one of Scottish football's biggest shocks and the biggest achievement in the Highland club's short history.

The next day, Barnes was sacked. Unable to bridge the financial gap between his club and Rangers, and a victim of the factional politics at the head of the club, black Britain's most decorated footballer was ultimately defeated by an environment where being second in a two-horse race wasn't enough. Given the size of the club and the difficulty of the task, his sacking wasn't particularly surprising. There had been intense speculation about this from the moment he was appointed to the job. Surprisingly, however, it would be nine years before he was offered another job in club football.

Barnes is philosophical about his experience in management. He believes that of course any manager who loses will be sacked, irrespective of race or nationality, but that black managers are given less time to fail. He cites Stan Collymore's assertion when discussing likely contenders for the managerial job at Wolves in 2013 that tough, combative Glaswegian Alex Rae would make the right impression in the dressing room as an example of British football's perception of what or who would make an ideal manager. As black managers don't fit the ideal, when they lose games and their capability as a manager is questioned, they are given less time.

At the end of the 2001/02 season, England participated in the 2002 World Cup and went into the tournament with a degree of optimism about the youthful squad that Sven-Göran Eriksson, England's first foreign manager, had assembled. The squad included David James and Trevor Sinclair of West Ham, Rio Ferdinand of Leeds, Arsenal's Sol Campbell, and Ashley Cole and Emile Heskey of Liverpool. Campbell scored the first goal of England's campaign in a 1–1 draw with Sweden, which was followed by an excellent 1–0 victory against Argentina. With Campbell and Ferdinand at the heart of England's defence and Cole at left-back, England progressed to the next round as group runners-up. They beat Denmark 3–0 in the last-sixteen game, in which Ferdinand and Heskey scored, and therefore progressed to the next round, where they were to meet Brazil. England started well and Heskey provided the pass from which England took the lead, but in first-half stoppage time Brazil equalised. Ronaldinho put Brazil ahead with an outrageous free kick from 40 yards out and then got himself sent off for a studs-up challenge. With Brazil down to ten men, the anticipated England onslaught never materialised. Unable to capitalise on their numerical advantage, England never really looked like getting an equaliser and went tamely out of the competition. Brazil went on to win the tournament and Campbell made the tournament's All-Star team, the only England player to do so.

Campbell's defensive partner in the England side Rio

Ferdinand had also had an excellent tournament and on the strength of that, in July 2002, Manchester United broke the British transfer record when they paid bitter rivals Leeds United £29 million for the centre-back. Ferdinand became the world's most expensive defender for a second time.

The following season, the underperforming West Ham United were surprisingly relegated, sparking an exodus of their best talent. Chelsea paid £6 million for nineteen-year-old defender Glen Johnson in July 2003, and later in the season, in February 2004, Spurs paid £7 million to take striker Jermain Defoe to White Hart Lane.

At Leeds United, Aaron Lennon, a local boy from Chapeltown and one of the brightest stars from the youth system that Ces Podd had helped to develop, made his Premier League debut, aged just sixteen, in a 2–1 loss to Spurs in August 2003. At the time, he was the youngest footballer ever to play in the Premier League.

Later that season, Ron Atkinson, describing a less than stellar performance from Chelsea player and former France international Marcel Desailly in a Champions League game between Monaco and Chelsea in April 2004, referred to Desailly as 'a fucking lazy, thick nigger'. His description had carried with it an element of real venom and he had uttered the statement during the half-time break, when he'd assumed he was off air. However, the comments were broadcast across television networks in the Middle East and resulted in the sacking of Atkinson as an ITV pundit and as a columnist for the *Guardian* newspaper.

Atkinson had played an important role in the history of black footballers in Britain. He had been the first manager to regularly field three black players in a top-flight side and had coined the name the Three Degrees to describe Batson,

Cunningham and Regis. When he was appointed manager of West Brom, he had brought Batson with him from Cambridge United, where he had made the classy right-back his captain. As manager of Manchester United, he had also signed Remi Moses, making Moses the first black player to play for United. At Aston Villa, Atkinson had fielded a side with nine black players in the starting XI.

As a successful manager, Atkinson signed and selected whoever he thought could do the job he wanted, and several of those players were black. His willingness to provide opportunities for black players not only to play, but to play with confidence and responsibility, was, at the time, almost unique amongst managers of his generation.

He had also encouraged several black players to take coaching qualifications and consider careers in coaching and football management; his record in nurturing black talent made his remarks about Desailly all the more shocking. Amongst black players, there exists a wide range of perspectives about the motives behind his comments. Inevitably, those who played under him were more likely to provide a sympathetic assessment of him. Some former black players, notably Carlton Palmer, were keen to defend him, but most found his remarks and subsequent behaviour unacceptable and demeaning, including both Regis and Batson. They acknowledged that Atkinson was distinctly 'old-school' in his attitudes and outlook and often indulged in banter and behaviour that was clearly the wrong side of offensive, aimed at a wide range of targets, not necessarily black footballers. Under his stewardship, Cunningham and Regis earned England caps, and many other black players he managed earned international recognition. His Aston Villa side of the early 1990s regularly included five or six black players.

However, by the time Atkinson had issued his remark, changing social attitudes had rendered the term as just about the most offensive in the English vocabulary. His often clumsy attempts to explain his remarks after the Desailly incident demonstrated what little understanding he had as to why his utterances were so offensive. A TV documentary with veteran black activist and broadcaster Darcus Howe further exposed Atkinson's attitudes on issues of race. When Howe confronted Atkinson on his remarks, he expressed contrition, seemingly believing that the incident should be viewed as little more than a minor blot on an otherwise highly successful career in the game. However, he appeared to possess little understanding as to why his description of Desailly was so unacceptable and preferred instead to blame a culture of political correctness and to present himself as the victim, rather than Desailly.

Atkinson was a product not only of his generation but also of the insular nature of English football. He had made his supposedly off-air remarks amongst those he assumed shared his perception of the game and, in doing so, forced a reassessment of his legacy in providing opportunities for black footballers; his comments have since come to redefine his career. Atkinson was never an anti-racist crusader; he was a football manager and selected black players because, ultimately, he thought they would add something to his teams that could make them successful. His support for black footballers extended as far as they were able to perform well, and when a player dropped below a level that was of use to the team, they were reduced to 'a fucking lazy, thick nigger'.

If the English FA paid barely concealed lip service to issues of racism, their Scottish counterparts seemed equally incapable of doing any more. The treatment of firstly Mark Walters and then later Paul Elliott should have been the catalyst for the Scottish FA to take action on the issue. While the English FA had agreed to fund the Kick It Out campaign in 1997, the Scottish FA had the opportunity either to fund the campaign to enable its activities to extend north of the border or to develop a similar campaign of their own. They did neither. In keeping with the increasingly global game, Scottish sides continued to sign black players, not only from England but from around the globe. For the few home-grown black players, like Kevin Harper, the experience at grassroots level and when starting out in the professional game illustrated how this lack of action on racist abuse left players feeling isolated and frustrated.

Harper was born in Oldham to a Scottish mother and Jamaican father. His father died before Harper was born and, after a year, his mother returned to her native Glasgow. He spent his first few months in Scotland in children's homes and eventually settled with his mother in Possilpark, a tough housing scheme in north Glasgow, amongst the poorest areas in the UK. Although the scheme was notorious for its social problems, every available space was usually taken up by a football game and Harper found himself in demand from other kids eager for him to join their makeshift sides. He would get home from school, have a quick piece and jam and be out playing football. This would eventually be interrupted by his tea, after which he would be out again until it was time for bed.

Although small, Harper was skilful and strong and, as one of only two black kids on the sprawling estate, football was an important part of his integration and acceptance into the world of his peers. However, while his proficiency as a footballer had gained him acceptance, it hadn't provided freedom

from racist abuse. Growing up in the 1980s, Harper constantly had to fight to defend himself from racist abuse from
other children. Furthermore, after he'd given another child a
beating for racially abusing him, their parents would often
seek him out to provide him with additional racist abuse.

His introduction to organised grassroots football came
when a game he was playing with a friend was suddenly
abandoned after his friend had been forced to leave to
attend football training. His friend invited Harper along and
Harper went to play for Celtic North in nearby Sighthill.
Sighthill would later become a housing location for asylum
seekers, refugees and other migrants, due to its low occu-
pancy rate and poor conditions. After a year at Celtic North,
he played for West Park in Bishopbriggs, an affluent area of
north Glasgow.

His manager at Bishopbriggs was to have a huge influence
on his childhood. Bert Rowan would pick Harper up from
his home and drop him off in his car. He organised a number
of trips abroad for the team to play in international youth
tournaments. Harper's mother worked three jobs to save
enough money to buy him football boots, so foreign football tournaments were out of the question. Rowan would
arrange sponsorship for Harper to fund his trip and provide
him with a little spending money.

Harper suffered constant racist abuse not only by opponents but also by coaches and parents on the sidelines. It
cut him deeply, particularly the experience of being racially
abused by adults, which he found especially horrific. Referees did nothing, unwilling or unable to address the behaviour. In the absence of FIFA directives or leadership amongst
grassroots administrators, he was left to deal with the situation pretty much on his own. As his mother couldn't drive

and had therefore never seen him play, she could offer him no support or protection.

By the age of thirteen he was constantly told how good he was and began to realise that he really was a talented footballer. As he became one of West Park's stand-out performers, opposition coaches and parents would constantly implore their charges to 'break the black bastard's legs'. As Harper was no shrinking violet, he would get into fights on the pitch and arguments on the sidelines, until Rowan took him aside and encouraged him to allow his football to do the talking.

He began to attract the attention of professional clubs. At a tournament in Paisley, Alex Miller, manager of Hibs, was watching his son play when his attention was drawn to an adjoining pitch, where a small black kid was ripping through opposition defences at will and helping himself to a hatful of goals. A couple of weeks later, Miller turned up at Harper's home, along with Hibs coach Martin Ferguson, brother of Sir Alex. At the time, Harper had been training with Hearts and had also received interest from Dundee United and Spurs, but was impressed with Hibs because their manager had made an effort to come round to a rough housing scheme that he would have heard about for all the wrong reasons. He also felt that he'd get the opportunity to get into the first team much quicker than at other sides, so he agreed to sign schoolboy forms with Hibs. A week before his sixteenth birthday, he signed professional forms and began his rise through the ranks. After a handful of reserve team appearances, he made his first-team debut at the age of seventeen. In so doing, Harper became the first home-grown black player to appear in the Scottish Premier League.

In 1991, the Scottish FA had belatedly condemned the boos and monkey chants suffered by Mark Walters after his experience at Tynecastle had been brought to national attention by Archie Macpherson's expression of shame on Scottish television. It continued to sit on the sidelines as racist behaviour and actions continued to blight the Scottish game. In August 1995, George Galloway, Labour MP for Glasgow Hillhead, had announced the possible takeover of Partick Thistle by a consortium of Asian businessmen fronted by Charan Gill, a businessman and restaurant owner. Thistle desperately needed investment in the team, while fan groups had voiced concern over the continued lack of investment in playing staff and over the Thistle board's running of the club. Days after Galloway's announcement, Partick Thistle chairman Jim Oliver stated that Galloway was trying to win support for Asian votes, the club was being hijacked and he would not sell it 'simply to satisfy the wishes of some Indian with a curry shop'. When Oliver was asked if his comments were racist, he replied, 'As I understand it he is an Indian and he owns a curry shop. If he is not an Indian with a curry shop, then I'll apologise … if they are Asians, Eskimos, or one-eyed black lesbian saxophone players, if they have the money we will talk to them.'

The media debate around the takeover – or 'takeaway', as it was often described – was full of racist language, crude stereotypes and racist 'humour'. The unashamed description of the club as 'Paki Thistle' by Ian Archer, a journalist from *The Herald* in August 1995, demonstrated the depths to which Scottish newspapers were prepared to sink. Meanwhile, the Scottish FA remained silent.

It was in an Edinburgh derby game at Hibs' Easter Road ground in September 1996 that the Scottish FA further demonstrated its craven attitude towards issues of racism. Harper had been subjected to monkey noises by Hearts supporters every time he picked up possession. Hearts were 2–0 up when Harper picked up a pass on the right-hand side. With a body swerve, he put one defender on his backside and picked up pace, and with a drop of the shoulder he pushed the ball past Hearts captain Gary Mackay. Comprehensively beaten for pace, Mackay brought him down. As Harper picked himself up and made his way towards the penalty area to wait for the resultant free kick, Mackay barged into him and got right in his face. As Harper continued on his way, Mackay allegedly made monkey noises at him (which Mackay has denied). The match ended with a 3–1 victory for Hearts, but the following day Harper was contacted by a journalist from *Scotland on Sunday* and asked for his comments on the issue. A subsequent piece appeared in the paper, in which Harper spoke about the need to integrate ethnic minority kids into the Scottish game and how the incident sent out the wrong message to them.

The SFA had an opportunity to undertake some kind of investigation into Harper's allegations, but chose not to. They also had an opportunity to bring charges of 'bringing the game into disrepute', or similar, but didn't. There were none of the channels to deal with issues of racism that should clearly have been put in place after Mark Walters and then Paul Elliott had been racially abused. Mackay was an established and high-profile Scottish international and was never questioned or called to account for the allegations, which he has always denied. Mackay undertakes high-profile anti-racist work within Scottish football, including with Show Racism the Red Card. Harper was only twenty years old at the time and was left frustrated and angered by the lack of action by the custodians of the Scottish game.

Pointedly, there was no support for Harper from his club or teammates, their inaction a reflection of simply not knowing how to react.

Hibs were relegated at the end of season 1997/98 and, as one of its brightest stars, Harper went to Derby County in the English Premier League for a week-long trial before being sold to them at the start of the following season as Hibs desperately sought ways to cut costs.

The now 22-year-old had been suspended as a result of a red card he'd received as Hibs' battle to stave off relegation faltered. Therefore, he hadn't played any games for Hibs and wasn't fit enough to feature for his new side in the immediate aftermath of his transfer in September 1998. Harper observed that Premier League players were bigger, fitter and stronger than he was used to in Scotland and, although Hibs were a professional outfit, the level of professionalism and the standard of facilities that existed at Derby were of an altogether different magnitude. His coach at Derby was Steve McClaren, future England manager, whom Harper describes as the best coach he's worked with. McClaren's sessions were geared towards honing preparation for matches. Sessions were short, sharp and high-tempo and were varied to maintain the interest of players and to focus on different aspects of their play. Just prior to matches, the squad would play fast-paced games of seven-a-side to increase sharpness for the game ahead. As well as specialist seven-a-side pitches, there were massage chairs, big screens to watch videos of games, and specialist training facilities – a far cry from what he was used to at Hibs. In addition, there were some great players and internationals at Derby such as the Croatian Igor Štimac, the Costa Rican Paulo Wanchope, the Italian Stefano Eranio, the Norwegian Lars Bohinen, the Argentinian

Horacio Carbonari, and Deon Burton, who had represented Jamaica at the recent World Cup, as well as home-grown black players such as Dean Sturridge. The multinational and cosmopolitan nature of the Derby side was a far cry from the overwhelmingly Scottish nature of the Hibs squad.

Some six weeks after signing for Derby, Harper was fit enough to be included in the first-team squad. He had been put on a weight programme as part of his fitness regime, and now, visibly heavier, he made his first start at Anfield against Liverpool. In spite of his small stature, Harper had always been a good header of a ball and had a prodigious leap. Employed on the right but with licence to drift infield, he got on the end of a deep cross from the left to employ his leaping ability to great effect and put a firm, well-placed header beyond David James into the Kop-end goal to put Derby 1–0 up. He also had a hand in Derby's second goal by Wanchope and, despite a late rally by Liverpool to pull a goal back, Derby ran out 2–1 winners.

However, Harper's move to Derby was a rather unhappy one overall. It was the first time he'd been away from his mother and he didn't settle well and wasn't sleeping. He was living in a hotel, where there were also other Derby players, including Rory Delap, with whom he got on well. He was also friendly with Deon Burton, but Burton lived in Nottingham and Harper felt largely isolated and had few friends, which in turn caused him to become too independent and seek out his own company far too readily.

Harper's form was affected and he failed to impress. His appearances were largely as substitute, and part way through the following season he was loaned out to Walsall. Initially, this was to be for the remainder of the season, but his loan period was cut short when he was sold to Portsmouth in March 2000. His time at Portsmouth was special and coincided with one of the most exciting times in the club's history. The club were embroiled in a relegation battle from the First Division when he joined and they managed to stay up on the last day of the season. Manager Tony Pulis, who'd signed him, was sacked in October 2000 and was eventually replaced by Graham Rix in February 2001. The side were languishing in mid-table when Rix was sacked and replaced by the club's Director of Football, Harry Redknapp, in March 2002. With newly acquired money from club owner Milan Mandarić, Redknapp brought in England internationals like Steve Stone and Paul Merson. He also signed high-quality players like Shaka Hislop and Nigerian international Yakubu. Harper played thirty-nine games at right and left wing-back during the 2002/03 season despite suffering a double hernia in October. He was on Voltarol consistently and played on until the last but one game of the season, when he finally had an operation to correct his hernia problem. Portsmouth won the First Division title at a canter to gain promotion to the Premier League.

He played a few games in the Premier League before he was loaned out to Norwich City in the First Division, where he helped the side to gain promotion to the Premier League. He then went to join his former manager Tony Pulis at Stoke City but suffered a number of injuries. He found he had a defect in his back that affected his calf muscles and put them under undue strain. His injury problems meant he was unable to hold down a regular club place and he moved around before returning to Scotland.

During his time at Hibs, Harper had made nine appearances for the Scotland under-21 side and had scored a hat-trick on his debut. Like Iffy Onuora, he should have got a call up for Scotland under Craig Brown. Brown had stuck with an older generation of players for the Euro 2000 campaign, mistrusting younger players and keeping the old for one tournament too long. The consequence of this was that a generation of Scottish players were denied the opportunity to gain international experience, which deeply affected the national side and the ability of subsequent managers, like Berti Vogts, to have an impact on the team's progress. During the period in which Harper had won a First Division winner's medal with Portsmouth, he was cruelly overlooked for an international cap. Brown gave the impression he thought the English First Division was not of a good standard and Scotland generally were going through one of their occasional periods when English-based players were being overlooked. Undoubtedly, had he played for Celtic or Rangers, Harper would have won a number of international caps.

Through his career, Harper was uniquely positioned to assess the main differences between Scottish and English football with regard to racism, and they proved to be overwhelmingly cultural. The more cosmopolitan nature of the English game and, in particular, the influence of more black players in English teams meant that home-grown white players had far more education and awareness of issues of racism than their Scottish counterparts. This, along with some prominent anti-racist campaigns, had had a significant impact on English society. Meanwhile, Scotland's lack of organised far-right racist groups within the Scottish political framework had allowed a narrative of complacency to develop within Scottish politics and society, giving rise to the idea that racism was somehow an English phenomenon and that Scotland was a far more tolerant and welcoming nation than England. Harper's experience as a child, growing up on one of Scotland's biggest estates in its biggest city, challenges that idea.

The Scottish game never experienced its watershed moment that would enable it to collectively draw the conclusion that issues of racism could no longer be allowed to blight the game. The failure of the Scottish footballing authorities to provide support for Walters, Harper and others reflected their complacency about racism within Scottish society and a degree of cowardice within football.

CHAPTER 13

DOING SWEET FA

MUCH OF THE focus of the media attention around racist activity had shifted as a result of some high-profile incidences of racism involving English clubs and national sides, particularly in southern and eastern Europe. Black players of English teams were being subjected to a type of racist abuse that had largely been eliminated from the English game. The incidents occurred throughout mainland Europe, but appeared to be worst in Spain, Italy and a number of countries in eastern Europe.

Of the European countries, Britain was amongst the first to exploit the footballing talent that emerged from its home-grown black communities. After the Second World War, it had been amongst the first European countries to exploit its former colonies as a source of cheap labour and invite black people to its shores, and other European nations followed suit. Portugal had a long history of inclusion of black players in its domestic game, both from within its shores and from its former colonies, such as Mozambique and Angola. France's dashing national side of the 1980s included Marius Trésor and future Fulham manager Jean Tigana, amongst others. The last all-white Dutch national side had played in the early 1980s and black players Ruud Gullit, Frank Rijkaard and Aron Winter had been regulars at

international level since the middle of the decade. Other
European countries such as Germany and Belgium didn't
feature black players on a regular basis until the late 1990s.

Changes in patterns of migration across Europe resulted
in a more diverse profile of home-grown talent playing
within European countries, particularly from those communities whose heritage was from footballing hotbeds in
sub-Saharan and northern Africa. At youth level, in particular, most national teams in western Europe were regularly
including black players within their squads. As Europe was
becoming more racially diverse, the backlash from sections
of host white football fans increased. The wholesale terrace
abuse that had become a common feature of English football was replicated in other European countries. Italy, Spain,
Germany, Belgium and others all had well-documented instances of terrace racism.

In eastern Europe, a different situation had arisen. Eastern
European countries hadn't developed colonies in the way
western powers had done. The end of the Soviet-dominated
regimes following the fall of the Iron Curtain in 1989 had
brought into being new political structures and the emergence of new nations. The development of these new nations
had ushered in nationalist and patriotic political trends, and
football became the arena where expressions of nationalism
were played out.

In the era of the global economy, Europe became the
centre of the global game. The best players from across the
world were playing in European leagues in a way that would
have been inconceivable in the era of Pelé, Jairzinho and
others, who undertook their footballing careers almost entirely in their home country of Brazil. For many countries in
Europe, a small number of black players, mainly Brazilians,

Nigerians or other Africans, began to turn out regularly within these leagues and suffered widespread racist abuse, not only in eastern Europe but in many parts of western Europe also.

This abuse wasn't confined to domestic games: in October 2002, for example, an England side containing Andy Cole and Emile Heskey was racially abused by Slovakia fans. To their credit, the Slovakian FA apologised to the English FA and to Cole and Heskey too. A year later, in September 2003, England's black players, Cole, Heskey and Sol Campbell, were racially abused by Macedonia fans.

However, racist abuse wasn't focused completely in one direction. In April 2003, the FA was fined £70,000 for a pitch invasion and racist abuse by England fans at a Euro 2004 qualifier against Turkey at the Stadium of Light in Sunderland. England fans had booed the Turkish national anthem and kept up chants of 'I'd rather be a Paki than a Turk' and 'Stand up if you hate the Turks' for the duration of the game.

Despite substantial evidence to the contrary, however, the media and football authorities were now beginning to peddle the narrative that English football had largely addressed its racism problem, which was now a relic from football's dark ages, along with football hooliganism and tackles from behind. The notion that racism had been eliminated from the English game was proving hollow, but they were promoting it with increasing conviction nonetheless – and with increasing success. What was needed was an opportunity to fully consolidate the illusion and this duly arrived in the form of an England international friendly against Spain.

The issue of racism had dominated the run-up to the game in November 2004. Spain manager Luis Aragonés had referred to Arsenal's Thierry Henry as a 'black shit' in an apparent attempt to motivate the Spain winger – and Henry's Arsenal teammate – José Antonio Reyes while preparing for a World Cup qualifier against Belgium in October 2004. His comments were widely reported in the British media and the issue was raised in press conferences with Aragonés in the build-up to the game, with repeated calls from the British media for the Spanish authorities to take action against their manager. For his part, Aragonés caused further controversy by declaring that his 'conscience was clear', asserting that it was the English who were racist, and criticising Britain's colonial past. On the night before the game, England's black players suffered racist abuse in an under-21 international between the two sides.

The game at the Bernabéu stadium in Madrid was marred by racist chanting directed at England's black players by large sections of the crowd. The chanting took place every time one of the black players took possession, and seemed to contribute greatly to what turned out to be a niggly, bad-tempered spectacle. The abuse seemed to particularly affect England left-back Ashley Cole's composure, but it was also clear that the white players in the side were affected by the general atmosphere within the stadium.

After the game, the English media were outraged. They denounced the racist behaviour of the Spanish crowd and the previous racist utterings of Aragonés towards Henry. They also correctly noted that the Spanish football authorities and large parts of the Spanish media had not acknowledged that the abuse had occurred, fuelling the belief that a failure to condemn previous racist incidents had contributed to the level and vehemence of the attacks on England players. The press, television pundits, the FA, the Prime Minister, the

Sports Minister and John Motson all condemned the monkey chanting and general racist abuse. An Early Day Motion condemning the incident was put forward in the British Parliament and enthusiastically supported by all sides of the House. Never before had so many both within and outside the game been so unanimous and explicit about condemning racism. It seemed to denote a new level of awareness and determination to finally tackle the issue.

The press reaction gave the impression that the kind of abuse meted out to Shaun Wright-Phillips, Rio Ferdinand, Ashley Cole and others was an entirely new and unique occurrence. A typical response came from *The Guardian*, which stated: 'The abuse, the worst example of racism at an England match in decades, was greeted with disgust and disbelief in the UK, which is acknowledged as leading the way in European football in the battle against racism.'

The abuse was indeed deeply unsavoury, but no more so than abuse given to John Barnes, Ruud Gullit and others at national games. Indeed, in the wake of the game, Barnes was moved to advise caution against the self-congratulatory tone of much of the press reaction. He implored, 'Please let's not all believe we're much better in this country. Because we don't hear it any more we think we're getting rid of racism. They might be less vocal but there are plenty of racists around in English football.'

Few in the media were prepared to deviate from the accepted line that Barnes had challenged. However, in another *Guardian* article, commenting on press hypocrisy around the events in Madrid, journalist Martin Jacques observed:

The condemnation carried more than a hint of the sanctimonious: the implication that somehow the English game was

no longer tainted with racism. An interesting trait of racism is
that the perpetrators – conscious or unconscious – are always
in denial. It was so in the 1970s and 1980s, when monkey
chanting and banana throwing were at their height in the
English game and it was rarely ever reported on. And it was
true again now as people in the game queued up to condemn
the events in the Bernabéu while remaining silent about the
racist practices that abound in the Football Association, the
clubs and the media at home.

The Bernabéu incident marked the point at which the media
placed itself firmly in the anti-racist camp and designed a
brand new narrative of racism as something that now only
took place in other European countries. In doing so, they
completely disregarded their role in ignoring and in some
cases pandering to issues of racism within the game. The
media had now reinvented themselves as defenders of the
dignity and human rights of black footballers, but they had
also realised that racism was a toxic issue that could maximise attention for media outlets.

The widespread condemnation of the abuse of England's
black players had travelled far beyond football's traditional
circles. Racism had developed into an issue that no right-
minded person would wish to be accused of and one they
would be keen to support efforts to eliminate. It was an issue
that could fill column inches, and everybody and anybody
could have an opinion on the matter. Their opinion would
then provide opportunities for additional column inches or
items on 24-hour sports news outlets. Issues of racism thus
became increasingly sensationalised and treated in the same
way as the press might report on a Premier League star falling drunk out of a nightclub or cheating on his wife with a

supermodel. From this point on, the media treated issues of racism as items of celebrity gossip to provide opportunities to berate, condemn and otherwise adopt a holier-than-thou attitude. The impact of this about-turn has been to treat each incidence of racism as a self-contained event, with the authorities under immediate pressure to undertake inquiries, hearings and investigations and then simply dispense fines, bans or other sanctions. Anyone with even a tenuous connection to the game is required to give their opinion, irrespective of their understanding or knowledge of the underlying factors. However, this approach does nothing to bring the game as a whole any closer to addressing these issues.

Away from international football, black players continued to have an impact on the domestic game. On 10 April 2005, James Vaughan became the youngest ever Premier League goal scorer when he netted one within a few minutes of coming on for his debut appearance as a substitute for his club, Everton, in a match against Crystal Palace at the age of sixteen years and 271 days. Meanwhile at Leeds, eighteen-year-old Aaron Lennon had just completed an exceptional first season after his club's relegation to the Championship and was attracting interest from top-flight sides. The club was in a dire financial situation and Lennon was sold in a fire sale for a paltry £1 million to Tottenham Hotspur in July 2005. Later that month, Chelsea signed Ian Wright's son Shaun Wright-Phillips, a product of Manchester City's academy, for £21 million and helped to ease City's considerable financial problems at the same time.

The FA once again showed its unwillingness to tackle issues of racism unless they were high-profile incidents or involved high-profile players. Bradford City keeper Donovan Ricketts was given a red card for making an abusive gesture to Southend fans, alleging racist abuse. Bradford appealed, citing the alleged racist abuse as mitigation, but the FA decided to limit the remit of the appeal to whether or not Ricketts had made the gesture and left the matter of racist abuse to the police, thereby absolving themselves of any responsibility.

• • •

The England squad for the 2006 World Cup in Germany contained Ashley Cole, Rio Ferdinand, Sol Campbell, David James, Jermaine Jenas, Aaron Lennon and, most surprisingly, seventeen-year-old Theo Walcott. Arsenal had paid £5 million to Championship side Southampton for the young striker as a sixteen-year-old in January 2006. Walcott hadn't yet made his debut for Arsenal when he was called up for the World Cup squad and would become the youngest ever player to feature for England when he appeared as substitute in a pre-World Cup warm-up game against Hungary in May 2006, when he was just seventeen years and seventy-five days old.

In their opening game, an England line-up featuring Rio Ferdinand and Ashley Cole beat Paraguay in an unconvincing 1–0 win. Their next match, against Trinidad and Tobago, was a sterile, turgid affair, with England finally overcoming their opponents with two late goals. Trinidad and Tobago, featuring a number of British-based players including Dwight Yorke and Shaka Hislop, were the smallest nation ever to qualify for the World Cup. England finished top of their group after a 2–2 draw against Sweden and were eventually to go out on penalties in the quarter-finals to Portugal. Walcott never got to feature in the tournament.

• • •

Knutsford is a quiet, affluent town in Cheshire, close to the M6 and within easy striking distance of Liverpool, Manchester and other towns within the north-west of England that form a key part of football's traditional heartland. The area has become a magnet as a place of residence for the wealthy young men who kick a football around for a living.

One of these young men was twenty-year-old Everton striker Victor Anichebe, who was out and about in Knutsford town centre with an old friend, Yeovil Town player Lee Peltier, in March 2009. The two had known each other for many years. Anichebe was a product of Everton's academy and Peltier had been through the Liverpool academy and had played a few games for the first team before eventually moving on to play for Yeovil.

The two had gone for lunch and then spent some time looking in a jeweller's shop window. After queuing at a cash machine, Anichebe went into a branch of Waterstones and began searching on the shop computer for a title he was interested in. At this point, members of Cheshire Constabulary entered the shop and took Anichebe outside. He had undergone an operation a few days earlier on a serious injury that eventually kept him out of the game for eleven months and was unable to walk without the aid of crutches. While outside, one of the officers tried to remove one of his crutches to prevent escape, to which Anichebe objected. Meanwhile, Peltier had been placed in handcuffs and the officers were heavy handed and aggressive. When, eventually, other officers arrived, one of them recognised Anichebe and the pair were released.

In this run-of-the-mill confrontation, many young black males would have considered their experience a lucky escape and would most likely have tried to put the matter behind them. Instead, angered and humiliated at being marched out of a bookshop and having his friend handcuffed in a busy street in broad daylight, Anichebe went public and informed the press of the incident. He demanded an apology and wondered out loud if their treatment at the hands of Cheshire Police had been racially motivated. The story was picked up by a number of media outlets.

A few days later, the Assistant Chief Constable of Cheshire Police made a personal visit to Anichebe's home in Knutsford to apologise for the behaviour of the officers. He explained that by looking in a jeweller's shop window they had been acting suspiciously; furthermore, they had gone to a cash machine, spoken to a woman (whom Anichebe had directed to an alternative cash machine) and looked up and down the street, and so had further aroused suspicion. The officer was keen to make Anichebe understand that race had not been a factor in his and Peltier's treatment.

Home Office research published in March 2006 found that black people were six times more likely to be stopped and searched in the street than white people, that the high levels of stop and search could not be explained by the greater police presence within black communities, and that black people are over-represented at every level of the criminal justice system, from being three times more likely to be arrested through to making up 24 per cent of the prison population, despite accounting for less than 3 per cent of the overall UK population. The report also found that Asians were twice as likely to be stopped and searched as whites.

Stephen Lawrence's murder was supposed to be a

game-changer. The authorities had expressed the view that something positive would come out as a result of his murder and the associated issues around Lord Macpherson's report. There was widespread agreement that Stephen Lawrence's murder would not be in vain – but, as the treatment of Anichebe and Peltier starkly illustrated, nothing had changed in terms of black communities' relationship with the police. The use of stop and search was still widespread – seemingly as an instrument of harassment and coercion, given that the Home Office agree it has little impact as a method of crime prevention and detection. Indeed, a Home Office report of 2002 estimated that searches reduced the incidence of 'disruptable crimes' by just 0.2 per cent. The repeal of the 'Sus' law had ultimately made little difference in preventing the abuse of stop-and-search powers, and the issue continued to shape the relationship between the police and young black males.

The status of Anichebe and Peltier as footballers was not able to protect them from heavy-handed, aggressive and discriminatory policing. Their detention, albeit brief, would likely have had a different outcome had they not had such a high profile and had they not had access to press contacts and high-quality legal representation. The two also received a personal apology from a high-ranking officer, which the vast majority of black males, with no such access to the trappings of Premier League stardom, would have been very unlikely to receive.

CHAPTER 14

BUT CAN THEY MANAGE?

'How is the FA, how is the PFA, how is the LMA going to help people like Michael Johnson, which are totally qualified and through no fault of their own, cannot get one foot on the ladder?' – Michael Johnson

THERE IS A point in a veteran footballer's career when their understanding, their ability to read the game, their powers of anticipation, their organisational skills, their ability to cope with pressure and their knowledge of how to play their position is at a level higher than any other time in their career. The point at which they know exactly how many minutes of a game have gone without the need to check the clock or know exactly what to say when the team is 3–0 up or 3–0 down. This is the stage when, mentally, their game is at a premium, but the body can't do what the mind wants it to. Inevitably, a player goes through a process of denial, but soon it takes its toll on their performance. Those players whose game relied on blistering pace experience the decline most acutely, but some manage this decline better than others. Some are able to work out what their body will allow them to do and adjust accordingly. If they have clubs or managers who value their experience, they may be able to reinvent themselves. As his pace dulled and he could no longer cope with a succession of young flying wide-men, Viv Anderson successfully reinvented himself as a centre-back, where his ability to read the game, his positional sense and his organisational skills extended his career in the top flight and won him honours with Sheffield Wednesday.

Every player thinks about going into management, if only because they are constantly asked about how much longer they can play and what their plans are once their playing days are over. Towards the end of his playing career, Iffy Onuora had a dressing room conversation with three or four teammates about the prospect of taking the UEFA B Licence, the first step on the ladder for a professional footballer to become a fully qualified coach. Agreeing that it would be a great way to accumulate their qualifications, and discussing how they could provide each other with mutual support to achieve it, they decided that at the end of the season they would all adjourn to some FA-approved venue to acquire their coaching badges and take their first tentative steps towards a career in coaching. When the end of the season came and Onuora reminded his colleagues of the agreement they'd made so enthusiastically, all of them made their excuses, citing family, time and other commitments for their inability to attend the course. With his enthusiasm undimmed, Onuora decided to go it alone.

Onuora had first taken basic-level coaching qualifications in his late teens and early twenties and had coached young footballers in and around West Yorkshire during his days as a student at Bradford University. He'd had an opportunity to work with Leeds United and had observed then Leeds manager Billy Bremner's first-team coaching sessions. Always something of a student of the game, his experience at university instilled a liking for coaching. As he became one of the senior professionals at his various clubs, he became a stronger voice in dressing room and started thinking about coaching. He'd played under a number of good managers. His first manager, Eoin Hand, had managed the Republic of Ireland. Tony Pulis went on to manage in the Premier League for different clubs. Neil Warnock had forged a successful career as an expert in getting teams promoted to the top flight, if not always able to keep them there. Peter Taylor had managed the England under-21 side and was later to become caretaker manager of the full England side. Some were great coaches, preparing lively and engaging sessions that were brilliant at developing technique, but struggled to manage people and individuals. Some had great knowledge of the game and very good tactical awareness but weren't the best at designing high-quality coaching sessions. Some were great motivators; others were nice but not always strong enough personalities to maintain discipline. Others were all too willing to blame the players for poor performances and sought to deflect attention from their own deficiencies. Some managers were egotists, others disciplinarians; some were untrustworthy, others were spiky characters; and some just weren't very nice people.

As he played under a succession of managers, Onuora carefully observed the way in which they operated, taking ideas about how things should and should not be done, gaining tactical insights and training tips, handling players and fellow coaches, delegating skills, handling pressure and getting to grips with all the other challenges of football management in preparation for becoming a coach. At the age of thirty-five, while playing at Sheffield United, Onuora snapped his Achilles tendon and, although he'd done well to come back to play later that season, and played a further

season, the physical demands of playing as a central striker
– the need to jump, spring and challenge for the ball – meant
that he was never quite the same. The constant toll on his
body, and the succession of loans, transfers and general instability of a veteran player, meant that football had become
too much like a job, and he decided to retire.

While playing, he had acquired a full set of coaching
badges, including the UEFA Pro Licence, the qualification
required to coach in the top flight across all of Europe's
top divisions and at international level, and he had also acquired an Applied Certificate of Football Management from
Warwick University, where he was the only current player,
alongside a number of established league managers, assistant managers and coaches, to complete the course.

Football is one of the few multi-million-pound businesses
where coaching jobs are almost exclusively determined by
who you know. Former Arsenal and England player Paul
Merson had taken over as manager of First Division Walsall.
His assistant at Walsall was Simon Osborn, who'd played
with Onuora at Gillingham and had bonded with him over
their shared experience of fragile Achilles tendons. Merson's
knowledge of the game was good, but neither he nor Osborn
had any coaching badges and they wanted someone who
was qualified. Osborn recommended Onuora to Merson
and, after meeting with him, Merson offered Onuora the job
of first-team coach at the start of the 2005/06 season.

The role was something of a baptism of fire as he crossed
the line from player to coach. Because he'd only just stopped
playing, he hadn't the experience of organising and delivering
coaching sessions on a daily basis. He had been able to take
the odd session here and there, but the responsibility proved
something of a culture shock. Slowly, however, he got used to

the challenge of the role, but the team weren't playing well. Losing games, they were sliding down the table; Merson had spent heavily and the fans had lost patience. Changes had to be made, and after only three or four months in the role, it was a case of last in first out, so Onuora was sacrificed for a more experienced coach. Eventually, Merson was sacked in February 2006, with the team in the relegation zone.

Before Onuora had had an opportunity to fully reflect upon his first taste of coaching, barely a week after his sacking by Walsall, a former manager, Andy King, offered him the job as head of youth development at his old club Swindon Town, who were also in the First Division. The job of an academy head is fundamentally an administrative position rather than overseeing the coaching of young players. The role includes attending regular meetings with every age-group coach, arranging trials for young players, liaising with scouts, speaking with other academy coaches, dealing with complaints from parents that their son isn't playing often enough or making sufficient progress, and the often heartbreaking job of releasing young players who aren't good enough to make the grade. He was, on occasions, able to put on a tracksuit and take the odd session with the under-18s, but it was a rare luxury when he was able to put his coaching credentials to good use.

However, Swindon Town were in crisis. They were in severe financial difficulties and were soon placed into administration. Results were poor, winter hadn't yet got into its stride and they were already embroiled in a relegation battle. A sizeable number of fans were calling for the manager to be sacked and opposition teams, sensing a fire sale, were eyeing up the team's best talent to try to get it on the cheap. The embattled manager had received some highly unsavoury personal criticism and, after losing their fifth game on the spin, he left the club.

Given the financial state of the club, the obvious replacement was player-coach Alan Reeves, but the veteran centre-back had broken his leg. Onuora was already helping out with first-team coaching duties when Swindon and Andy King parted company. The day after King's departure, Onuora received a phone call from a Swindon board member and was offered the job as caretaker until further notice, making Onuora one of only a handful of black managers at the time.

Two months into the job, the freefall that had befallen the club's league fortunes had been arrested, but results were still poor. At this point, the club was offered a much needed cash injection of £120,000 to participate in a TV documentary. The documentary would see a young, inexperienced football manager being mentored by an older guru-type, who would impart his knowledge and wisdom for the benefit of the fledgling manager. The management guru would be Ron Atkinson, barely twelve months after leaving his job as a TV pundit in disgrace.

It is difficult not to view the programme as a highly cynical manoeuvre on the part of Sky TV to assist in the resurrection of the disgraced Atkinson's career and repair accusations that he was racially prejudiced by placing him in the role of trouble-shooter in support of a black manager. Onuora was given the opportunity to reject Sky and Atkinson's overtures by the club, but the state of the club's finances meant that he had far greater responsibilities than his own personal feelings on the matter. In the run-up to Christmas, there were rumours around the club that many of the staff wouldn't be paid. While the players' wages would have been prioritised, there was an army of loyal personnel who were also fans and were helping to keep the club afloat. Ground staff, catering, retail, admin and other staff all had bills to pay, families to feed and other responsibilities, so, in spite of reservations about assisting in Atkinson's rehabilitation, Onuora agreed. Filming was to last from January till the end of the season.

He insisted on some conditions. He refused to wear a microphone on match days and refused to allow the TV cameras to film inside the dressing room. However, he was also unsure about Atkinson and his motives. Atkinson's role as mentor and trouble-shooter involved little more than trying to arrange loan signings from contacts in the game and he spent two weeks of the four the film crew eventually stayed at the club on holiday. Thrown together for the purposes of a TV documentary, rather than the day-to-day needs of a manager struggling to turn around the fortunes of a team languishing in the relegation zone, Onuora and Atkinson had radically different ideas as to how Atkinson should carry out his role. This might actually have made for good TV viewing but Onuora's refusal to wear a microphone and the film crew's lack of access to the dressing room rendered the project unworkable. It ended after barely a month.

Barry Fry, now the owner at Peterborough United, was keen to bring some publicity to his club, so Sky and Atkinson were invited to film the programme at Peterborough's London Road ground. Given the access they were denied at Swindon, Sky and Atkinson's presence destabilised the club. With the players unsure as to who was in charge, and undermined by Atkinson's presence and by the lack of support from the owner, Peterborough's manager Steve Bleasdale famously resigned an hour before a vital promotion clash with Macclesfield. The club, who'd been well placed for a push for the play-offs when the Sky cameras turned up, saw their promotion chances flounder under the weight of the pressure.

In most circumstances, a new manager will take over a side that is struggling. In Onuora's case, he didn't have a budget to acquire new players and was reliant on loan signings. Although they were still deeply in the relegation mire, Swindon had rallied to give themselves hope that they might yet avoid the drop. The team had been struggling to score goals and they lost their best player and main goal scorer when the board accepted an offer for the services of New Zealand international Rory Fallon. When the transfer window loomed and they had the chance to bring in some loan signings, the defence, which was made up of young and inexperienced players, had steadied somewhat and were performing well. Given a limited budget, Onuora decided to ensure that any loan signings he would bring in would be strikers, in order to replace Fallon and add to his overall strike force.

As the season progressed and the games increased in importance, the defensive frailties the side had displayed earlier in the season returned and in the end this was the key factor that ended the club's difficult struggle to avoid relegation. With hindsight, Onuora would have tried to sign a decent, experienced centre-back with good organisational skills to help the youngsters solidify the defence. In this he'd learned a valuable lesson, but it had come too late. What Onuora had needed was a mentor; what Atkinson had offered was showbiz. Their relationship was doomed from the start.

That experience, however, would have stood him in good stead in his bid to get the side immediately promoted to Division One. Instead, new owners came in and offered the job to Dennis Wise, the former teammate of John Fashanu at Wimbledon, and provided him with one of the biggest transfer budgets in the division.

One of the arguments against the implementation of any scheme that will specifically support the development of black coaches is the notion that football is a meritocracy and therefore any coaching or managerial appointments should be based on merit. However, managerial appointments are very rarely made in this way. Only in exceptional circumstances do clubs make a reasoned decision as to the type of manager they want and then carefully consider a list of likely candidates, assess their relative strengths and weaknesses, invite a number of candidates for interview and select the most favourable candidate after careful consideration. It is hard to imagine any other multi-million-pound company appointing a key member of staff in the way in which clubs choose to make appointments. Chairmen and chief executives identify future candidates for managers at a series of small exclusive network opportunities and events. A capacity for golf can assist in gaining access to a chairman's inner circle and wider network, which helps keep a potential candidate on a decision-maker's radar when a job becomes available.

Some clubs offer coaching roles to players as an inducement to sign. Former players, especially captains or star performers, are often given managerial positions. Former managers, especially those who had some success, are reappointed by the very people who sacked them first or second time round. When a manager is sacked or resigns, it's often the case that clubs are bombarded with requests by agents to promote their clients. Newspaper articles are strategically placed linking out-of-work managers with jobs, with managers at other clubs expressing flattery at being linked with such a fantastic job but explaining that they have no plans to move from their current role, so that within twenty-four hours, the chief executive has already decided on the identity of the new manager.

The current rate of attrition of managers outside the Premier League should be a warning to the game that successful appointments cannot be made when a manager is in place for an average of only thirteen months. This is particularly true when, as is sometimes the case, managers are given responsibility for vast areas of the club that require long-term development and attention. As head of youth development at Notts County, Michael Johnson created a youth system from scratch and developed a successful programme, only for a new first-team manager to be appointed and be allowed to overhaul the system. When supporters express concern about boardroom decisions or lack of investment in the side and demand the sacking of the board, the board responds by sacking the manager. Onuora has pointed out that top European sides have a philosophy of recruiting former players into senior administrative roles. Bayern Munich have a number of former players who are key administrators for the club, while Barcelona, Real Madrid and Ajax all have similar structures allowing former players who are familiar with the traditions of the club to be involved, thus harnessing their expertise to make good football decisions.

And when a manager is appointed they usually bring their tried and trusted lieutenants with them, who share their footballing philosophy and outlook. All this renders absurd the idea that managerial appointments are based on merit – and, clearly, this militates against greater numbers of black coaches being employed within the game. There are few black decision-makers in boardrooms and in administrative roles to see past stereotypes and consider a black coach as a viable candidate. At the present time, the system dictates that very often the appointment of the most important employee of a multi-million-pound concern is made on the whim of an individual owner, not all of whom understand the game.

As Iffy Onuora said,

> When I go and see a bunch of scholars, I will guarantee that I'm the first black coach they will ever see in their entire professional career ... You almost see the same in education, or in TV with black producers, that's just the failure of society, they say you can go so far but not far enough.

The lack of black coaches is mirrored by the lack of black faces in senior positions across British industry and institutions. What they lose is the potential for good ideas, talented people and different perspectives – not to mention vital role models. When, in 2008, Paul Ince was appointed as manager of Blackburn Rovers, becoming the first black British manager to manage a Premier League club, there was hope that his appointment would leave the door open for others to come through. In hindsight, however, for this to have happened, Ince would probably have had to achieve unprecedented success at Blackburn, as unfair as it seems to add the responsibility for the future of black British management to the considerable pressures of Premier League management. In the event, he lasted less than six months in the job and was sacked.

• • •

On 22 July 2005, Jean Charles de Menezes was shot seven times in the head on a crowded Tube at Stockwell station after being mistakenly identified as a terror suspect by armed police. In the immediate aftermath of his death, police reported Menezes had acted suspiciously and was wearing a padded coat with wires sticking out on a summer's day; that police had challenged him and he had refused to co-operate; and that he had vaulted the ticket barrier to escape police in pursuit of him. Over a period of several months, it emerged that none of the allegations were true and that, in the words of his family's solicitor, 'He was just unfortunate enough to be living in a block of flats that was under surveillance and to look slightly brown-skinned.'

With the de Menezes family continuing to seek justice, and with the shooting and other instances of alleged police brutality ingrained in the consciousness of a sizeable section of young people in London and beyond, the shooting of Mark Duggan, a resident of the Broadwater Farm estate, in August 2011 was the spark that ignited the biggest and most widespread disturbances ever seen in the UK. The disturbances began in Tottenham and quickly spread across London and the rest of the country and, after a week, there had been five deaths, several injuries and millions of pounds of damage and looting to property.

As in the de Menezes case, police briefed journalists with misinformation that there had been a shoot-out and Duggan had fired first and that he was a senior member of a street gang with links to Yardies and Manchester gangsters.

The events of the summer of 2011 and the disturbances that had occurred in the 1980s were similar in terms of police action. While the 1980s disturbances could never be characterised as 'race riots' in the sense of pitched battles between black and white people, or a white police force, there had been a racial dimension in so far as the protests were a result of police racism. Although issues of police racism also appeared to be a factor in the later riots, the issue of general policing of inner-city communities and the view of the police as a visible and hated embodiment of the establishment singled the force out for the fury of large numbers of young people, united less by issues of race than by commonality of geography and social class. The speed at which the disturbances spread was fuelled by mainstream media outlets, 24 hour rolling news reports and social media. However, the ferocity of the pitched battles by young people against the police, which 21st-century media development helped to convey, gave an insight into the mindset of those who took part.

A year later, all across England, a very different kind of protest took place. The protests were precipitated by the accusations of racism against Luis Suárez and John Terry, and the reactions of the two players' respective clubs raised questions about English football's commitment to fighting racism. Chelsea had supported their captain, Terry, in allegations that he had racially abused Anton Ferdinand, QPR defender and brother of Terry's centre-back partner in the England team, Rio Ferdinand. Terry had been cleared in the High Court of racist abuse, but was subsequently fined and banned by an FA hearing after an inquiry. The report highlighted the lengths Chelsea would go to defend their player, as illustrated by allegations that their chief executive had encouraged Terry's teammate Ashley Cole to provide false information to the subsequent investigation.

As the annual fortnight-long Kick It Out campaign began in October 2012, a number of prominent black players refused to wear the organisation's warm-up T-shirts, in protest at the lack of action against racism on the part of football's authorities. The previous October, Liverpool had proudly sported the T-shirts during the weeks of action, only to wear new T-shirts in support of Luis Suárez, who had been accused of making racist remarks, two months later. That example illustrated how the weeks of action had become little more than a photo opportunity in many cases, allowing the wider game to congratulate itself on its commitment to promoting T-shirts, without actually taking action over racism.

Led by Jason Roberts of Reading, the nephew of Cyrille Regis, the dissidents were supported by others including the Ferdinand brothers, Joleon Lescott and Victor Anichebe. The older generation of retired players, many of whom were by now involved in a number of anti-racist initiatives with the PFA, Kick It Out and others, were caught off-guard by the actions of their younger and distinctly more impatient counterparts. It was the first time that black footballers had taken a co-ordinated stand against racism in the game's history and their actions brought them briefly into conflict with the older generation who had sought to bring about change through the traditional channels of negotiation and discussion via the FA, Football League and Premier League's committee structures and formal and informal networks. Frustrated at the slow progress being made against racism at home and abroad, the leaders of the boycott generated wide discussion as to how much progress English football had made. In the immediate aftermath, there was talk of a breakaway black players' union, although the idea was never seriously promoted. Sir Alex Ferguson spectacularly backed down in the days following the boycott after it had initially seemed that his captain, Rio Ferdinand, would be censured for his part in it. After a meeting between the two, Ferguson was backtracking at a rate of knots.

• • •

Michael Johnson is convinced he would not still be in the game if it weren't for the fact he had a nine-year relationship with Birmingham City, thus proving the old adage of 'it's who you know'. This culture militates against black players, because their contacts are limited, but it also militates against actively seeking to hire the best.

After his career at Birmingham City, where he had proved to be a popular figure amongst the fans, Johnson was transferred to Derby County, then of the First Division, in 2004. A good organiser and vocal presence in the City dressing room, he had captained the side during their 2001 League Cup run against Liverpool, when they'd lost the final only after extra time and penalties.

He was captain of the Derby side when they were promoted in 2007 under manager Billy Davies. Even as Derby were beating West Brom in the play-off final there was considerable tension between Davies and the Derby County board, which derailed the start of their Premiership campaign. County's season had been extended due to the play-off campaign and they weren't in a position to take the gamble of buying new players in order to meet the considerable challenges of a Premier League campaign. By the time of their Wembley final defeat of Albion to win promotion to the Premier League, their rivals already had four or five weeks' head-start on Derby in making plans to bring in new players to strengthen the squad. This lag was further compounded as the internal tension between Davies and the board descended into out-and-out warfare, with the result that an additional two weeks went by without any plans being made to add to the squad.

The play-off final and Premier League promotion had been one of the greatest moments in the club's recent history.

Derby had a proud history and had reached the semi-final of the European Cup in 1973. The club were entitled to feel that given their history, traditions and fan base, the Premier League was where they belonged. In keeping with most promoted teams, Premier League survival was Derby's number one priority and they would be favourites for relegation. Everyone associated with the club would need to pull together to successfully negotiate what was undoubtedly going to be a difficult campaign, but valuable time was already being wasted as individual egos enveloped the needs of the club as a whole. Things looked ominous.

They eventually brought in Zambian-born, Wales-raised Rob Earnshaw, a Welsh international, amongst other signings, but the new signings were either of questionable quality or were unproven at Premier League level. Nonetheless, the league campaign started reasonably well, with a hard-fought 2–2 home draw against Portsmouth. In their next game they narrowly lost 1–0 away at Manchester City and then suffered a 4–0 defeat at Spurs, at which point the club dropped into the bottom three relegation places. They lost their next game at home to Johnson's former club, Birmingham City, and then were thrashed 6–0 away to Liverpool. At this point one bookmaker agreed to pay out on bets for Derby to be relegated. They were only five games into the season and it was only September in a campaign that would last till May.

Off the pitch, there were additional tensions and arguments within the boardroom itself as various parties wrestled for control of the club. In circumstances where boardroom strife exists, the instability eventually filters through to the players, even when they rationalise that the boardroom situation is out of their control and they should concentrate on playing and performance, which is within their area of influence. Players begin to wonder about which direction the club is heading. Some are being offered opportunities at other clubs; others wonder what impact the instability will have on their contracts, particularly if new management is brought in. Eventually, the instability began to affect Derby's performances and the team went from bad to worse. Amazingly, immediately after the disastrous Liverpool result they won their first game of the season at home to Newcastle, but from then on, confidence drained from the players. Of their next eight games, they drew two and lost six, including two 5–0 defeats, one of which was at home to West Ham.

At this point, fans were openly demonstrating against the board for lack of investment in the club and, by way of a response to this, in time-honoured fashion, the manager was sacked. New manager Paul Jewell came in and couldn't stop the rot. They lost five of the next six games and, by the end of the calendar year, they knew it was all over. The players still had much to play for: fans were desperate to see another win; players were playing for professional pride; some were playing for new contracts. In the January window, a raft of new players were brought in, as the manager tried new personnel and different formations to stem the tide. On 29 March, Derby drew 2–2 with fellow strugglers Fulham to confirm their relegation, making them the first team in Premier League history to be relegated in March. As club captain, Johnson had overseen a league campaign that was a source of personal and professional embarrassment. They ended the season with just eleven points – a record – and just one win in thirty-eight games – also a record.

At the start of the season, Johnson had been informed that he was to be fifth choice centre-back and in September, with Derby already struggling, he was loaned out to Sheffield

Wednesday. Johnson had been a regular in their promotion-winning season and had been a fans' favourite. The decision to loan him to Sheffield Wednesday became increasingly baffling as Derby's defence proved very accommodating to Premier League sides.

When he arrived at Wednesday, they had made the worst start in their history, losing the opening six games. Johnson was thirty-four and manager Brian Laws showed tremendous faith in him, allowing him the responsibility of making organisational changes on the pitch. With regular playing time, Johnson played some of his best football for many years. Wednesday won their first two games with their new defender in the side and would go on to avoid relegation on the last day of the season. His impact was such that he had begun to discuss a permanent eighteen-month contract with Wednesday, which Johnson, now approaching thirty-five, would have given his right arm to sign. However, these plans had to be shelved as a number of events conspired against him. Derby, shell-shocked and unable to string together decent results and performances upon their return to the Premier League, faced an injury crisis and Johnson was recalled in December 2007, thus ending what was supposed to be a six-month loan after only three months. On his return, he appeared as a first-half substitute and was met with rapturous applause from the Derby faithful and chants of 'One Michael Johnson'. The following week threw up one of those anomalies that seem to appear regularly in football and he again made a first-half substitute appearance as Derby were drawn away at Sheffield Wednesday. Johnson received his second rapturous welcome in two games, this time from Sheffield Wednesday fans.

However, things had changed at Wednesday. The chairman

had resigned, so the discussions on the possibility of a permanent contract at the club had been curtailed without any formal offer on the table. He was loaned out to Notts County, where he had started his career, but his experience at Wednesday had made him think seriously about impending retirement and how he was going to spend it.

The responsibility he had been given under Laws at Wednesday had made him keen to pursue a career in coaching. He remained at Notts County until the end of the 2007/08 season and in the process scored his first goal for the club, some sixteen years after making his debut for the team. He was now out of contract at Derby and signed a twelve-month deal with County on condition he would coach the under-21 squad. At the end of the 2008/09 season he retired to take a role as head of youth development at the club.

County had abolished their youth system as part of a cost-cutting exercise some two years earlier and much against the wishes of its supporters, so Johnson's first task was to establish a structure that could nurture young players and provide home-grown players for the youth team.

He had no players and no coaches, so first set about identifying and hiring good-quality youth coaches. He then established a number of training camps in Nottingham and the surrounding area to identify young talent and recruit them to the programme. The first year was a struggle as the programme was being established, but by the second year the youth team missed out on winning the league by a single point and reached the quarter-finals of FA Youth Cup, where they were knocked out by a Liverpool team featuring Raheem Sterling and Andre Wisdom.

In spite of his success, Johnson was soon removed from his post. The club recruited Martin Allen as first-team

manager and, naturally in those circumstances, a new manager would wish to bring in his own backroom staff. Allen
was no different, but, critically, he wanted to bring in his
own people not just for the first team, but also to oversee
the youth set-up, a move that in this day and age is highly
unusual. Youth development at the club was in dire need of
consolidation and stability, given that the existing structure
was only two years old, but nonetheless, the chief executive of the club agreed to Allen's requests, Johnson was paid
up for the few months left on his contract and he left to
be replaced by the under-12s coach, who had less experience and fewer qualifications. Six months later, Allen was
sacked and before long the youth set-up that Johnson had
worked so diligently to establish was in tatters, mired in controversy and facing a police inquiry and the intervention of
social services.

In May 2013, Brett Adams and Lee Broster resigned from
their posts as youth coaches at Notts County following allegations of racist bullying and abuse. Adams was alleged to
have thrown a banana at a black youth team player with the
words 'fuck off' written on it, before telling the youngster to
'fuck off and eat it'.

In response to hearing rap music in the changing room,
Broster is alleged to have said, 'No wonder you black lads
always go around stabbing people when you listen to music
like that,' and, on another occasion, switched off the lights
in a room and said, 'Make sure you black lads smile so I can
see you.'

Adams and Broster resigned after an internal club investigation but the club was subsequently criticised by Nottingham Social Services for the way it carried out its inquiry, in
particular for paying insufficient attention to protecting the

children and young people who had made the allegations and for not involving the local authority sooner.

The incident is amongst the most serious issues not just of racial prejudice but of safeguarding and child protection, and while the club acted promptly, the FA didn't use the opportunity to provide guidelines to clubs in handling such matters.

Since leaving Notts County, Johnson has applied for numerous jobs and has been unsuccessful in obtaining a coaching role. He has the UEFA A Licence, B Licence and Pro Licence, the highest-level qualifications in professional football. He has established a youth academy at a professional football club from scratch and made it competitive and successful. He has applied for roles as first-team coach, assistant manager and as youth team coach and has never had an interview. His applications for jobs have also been realistic in so far as he hasn't applied for roles vacant at Manchester City or United, Arsenal, Chelsea or indeed any other Premier League club, but rather for roles at Championship level and below. He has taken advice to update his CV, developed new networks, attended workshops, participated in forums, taken additional professional development opportunities, attended training courses and gone and watched training sessions to pick up fresh ideas and tips and to increase his profile, but to no avail. His experience as a Premier League player, international footballer and successful and qualified youth coach leaves the game shorn of his talents, and Johnson himself frustrated.

Johnson has since gone on to become a vigorous campaigner for more black coaches in the game. He was appointed to the FA's Inclusion Advisory Board in January 2014, but resigned when it emerged that he had said in a BBC interview in 2012 that he would not support a Football

Association campaign against homophobia 'because of my beliefs, because of the Bible that I read, in the Bible it does state that homosexuality is detestable unto the Lord'.

Johnson has since changed his position. At the time, he had just started his Christian journey and was reading Old Testament scripture. He now believes that homophobia is incompatible with Christianity and that Christian teachings mean that God made man in his own image, which can mean gay or straight, black or white. He asserts that the FA could have used the incident to highlight the problem of homophobia, and that he would participate in any initiative to tackle the issue.

Along with Jason Roberts, Johnson launched a report in November 2014 entitled 'Ethnic Minorities and Coaching at Elite Level in England: A Call to Action', based on research by the Sports People's Think Tank. The report found that at the ninety-two professional clubs there were nineteen BME coaches out of 552 senior positions, representing 3.4 per cent of the total.

Amongst much else, the report recommended that 20 per cent of coaches in professional football in England should be from BME backgrounds by 2020 and that urgent action was needed to address the fact that less than 1 per cent of senior administrators and governors are black.

For Johnson and other black players, they feel the game demonstrably wants their talents as footballers but doesn't view them as managers. The stereotypes that the early generation of black players did so much to challenge – those images of them as lacking the intelligence to be given the responsibility to provide the tempo and creative hub of a side – now appear to work to prevent them from progressing into football management.

• • •

Upon retirement, Paul Davis could have continued his career in someone's midfield, trying to get on the ball, moving it along, picking the right passes, making himself available and occasionally watching the net bulge as he put that sweet left foot to good use or employed that somewhat underrated heading ability. He had offers to continue playing, but he'd always wanted to be a coach at Arsenal and wanted to work at the top end of the coaching hierarchy. He got his preliminary coaching badges at age seventeen, even before he got into the first team, and completed his coaching training towards the end of his playing career. He got a job at Arsenal's academy, where he would help in overseeing the development of players like Ashley Cole, and he was happy to have such a great experience. He was doing well and was confident in his ability to transfer his talents to the elite players. After seven years in the same role at Arsenal's academy, the ambitions Davis had to move up the coaching ladder were continuously frustrated by the club hierarchy. Pigeonholed as a developer of the youngest players, and constantly overlooked for higher-level coaching roles, he couldn't see any way out of the impasse and he walked away from the club he loved, where he had been since he was thirteen.

Davis has been unable to find a coaching job, except for a brief, ill-fated stint as Paul Gascoigne's assistant at non-league Kettering, and his talents and experience have gone criminally to waste. Davis has long since given up trying to find a coaching role and now works for the PFA in a coach education role, where he puts former players through their qualifications and get them employed.

Davis's experience of the glass ceiling that affects black

coaches is borne out by the Sports People's Think Tank re-search, which showed that black coaches are overwhelmingly operating at academy level or in community programmes, rather than in high-level coaching positions. The higher up the coaching ladder you go, the less likely you are to see black coaches or managers.

CHAPTER 15

COACHING FAIR PLAY
AND FURTHER

*'We have a right to be involved in the decision-making of
this game.'* – Paul Davis

IN APRIL 2014, Norwich City manager Chris Hughton
was sacked from his job. This would have been a relatively
unremarkable event in a season that had seen a number of
high-profile sackings in an increasingly impatient club management culture. Hughton's side had been languishing near
the bottom of the Premier League for most of the season
and the sacking was a last ditch and ultimately futile attempt
by the board to keep Norwich in the top flight. However,
what was distinguishable about the event was it now meant
that there was not a single black manager in any of the four
divisions within English football.

At the start of the 2013/14 season, a decision on the
proposal for an English version of the 'Rooney Rule' had
been quietly dropped from the debate amongst the seventy-
two Football League chairmen, without resolving the issues
behind the under-representation of black coaches and
managers that had led to the promotion of the rule. The
Rooney Rule was named after Dan Rooney, the owner of
the Pittsburgh Steelers of the US National Football League.

In response to the fact that, while some 70 per cent of pro footballers were black, that figure dropped to only 28 per cent amongst assistant coaches and 6 per cent amongst head coaches, the NFL introduced a rule requiring that for each coaching position, a minority candidate had to be interviewed. Since the rule was introduced in 2003, the number of black head and assistant coaches has increased dramatically. Cyrus Mehri, a US-based lawyer and the architect of the scheme, has spent a great deal of time discussing how such a scheme might be implemented in the UK, helping to promote the Coaching Fair Play strategy, designed to work along similar lines.

If the Football League's lack of action was designed to end these discussions, it was to fail miserably.

The same circular counterarguments rumbled. Some arguments against the rule were legitimate, but its opponents were unable or unwilling to put forward any viable proposals to address the under-representation of black footballers at managerial level. The counterarguments could be characterised as falling into four broad categories. These were: that there was no real problem; that some form of footballing meritocracy would see black managers emerge in the future; that the proposals were discriminatory; and that the proposals were tokenistic. Of these, the issue of tokenism was a genuine and legitimate argument for abandoning the rule, given that it opened the door for black managers being invited for interview merely for show, abiding by the letter but not the spirit of the new rule.

There have been some desperate arguments put forward in the press. Those of the *Daily Mail*'s Martin Samuel are only examples and it would be unfair to suggest that he is the sole culprit, but his arguments require some dissection.

His main argument is that chairmen need to hire quickly as the wait could cost points that could ultimately be the difference between success and failure.

However, the manager is the most important employee of the club. It's crucial to get the right person for the job, and perhaps if the hiring process were more rigorous, with more attention paid to meeting specific skill requirements, chairmen would be more likely to make the right appointment in the first place. In those circumstances, black coaches would be less frustrated, happier that the process was open and transparent, and more easily persuaded to consider a career in coaching. Secondly, a proper selection procedure might make chairmen less trigger-happy. They might learn from the example of Charlton from 1991 to 2006: Alan Curbishley took them into the top flight early in his leadership, only to face relegation at the end of the season. The board gave a lesson in sticking by a manager, and Curbishley repaid the favour by taking them back to the top in 2000. Since then the club have had seven managers and are no nearer getting their status back.

According to Samuel, for the lack of black managers to be the result of prejudice, 'we first have to believe one thing: that the chairmen of football clubs would deliberately undermine their chances of success rather than employ a black man'. Here he gives chairmen and other decision-makers far too much credit. As Samuel himself pointed out when he severely criticised the FA appointment of Roy Hodgson over Harry Redknapp to the England manager's role because Hodgson was safe and mediocre, the wrong person can easily be employed, not least when an organisation is 'devoid of ambition', to use Samuel's description of the FA.

• • •

Almost twenty years had passed since Frank Clark had asked black coaches to bide their time and it had been over twenty-five years since Viv Anderson had been appointed as the only black manager. In the intervening years, the number of black coaches remained chronically low. The sacking of Hughton immediately reignited the debate as to how to address the lack of black coaches in the game.

As we have seen, the 2014/15 season kicked off without a single black manager in any of the four English divisions. In September, Chris Powell was appointed as manager of Huddersfield Town and later that month Keith Curle was appointed as manager of Carlisle United.

The first group of black British footballers had struggled to break down the stereotypes that had been foisted upon them and had challenged the perceived notions about them. Black footballers had been cast for their skill, speed, strength and athleticism. The compliments they received for their 'natural athleticism' barely masked the racist undercurrent of blacks as primal, exotic and operating on instinct alone. They were perceived as lacking discipline, 'bottle' and the required intellect. It was this perceived lack of intellectual skills that continued to impede the progress of black managers. Leadership, delegation, relationship building and, above all, strategic thinking and tactical awareness were the qualities that were thought to be missing from the make-up of black managers, and that a slew of coaching and managerial qualifications failed to make up for. Today, a game in which the participation of black people as players is celebrated and promoted cannot seem to bring itself to apply the rules it promotes on the pitch to the level of club management and the boardroom. A number of highly respected and extremely capable black administrators have proved their ability, yet their talents are rarely called upon. Despite their knowledge and experience in the game, their ability to manage areas of significant responsibility and the management of large budgets and of colleagues, their experiences are very rarely acknowledged as something that would be beneficial for clubs, associations and governing bodies.

It was for all these reasons and more that the Coaching Fair Play initiative gained support when it was first touted.

The campaign to address the under-representation of black managers has highlighted other inequalities in the game. The issue of black fan participation remains one of the game's biggest challenges and is linked to issues around grassroots football. The other issue of representation at ad-ministrative and boardroom level is likely to emerge as a key concern when the dust begins to settle over the issues of black managers. The same arguments that were used to oppose strategies to increase the representation of black footballers will be familiar to those currently campaigning to increase the racial diversity of football coaches. The football authorities have, with a few honourable exceptions, always demonstrated a reluctance to embrace change as far as the increase in diversity is concerned, but they have shown they are able to move rapidly when commercial interests dictate. All-seater stadiums and moving match kick-off times to suit broadcasters are two examples of how quickly change can be implemented, when there is the will to do so. Change in the diversity of those charged with making the key decisions as to how clubs or the sport are managed is likely to be met with similar levels of resistance.

The early support for Coaching Fair Play demonstrated in microcosm how far issues of racism have developed within the English game. On one hand, the issue is a hot topic within football circles, due to the refusal of anti-racist campaigners to allow the issue to die. Instances of overt racism are largely dealt with, albeit often crudely or tentatively: football culture is no longer willing to tolerate such behaviour and, in that sense, football has progressed. On the other hand, black people within the game still require progress around equality and access to roles within the game, outside of the pitch, training ground and dressing room.

Coaching Fair Play offers a path for promoting more lasting equality in the game and providing former black players with an opportunity to prove they possess the requisite intellect to coach and manage – and that battle continues, both within the game and outside it. Those opposed to the Rooney Rule have offered no alternative ideas on how to tackle under-representation at coaching and managerial level, other than to wait for some, as yet undefined, period of time. And where the football authorities have consistently failed ever since black footballers became a feature of English football is in the area of leadership. They have always been reactive and always been embarrassed into taking action in tackling racism, so much so that they have always been a key part of the problem. The game's leadership, the FA, the Football League and the Premier League, have failed to take the lead in furthering and promoting issues of anti-racism and equality and generating a healthy debate and discussion around representation. As the lead custodians of the game, it is ultimately their responsibility to provide a culture within the game where black people can play with dignity and respect, without vile abuse from the terraces or lazy pronouncements about their ability from managers, chairmen or fellow professionals. It is also their responsibility to support equality and take the lead in ensuring their committees and structures are sufficiently diverse to ensure that a range of different perspectives are brought to bear when key decisions are being made. They are not in a position to demand that clubs address issues of racial inequality when they fail to put their own house in order, and therefore, in the absence of any such leadership worthy of the name, the Rooney Rule will almost certainly be adopted in some form, in spite of its flaws.

Football has had a huge impact on race relations in this country, sparking parliamentary inquiries into racism and causing public figures across the political spectrum to publicly condemn racial abuse. Through formal initiatives, such as Kick It Out and Show Racism the Red Card, and informal discourse, football has been responsible for drawing widespread public attention to issues of race. For all that still remains to be done in order to mirror black players' participation on the pitch with that off it, fundamental changes have been made. The far-right groups who have used football as a means of increasing their profile and to recruit to their ranks have been utterly and thoroughly routed. They may still occasionally come out of retirement to wreak disquiet when the England team play abroad, but the days of publishing racist league tables are over. More casual racists can no longer hide behind the activities of the organised far right, and are now policed by more enlightened stewarding and fellow fans unwilling to tolerate racist abuse. In fact, for football supporters, racist abuse is likely to be vilified on fan forums and message boards where it occurs at games; the accusation of racism is now a stick with which to attack your opponents and to denigrate your fiercest rivals.

While the football authorities and the media claim progress has been made, the reality is that both the football authorities and the media have, to a large degree, been part of the problem. The movement, such as it was, came from black players themselves, and the impact of that movement has extended beyond football and sport more generally. Football exerts a huge cultural and social influence in Britain and beyond. Whether that influence is too great is a fruitful debating point, and its influence on the career and educational aspirations of black boys and young men is another important discussion to be had about the game's impact, but there is no question that that influence can be used for good as well as evil. The stereotypes that continue to bedevil black footballers – that they aren't clever enough, they can't lead, they don't work hard, and can't handle the pressure – will continue to be confronted and overcome, because black footballers have come too far to stop now.

The authorities once tried to characterise racism as a normal part of the game: seeking to make it normal absolved the authorities from having to deal with it, putting the onus back on to black players.

• • •

When Bobby Barnes was an apprentice at West Ham, like the other apprentices, he received free tickets for home games. Barnes was so concerned about the possibility of being racially attacked as he left the ground, he used to leave early and sprint all the way along Green Street, not stopping until he got a mile away from the ground, where he could relax. Upton Park was one of the grounds where black players knew they were going in to be for a stormy time. It was an intimidating place, with the crowd close to the pitch, and a belligerent welcome was routinely generated for opposition teams. For black players there was a particularly hostile reception.

Barnes grew up idolising Pelé and the great 1970 Brazilian side – the team that had the single most important impact on the progress of black footballers in Britain. There isn't one black footballer who began playing professionally in the 1970s and early '80s who wasn't inspired by their achievements. They were a predominantly black team who played a brand of football radically different from anything around at the time; they were all-conquering and their best player was black. For budding players raised on the increasingly sterile, functional and bland version of the game that was usually served up in Britain, Brazil provided a blueprint for a different style of football. A generation of players found inspiration on sunny fields in Leon and Mexico City. But although Barnes was inspired by Brazilian flair and had Jamaican parents, he was also an east London boy from Leytonstone and his local team was West Ham. Improbably, on 1 April 1972, the Hammers fielded a team that included three black players in Clyde Best, Ade Coker and Clive Charles – an event not emulated in the top flight until the Three Degrees took The Hawthorns, forming the backbone of the best West Brom side since the 1960s. At the time there were probably fewer than ten black footballers playing professional football in England or Scotland, so for three players to be included in one side was quite an achievement.

When West Ham played away, Barnes went to see his other local side, Leyton Orient, who themselves have been pioneers in providing black players with opportunities to play football. At Orient, Barnes could watch Laurie Cunningham, Bobby Fisher, John Chiedozie and Tunji Banjo, at a time when black players were a rarity. Inspired by heroes in Brazil, the Boleyn Ground and Brisbane Road, Bobby Barnes had no shortage of role models to call upon.

He also had other heroes from the world of sport. Barnes's father used to drag him and his siblings out of their beds to watch Muhammad Ali's fights and, like many of his generation, Barnes senior was a big cricket fan, imparting his love of cricket to his son. The West Indies touring team of 1976 inflicted a humiliating defeat on England after the latter's captain, Tony Grieg, arrogantly declared that England would make the West Indies grovel. His comments were widely interpreted as haughty and colonial. Barnes and his father attended Test matches during the long hot summer of 1976, in which the West Indies won the series 3–0 and England never really got close. A full fourteen years before Norman Tebbit introduced his cricket test, Barnes proudly failed it.

However, Barnes's first love was always football and, as a kid from Leytonstone, football meant West Ham. After being spotted playing schoolboy football, he was signed by West Ham and invited to train during school holidays. His deep affinity with West Ham had already started by the time he began to train with them at the age of eleven or twelve and hardened as the club made a point of looking after all the young players. The chief scout of the club, Eddie Baily, used to pick him up and drop him off at his home in Leytonstone, and manager John Lyall made a point of taking an interest in the youth players, trying to identify potential recruits for the first team. Barnes was one of the star performers in the West Ham side that won the FA Youth Cup in 1981 and included Keith Macpherson, Chris Ampofo, Dale Banton and the brilliantly monikered Everald La Ronde as captain, all of whom were black kids from east London.

After doing well in the reserves, Barnes made his debut aged seventeen in the Cup Winners' Cup against Castilla, the nursery club of Real Madrid at the Bernabéu. The game itself was marred by crowd trouble, forcing West Ham to play the return leg behind closed doors. However, on his home debut he scored a stunning goal against Watford to raise the roof at Upton Park. He'd fulfilled the dream he'd had for as long as he'd been able to kick a football.

Barnes was nicknamed 'Superwog' by the West Ham fans, a term so offensive it's difficult to believe it was a term of acceptance by a group of fans well known for their racist following. Whereas black players who played for opposition teams were mere wogs, Barnes was the claret and blue version. It's a reminder of what his generation had to face.

> When I think about it now ... in those days ... we really did brush so much off ... Our generation were not going to be beaten, we were going to be professional footballers. You weren't going to boo us off the field, you weren't going to abuse us off the field ... and a lot of us did actually blank a lot of stuff out.

Barnes is uniquely placed to assess the progress of black footballers and the journey they still have to make to gain acceptance. He had bananas thrown at him at St James' Park in the 1980s, when he went there for an away game with West Ham. He received hundreds of letters of support from Newcastle fans, and West End theatre tickets from the Newcastle Supporters' Club. He suggests now that 'if Chris Hughton had been appointed to the Newcastle job in the 1980s they'd have been out on the streets, protesting against his appointment'. As it happened, they were out protesting when he got sacked. There has been a world of change over the past thirty years, but most of the re-education that has taken place has occurred amongst fans. Many fans who chanted racist abuse, made monkey noises and even threw bananas are now the same fans who would happily report incidents of racist abuse to a steward or the police or condemn it on social media. A process of re-education has occurred and its impact has been profound. While the numbers of black and Asian supporters are still chronically low, football grounds are now much more welcoming places for black and Asian fans to attend. When Barnes played, his parents refused to attend the majority of his games as the level of racism meted out to their son and other black players was too difficult to bear. Barnes's wife also refused to attend and struggled to come to terms with sitting through matches and watching her husband be abused.

Like most of his generation, Barnes didn't allow himself to dwell on it for too long: to do so would make you question why you put up with it and if you ask yourself why, you might not be able to find the answer. That earlier generation are owed a debt of gratitude for not asking themselves those soul-searching questions, sticking with the game to pave the way for future generations of footballers. It is noticeable today that when black players are occasionally subjected to abuse, for example in Champions League games or while on England duty, it seriously affects their composure. Ashley Cole, Nedum Onuoha and Danny Rose have all suffered racist abuse and have all been visibly shaken by it, struggling to regain their composure during games. For the earlier generation, visibly reacting simply wasn't an option.

There have also been changes in the way that white players are more than happy to support and protect their teammates when they receive abuse. Pat Nevin and the Crazy Gang's actions were remarkable because despite the fact that team spirit and camaraderie were highly prized in the game, there were very few examples of the kind of solidarity that Nevin showed towards Paul Canoville. Usually teammates said or did nothing and allowed black players to deal with it in their own way, though occasionally they would find a way of making light of the issue.

West Ham had travelled to Elland Road and, as expected, Barnes, who was nineteen or twenty at the time, was, in his own words, 'getting dog's abuse'. However, he happened to be playing extremely well and at half-time his teammate Tony Gale made a dressing room plea. Gale explained that in spite of the abuse Barnes was getting, he was having a great game. Imploring the team to 'show these bastards', he urged Barnes to lead the team out for the second half with his head held high and his chest out. Feeling on top of the world, the young Barnes led the team out, got to the centre circle, noticed that the abuse was even louder, and turned round only to find he was completely on his own and his teammates were laughing at him in the tunnel.

Amongst black players, however, there was a camaraderie born out of a shared experience. Both Bobby Barnes and Brendon Batson bear testimony to the practice of giving a nod of acknowledgement to another black man, whether you're in an airport lounge or hotel reception, whether you're in New York or Northampton. Mo Johnston, a former teammate of John Barnes at Watford, was amazed at the practice. On an away trip to play Arsenal at Highbury, the coach travelled along the Holloway Road and Barnes nodded to a succession of black people going about their day. For Glasgow-born Johnston, the penny dropped when he realised that Barnes couldn't possibly know that many people.

The nod of acknowledgement formed part of the shared

experience on the pitch, and maybe it would turn into a few words exchanged while warming up, or just before kick-off, or in the players' lounge after the game. The bonds were also forged at social events, such as PFA dinners or charity events, while, particularly in London, Birmingham and other big cities, the players from different teams frequented the same bars, pubs and nightclubs. Often they would be the only black people in the club, their status as footballers allowing them entry to the most exclusive of places, whereas friends and brothers would be denied entry.

Occasionally they bonded at testimonials, like those held for Len Cantello and Ces Podd, or when a British-based Jamaican side played the Jamaican national side during a close season in the summer of 1987. In the British Jamaican team were Alex Williams, Bob Hazell, Clive Wilson, Luther Blissett, John Barnes and Franz Carr, as well as Bobby Barnes. As he was forbidden to play, being Grenadian, Brendon Batson managed the team. They were able to spend some time in Jamaica and received a brilliant reception everywhere they went on the island. The British Jamaicans ran out 3–2 winners over the home side, in a game played at the national stadium. Bobby Barnes was struck at how popular John Barnes was. After a few days, the accents and speech had slipped into patois, so much so it was impossible to work out who were the Jamaican Jamaicans and who were the British Jamaicans.

Barnes is perhaps the highest-profile and most powerful black administrator in football – perhaps even in British and European sport. Having studied business while still a player, he later qualified as a financial advisor for Friends Provident, doing well enough to be one of their top earners. Brendon Batson was managing the PFA financial services company and invited Barnes to run the business in the Birmingham office. After joining the PFA he held a number of positions and a few years ago was responsible for establishing their London office.

The PFA has been the avenue through which many of the issues of racism have been channelled throughout the last thirty or so years. Garth Crooks, Chris Powell and Clarke Carlisle have all been chairmen of the PFA and Brendon Batson was once deputy to Gordon Taylor, the role that Barnes now holds. As such, when tensions have arisen over how issues of racism, under-representation and discrimination have been addressed, the PFA has often been at the forefront of events.

• • •

Bobby Barnes first started looking at the issue of under-representation of black managers in 2003, at a time when, including caretaker managers, there were seven black managers in post. The most difficult task then was to persuade black players to gain qualifications, in order to ensure that charges of lack of qualifications couldn't be levelled at them. Now those same players are frustrated at being persuaded to study coaching qualifications for which they cannot find a job.

Barnes has been instrumental in liaising with the architects of the Rooney Rule in the USA in order to win support for the scheme and develop an English equivalent. The PFA's credentials as an ethnically diverse organisation and its commitment to open and transparent recruitment practices are not coincidental. If clubs adopted the same principles, they would increase their diversity and bring benefits for all. All coaches, both black and white, face the same problems in trying to find a coaching or managerial job within a culture that employs people based on who they know rather than their skills and aptitude for the job. In these circumstances, those under the radar of a club chairman or chief executive cannot get on the ladder and this militates particularly against black coaches and managers. The benefit for the clubs of introducing a Rooney Rule is that they might increase their diversity and therefore widen their potential pool of talent – and, more importantly, employ someone they might otherwise have missed. The impact will be that those who are interviewed, whether they are black or white, may be unsuitable for that post but may be suitable for another, or may be invited back in six, nine or twelve months' time, when the previous manager finds himself out of a job.

Barnes concedes that as a global recruiter of coaches and managers, the Premier League is a special case, and until there exists a groundswell of experienced black coaches, plans for the scheme to promote more black managers should apply only to managerial appointments outside the Premier League. Other than head coaches and managerial positions, there are a number of Premier League roles that might provide experience of operating at a Premier League level, but in managerial terms, the Championship and Football League are where black managers will be able to prove their worth.

Barnes sees the key barriers to the initiative as a lack of understanding combined with deliberate misrepresentation, not least because of the amount of time it takes to make the same arguments to the same people over and over again. He states that, 'Football is very conservative and doesn't want to embrace change ... If you don't understand it, the easiest thing to do is misrepresent the idea.'

Both Barnes and Upton Park have come a long way since the days when he had to leave the ground early to avoid the prospect of a racist attack. He attends matches at Upton Park with his wife and children and always receives a rapturous welcome from the fans whenever he is presented to the West Ham faithful. Undoubtedly, the older supporters will include some of those who chanted 'Superwog' at him during his playing days, but today the club is finally beginning to attract black and Asian supporters from the local area, which is one of the most ethnically diverse in the country. The working class black kid from Leytonstone who pulled on the famous claret and blue has risen to become deputy head of the world's richest trade union and European president of FIFPRO, the worldwide umbrella organisation of footballers unions and associations, and he participates in a number of UEFA committees.

However, as Barnes says, 'You could have a meeting of black administrators in a phone box.' And that is one of the fundamental issues facing the game as far as black footballers are concerned: gaining access to how decisions are made.

When a senior official of a large business knows little about a subject, before going to the press he or she is extensively briefed on the specifications of the new product or impact of the new development so that they are able to convey the company's new product or activities from a position of authority.

Wigan chairman Dave Whelan's announcements that 'chink' wasn't offensive and Jews did indeed chase money were remarkable only in so far as he had been allowed yet another opportunity to stand in front of a media scrum and give his opinions on an issue about which he was so insensitive and offensive. Whelan had previously stated in October

2011 that players who complained about racism were 'a little bit out of order'.

After being widely condemned and after losing two sponsorship deals, Whelan provided an apology and stated that he meant no offence, and indeed had many, many Jewish friends. He received a six-week ban and a fine from the FA.

Whelan's comments had been made after Wigan's appointment of former Cardiff City football manager Malky Mackay in November 2014, when Mackay was under investigation from the FA for sending emails containing racist, sexist and homophobic comments. Mackay had been ousted from the manager's job at Cardiff City in December 2013 following a public row with the club's owner, Vincent Tan, and was about to be appointed as manager of Crystal Palace in August 2014 when a dossier was sent from Cardiff City to the FA with the allegations. The texts included derogatory comments about Jewish and Chinese people and, as a result, Mackay was charged by the FA.

The FA's inquiry seemed to drag on and while it prepared its response, a discussion ensued as to whether racism was a product of society. The catalyst for this occurred in February 2015. Chelsea were playing a Champions League group stage game against Paris St Germain, and video footage emerged of Chelsea fans pushing a black commuter off the train on the Paris Métro while singing, 'We're racist, we're racist and that's the way we like it.'

On the surface, the Chelsea fans' unashamed celebration of their own bigotry was an act of defiance, but scratch the surface and what actually occurred was anger at the fact that the world they inhabited has now gone and isn't coming back. To describe them as dinosaurs would be an insult to the curmudgeonly old grandfathers to whom the term is usually applied: these fans weren't floundering around in a world that was passing them by; rather, it was a desperate cry from those who know the game is up but refuse to give up the fight to turn back the clock, because to do so would spark the need to find new values, and they have no idea where to look for them. Their behaviour was like that of fans who cheer wildly, ecstatically and without a hint of irony when their team, 6–0 down in stoppage time, scores a consolation goal.

Chelsea immediately distanced itself from the behaviour of this group of fans and promised life bans. Manager José Mourinho seemed dumbfounded by their behaviour. The previous October, he had stated there was no racism in football when responding to questions asked of him about the Rooney Rule. For a few days, the club was under intense scrutiny, anxious to get this one right. Captain John Terry condemned the behaviour of the fans in his notes in the next match programme, the search for the culprits continued and the incident blew over.

• • •

At the start of the 2014/15 season, Chris Powell was appointed as manager of Championship outfit Huddersfield Town. A few weeks later, Keith Curle's appointment at Carlisle doubled the number of black managers working throughout professional football to two and their appointments immediately re-energised the debate around how best to address the under-representation of black managers.

Of the black coaches who were in the frame to gain managerial appointments, Powell represented the best opportunity for a black manager to smash the glass ceiling, opening the way for others to be given managerial opportunities. Paul Ince's short, but ultimately ill-fated, tenure at Blackburn Rovers proved to be a disappointment as the hopes and goodwill he generated ultimately gave way to Ince being sacked after just six months in charge, having won only three games. Powell's credentials for the mantle of black managerial prospect were built on solid foundations, given his impressive record to date and the general consensus that he had been unfortunate to have been sacked from his previous managerial post.

Powell was an England international, had been chairman of the PFA and had made over 600 league appearances in a playing career spanning twenty-four years. He had enjoyed a successful first stint at management until a combination of change of ownership, internal club politics and circumstances beyond his control contrived to cost him his job just as he felt he was on the verge of producing something special.

Powell's father had arrived from Jamaica in the 1960s and immediately adopted West Ham as his team because he'd seen Clyde Best play for them. Powell's older brother was a football fan, although not a player himself, so a love of the game was instilled into him from an early age. Despite living in south London, Powell was a Spurs fan. As a child, he regularly travelled to north London to visit extended family and was overawed by the sight of Tottenham's White Hart Lane stadium, eventually adopting them as his team. From the age of thirteen, Powell regularly travelled by himself to White Hart Lane from his home in Tooting, paying his £1.10 entrance fee to stand on 'The Shelf' and be inspired by the exploits of Garth Crooks and Danny Thomas.

By this time, Powell had already shown promise as a left-winger and had been further inspired by the Three Degrees, particularly Laurie Cunningham, who, as a fellow left-winger, became the blueprint for how Powell wanted to develop.

He also, on occasion, went to watch Crystal Palace, the nearest side to home, where he sought to emulate another left-winger, Vince Hilaire. At school, Powell's team had reached the final of the English Schools Trophy and won a share of the title after a draw, so bringing its players to the attention of a number of professional clubs. However, it wasn't until shortly before he left school in 1986 that he and two others from his team were invited for a trial at Crystal Palace. In the event, of the three trialists, only Powell was offered an apprenticeship.

He considered his apprenticeship a good, tough schooling for life as well as for professional football, with discipline being very high for apprentices. A number of practices that in later years would almost certainly have violated health and safety regulations were commonplace, as were bullying and harassment. However, under the regime, Powell flourished and did well enough to earn himself a professional contract. By this time, he'd been converted from a left-winger to a left-back and had made his debut against Newport County, when he made a substitute appearance with ten minutes remaining of the League Cup tie.

His conversion to left-back had come about in a youth team game against Southampton, which included in their side the talented Wallace twins, Ray and Rod. Due to injuries to the regular left-back, Powell's first game in his new position required him to mark none other than Matt Le Tissier. As he progressed into the Football Combination with Palace's reserve side, he had to get used to the quicker pace, increased physicality and racist abuse from opponents as part of his footballing education.

Powell never experienced the sense of isolation that often characterised the dressing room experiences of many of

the earlier generations of black footballers. The Palace first
team included Wright and Bright, John Salako, Richard Shaw,
Andy Gray and Eric Young, and the multicultural nature of
the team reflected Palace's south London environment. There
were also a number of black players at all levels of the club,
from apprentices through to the first-team squad, and although, socially, the black players tended to gravitate towards
each other, there was an easy mix between black and white
players and a good spirit within the first team. The team spirit
and collective ethos so carefully fostered by manager Steve
Coppell was a key element of the team's promotion to the top
flight, FA Cup run and general success, so when Palace chairman Ron Noades made his remarks about his black players'
lack of intelligence and disinclination to perform in the winter
months, Powell regarded his comments as ill judged at best
and a cheap comment at worst. By this time, Powell had left
Palace in search of first-team opportunities, but had listened
to Noades's comments in amazement, knowing the enormous
impact they could have in the Palace dressing room.

Powell had moved to Southend at the end of the 1989/90
season, after a short period on loan at Aldershot, where he'd
gone after only a handful of appearances in Palace's first
team. At Aldershot, he had played regular first-team football,
but the club's financial problems meant they were unable
to sign him on a permanent basis. At Southend United he
knew Andy Ansah, who would go on to become a football
choreographer and consultant for TV and Hollywood films,
and who helped convince him to sign for the club.

At Southend, he learned his trade and began to learn a
little about management. At the time, managers were still
able to rule by fear and intimidation and it was not uncommon for them to be merciless bullies. It wasn't until players

began to receive more lucrative contracts, negotiated for them by agents, that this tactic fell out of use. At the end of his first season at Southend, Powell received a £75 a week pay rise, given by his manager David Webb as a bonus for promotion, which was done without negotiation by an agent or any other intermediary.

He began to attract the attention of bigger clubs and at the end of the 1993/94 season he was out of contract at Southend and about to go on holiday to Portugal when he received a phone call from Steve Perryman, the assistant manager at Spurs, who told him that the club had been watching him, they were keen on him and they had one or two deals to do but they definitely wanted him to come to White Hart Lane. Powell left for his holiday on a high, unable to quite comprehend the imminent dream move to his boyhood team, with the associated prospect of playing for Spurs at Highbury, Old Trafford, Anfield and elsewhere.

He returned from his best holiday ever having had no word from Spurs and began pre-season training with Southend. When he finally got the call, it wasn't the news he was hoping for. Spurs had blown their entire budget on securing the signature of German World Cup winner Jürgen Klinsmann, and so the deal to sign Powell was now off.

During the following season, in December 1995, he received an offer to move to Manchester City in the Premier League. By this stage he'd had five and a half years at Southend and he was ready for a move to a bigger club, but again he was heartbroken as the move fell through when the clubs couldn't agree a fee.

However, the following month he moved to Derby County, who were riding high in the Championship and challenging for promotion to the Premier League. In the event, Derby

won promotion to the Premier League and City were relegated to Division One, where they stayed for one season
before being relegated to the third tier.

Derby converted Powell to a left wing-back, a position they
felt he could adapt to comfortably given that he had been a
marauding full-back and had formed a potent, eye-catching
partnership down the left-hand side of the Southend team
with Ricky Otto. Derby had a young dynamic coach in
Steve McClaren, and manager Jim Smith was a tough and
demanding presence around the club. The move as a whole
was a significant change from Powell's time at Southend, as
Derby was a one-club city that had just been promoted to
the Premier League and there was a genuine buzz around
Derby and the surrounding area. The club's promotion to
the Premier League coincided, fittingly, with Derby's final
season at their famous Baseball Ground stadium before
moving to their shiny new home at Pride Park. Personally,
Powell had just got married and had moved to Derby to
finally play in the top flight, ten years after becoming a
professional footballer.

He played for Derby for just over two seasons before being
moved on after a humiliating 4–0 defeat to Leicester City in
a local derby at Pride Park. Leicester's four goals had come
inside the first fifteen minutes, and had all come from crosses
from Derby's left side. Although none of the goals were directly Powell's fault, he was blamed and was subsequently
dropped from the starting line-up. He eventually regained
his place in the side but, in Smith's mind, Powell wasn't right,
and when newly promoted Charlton made a bid for him, it
was accepted and Powell was on his way. For Smith, the
deal represented good business, given that he got a fee from

Charlton and he signed a replacement from Germany on a free transfer, but for Powell it was heart-breaking. He and his wife had settled in the East Midlands and he had become something of a fans' favourite, but he returned to London determined to make the most of his time at Charlton. As for Smith, later he publicly admitted in a meeting with Powell, when Derby visited Charlton, that he'd made a mistake and that the deal had ended up being a piece of poor business.

At Charlton, he played alongside John Barnes, then towards the end of his playing days, who was, in Powell's words, 'a class elegant player in the centre of the park' who helped to raise the profile of the club and proved to be inspirational in the dressing room. At the end of the 1998/99 season, the club was relegated, but, crucially, stuck with their manager, Alan Curbishley, won promotion as champions the following season and became Premier League mainstays until Curbishley resigned at the end of the 2005/06 season. On their return to the Premier League, they set about confounding critics, who expected them to spend the season battling against relegation. In fact, they started the season well and were to finish the campaign in ninth position, not too far from a place in Europe. Powell himself was playing extremely well, adding much needed solidity to an indifferent defence and valuable Premier League experience to the team as a whole.

He was driving into training one Friday, as the team were making their final preparations before travelling to Coventry for an important away fixture against the West Midlands outfit. As he drove into the training ground he noticed a few journalists hanging around, which was an unusual occurrence for Charlton, and was informed by the club press officer that the journalists were there following up an article on the back pages of the *Daily Mail* that had stated that Powell was to be included in the England squad. He was surprised, as he'd heard nothing, and quickly dismissed the idea, but later he got a call to go to the manager's office. Reckoning that, as it was the day before Saturday's game, a summons to the manager's office could only mean that he was to be dropped, he was stunned to be informed by Curbishley that a fax had been received from the FA and that he was to be included in Sven-Göran Eriksson's first England squad.

As his shock turned to disbelief and then happiness at the prospect of gaining an England cap at the age of thirty-one, the media interest in Powell and Charlton became unprecedented. On the journey up to Coventry his phone never stopped ringing as seemingly every journalist and radio station were keen to speak to him, intrigued by his age as a debutant, not to mention the prospect of him becoming the first Charlton player to be capped by England for thirty-six years, making him the biggest surprise of the new manager's first squad.

The FA contacted him to make all the necessary arrangements and he offered to get a train up to Birmingham, where the team was to play at Villa Park while Wembley was being re-developed. Instead, they informed him, a car would pick him up from his home and drive him to Birmingham. He asked what he was expected to wear and he was told that he could wear what he liked and wasn't required to bring anything with him except boots and shin pads.

On arrival, he was assigned to a hotel room and when he walked in, his training kit and tracksuits were all laid out in readiness for him. He studiously examined his training kit, amazed it wasn't the same kind of replica kit that might be available in Sports Direct, but rather authentic training gear with embroidered badges. The other players made him feel welcome and in Peter Taylor and Sammy Lee he had coaches whom he had worked with at club level. Everyone in and around the squad was encouraging and inclusive and he sought to nullify any signs of an inferiority complex by reminding himself he'd been selected, he belonged and he was there on merit.

Eriksson had selected a bigger squad than was usual and intended to give playing time to as many squad members as possible. The training sessions were sharp and precise and he was greatly impressed by the quality of the players in the squad; Powell performed well and held his own amongst England's finest footballers.

At the final training session, the squad practised set pieces in preparation for the evening's game, and as the training bibs were handed out he realised he had the same colour bib as Beckham, Ferdinand and Owen and so it dawned on him that he was in the starting XI to make his England debut against Spain.

On the evening of the game, the most noticeable feature of the pre-match routine was the quietness of the dressing room. Every dressing room at Charlton and at other places was full of noise, but this particular dressing room was deathly quiet. There was no loud music and no rabble rousing; Eriksson spoke quietly and carefully, stressing that this was the start of a new era, that they should be very proud of themselves and that he wished them all good luck. As Eriksson completed his remarks, the silence was punctuated by the usual exhortations of encouragement and the players left the dressing room to line up in the tunnel with their Spanish counterparts. Each player led out a mascot and Powell held the hand of a young girl aged about nine or ten, spending the long walk from the tunnel to the pitch talking with his mascot. As he went, he remembered all the people who'd helped him get to this point in his career and who had come to Villa Park to watch him make his debut. In the crowd were his mother, his wife, old school teachers and his coaches from Charlton, Palace, Aldershot and Derby.

The game itself went well for England in general and for Powell in particular. He looked extremely comfortable on his debut, playing like an England regular rather than a debutant. In his best moments in the game, he nutmegged Spanish midfielder Pep Guardiola and had a rampaging run down the left to get in a dangerous cross. A tight calf necessitated his substitution as a precaution at half-time, but Eriksson expressed pleasure at his performance and told him he'd done enough to gain inclusion for his next squad, something that gave Powell immense satisfaction: he was determined not to be a one-cap wonder and, as he put it, 'the subject of a quiz question'.

Powell was to retire at the age of forty after twenty-four years as a professional, a more than decent career. He had amassed over 650 league appearances, gaining five caps for England, and had spent the previous five years as chairman of the PFA. Fitness-wise, he had looked after himself but had begun preparing for retirement. His experience at the PFA provided him with options to go into football administration and he gained considerable experience undertaking media work, but his experience at his last club as a player tipped the balance in favour of a career as a coach.

His last manager was Nigel Pearson at Leicester City in League One, where, at the age of thirty-eight, he'd signed initially for six months in August 2008. When Leicester won promotion as champions, this was extended till the end of the season, which Powell thought would have been a fitting point to retire. However, Pearson offered him a role as player-coach, impressed with Powell's habit of taking the full-backs for ten minutes or so at the end of training for an extra session, as well as how he dealt with young players. Pearson offered to keep him registered as a player, wanting Powell to help create the right atmosphere in the dressing room. After cautiously requesting time from Pearson to think about his offer, Powell realised that this was a great way to begin the next chapter in his career and agreed to take the job.

In the following season in the Championship, he played around five games, each of which, in his own words, 'took me about a month to recover from'. His last game was at Pride Park, where he played the full ninety minutes. Leicester had a great season, eventually missing out on promotion after a semi-final loss, but Pearson moved on to Hull City after falling out with the Foxes' chairman.

In spite of Pearson's departure, Powell was asked to stay on when new manager Paulo Sousa was appointed and, after a brief spell as manager, Sousa moved on to be replaced by Sven-Göran Eriksson, who had given Powell his England debut. Eriksson's management style was very open, valuing the input of all the coaches, and although Powell's main duties were in coaching the under-21s, Eriksson allowed him the responsibility of taking some first-team training sessions. Learning much within that ideal coaching environment, Powell received an offer from former Palace teammate Alan Pardew to become assistant manager at Newcastle United. After some thought, he rejected the offer, considering himself too inexperienced and not yet ready to take on such a massive job.

Two weeks later, Phil Parkinson was sacked from Powell's old club, Charlton Athletic, and Powell was offered an interview for the vacant post. If he was going to start anywhere in management, Charlton was a good place to begin his career. He was a former player and Charlton legend and, as a new and inexperienced manager, this status would provide him with a little cushion from the trigger-happy managerial merry-go-round that characterised league appointments. Within a few hours of his interview he was appointed as manager in January 2011, and took time to take stock and assess his squad as the rest of the season petered out unsuccessfully for the club. At the start of the following season, he brought in eight new players and went on to win promotion, with Charlton finishing as League One champions in his first full season as a manager, losing only five games and gaining over 100 points. He also won League One Manager of the Year into the bargain.

The following season, 2012/13, he led Charlton to ninth place in the Championship, only three points from the play-off places, and his successful tenure at Charlton had brought a feel-good factor to the club. Charlton were on a high, with fans, players and everybody associated with the club in an optimistic mood for a successful campaign in a season in which a push for promotion to the Premier League was a realistic goal.

However, the sense of optimism soon gave way to disappointment as Charlton's owners effectively sabotaged the new campaign. They had informed Powell that they would make between £4 million and £5 million available for new signings in order to support a concerted push for promotion to the Premier League. In the event, they didn't renew any of the existing players' contracts and the £4–5 million transfer budget never materialised, with Powell only able to bring in cheap free transfers. It was going to be a tough season: he knew it, and he warned the fans that the side were likely to struggle.

The club had been sold club to a Belgian consortium, which forced Powell to sell his best players, and brought in inferior replacements, and the club became embroiled in a relegation battle. It was during this season that Powell learned some valuable lessons about the harsh realities of football management. From the perspective of fan forums, radio phone-ins and media pundits, the art of football management is an easy one, confined solely to selecting the right line-up, buying and selling the right players, selecting the most appropriate tactics and making the right substitutions. Powell's experience as a manager in that difficult, fateful season highlighted the complex nature of modern football management; the responsibilities associated with the role extended far beyond preparing the first team.

The manager acts as the public face of the club and is expected to comment not only on the fortunes of the first team, but also on a range of off-field issues, irrespective of whether or not they fall under his remit. The club's failure to renew players' contracts meant that Powell constantly had to deal with enquiries from agents wanting to know about contract negotiations on behalf of their clients. Powell wasn't in a position to provide the answers to contract questions and had to remind agents of their clients' need to keep playing well and be professional while they were at the club, even in situations where deals were being negotiated to move to other clubs. There were other problems that were also outside of his control. The drainage system at Charlton's Valley ground had collapsed and wouldn't be repaired till the end of the season, letting water sit on the surface and leaving the pitch in a bad way. Games were cancelled and one was abandoned, leaving the side with a fixture backlog.

The one bright spot, however, was the side's FA Cup run. They had reached the quarter-finals of the competition, where they would meet Sheffield United, and they could feel confident about progressing to the semi-finals, which would have been rewarded with a Wembley appearance. However, the relationship between Powell and the club's owners had reached the point where Powell felt that they were looking for the first opportunity to sack him. He told staff that he would likely be sacked if the club lost their FA Cup tie. At this stage of the season, Charlton were fourth from bottom. During the weekend of the FA Cup tie, amazingly, all the other teams around them won, putting Charlton bottom of the league with four games in hand. They lost 2–0 to Sheffield United on the Sunday in the FA Cup and Powell was sacked the following day.

For the next six months, he filled his time by doing radio and other media work and took the opportunity to take his Pro Licence. He was invited to the World Cup but couldn't go due to his Pro Licence commitments. Instead, he helped coach the England under-17 squad in preparation for the European Championships in Malta, in which they were ultimately victorious. The under-17s' coach, John Peacock, ran the Pro Licence course and had asked him to come in for three days to coach ahead of the competition.

At the beginning of the 2014/15 season, Powell received a call completely out of the blue with an offer to manage League One's Huddersfield Town, making him the only black manager in the league until Keith Curle was appointed at Carlisle United a few weeks later.

His brief at Huddersfield was clearly laid out by the club chairman: to overachieve within a fairly tight budget while introducing young players from the club's academy. In over 600 first-team appearances under a succession of coaches and managers, Powell learned that, as the public face of the club, what a manager says and how he carries himself is of critical importance. At Charlton he felt he had an overall duty to protect the club's image and therefore had to protect fans from much of the boardroom machinations, whereas at Huddersfield he was able to be far more open with information provided for fans. The squad at Huddersfield was as yet not his own and he was keen to bring in his own signings to better reflect his footballing ideas and philosophy. This would take time, providing that he was given it.

Powell was acutely aware of his position as a role model for aspiring black managers, and for the wider black community. At meetings in the street and in the barbershop, in London and in Yorkshire, he was regularly approached by black people who wished him well and informed him that Huddersfield had become their second favourite team. He had always been a strong advocate of football's anti-racist initiatives and was a patron of Kick It Out. The campaign had started when Powell was at Southend, at a time when no one had ever spoken out against racism, and he had seen the campaign grow to organise weeks of action. As Charlton manager, he had insisted his players wore the T shirts that had been boycotted by Roberts, Ferdinand, Lescott and others. He was dismayed by, rather than hostile to, the boycott, believing that the players were targeting the wrong organisation.

Powell considered that there had always been a large number of black coaches but their presence had been limited to the grassroots game and therefore many coaches had the mindset that grassroots was it as far as coaching opportunities were concerned. The black coaches who came first, such as Keith Alexander and Leroy Rosenior, never got the opportunity to manage at a higher level even though they had good records, and there had been a general reluctance on the part of clubs to employ black coaches at anything higher than community or academy level. Powell therefore welcomed the implementation of a form of the Rooney Rule as an opportunity to increase the numbers of black coaches and allow others to raise their profiles through the interview process. Therefore, for Powell and his assistant Alex Dyer, who was with him at Charlton, the responsibility of being amongst a tiny number of black coaches provided inspiration to achieve success rather than a burden laden with expectations. Given the dearth of black coaches and the perpetual debate as to how the problem could be addressed, Powell was constantly sought by the media to express his views on the subject, but ultimately, he wanted to be judged on his success as a football manager, hoping that he could leave a mark that would open doors for others. He had been speaking on the Rooney Rule for over two years and hoped that in two years' time the debate would be over. That, however, remains to be seen. Powell has always been an optimist.

After Luis Suárez had served his ban for racially abusing Patrice Evra, an FA Cup fourth-round tie on 11 February 2012 provided the first opportunity for the two teams to meet since his return. Liverpool and Manchester United lined up to perform the traditional pre-match handshake, with the world's media keenly watching for any signal or reaction that would provide them with further opportunities to comment on the relationship between Suárez and Evra. Here was a chance to close the chapter on the long-running saga and concentrate on the football, but Suárez petulantly refused to shake Evra's hand and immediately re-ignited the whole affair. That afternoon on the radio station Talksport, the incident was the main item of interest, and during the course of the studio discussion, John Barnes accused Patrick Barclay (a football writer for the *Evening Standard*) and many of his fellow journalists of hypocrisy for ignoring racism when Barnes himself had suffered it during his playing days, and for treating it as a feature of the game that was acceptable at the time, in comparison to their over-sensationalised approach today. Barclay was taken aback, not expecting to be on the receiving end of a minor interrogation, and spent a few flustered seconds tripping over his words and finally offering the defence that he would defer to Barnes's greater knowledge, given his own status as a white journalist. A fellow journalist in the studio came to Barclay's rescue and moved the discussion on to a related topic, saving Barclay from further embarrassment.

The unwillingness of the media generally to address in any great depth the endemic racism of football's past may reflect an unwillingness to acknowledge the role they played in contributing to the culture within football at the time. In discussions of historic racist incidents, the blame is usually placed firmly at the feet of fans. With the examples of terrace behaviour cited, this conveniently ignores the media's complicity.

Throughout the 1970s and '80s, much of the media actively employed the myths and stereotypes that flew around the game, questioning the attitude and temperament of black footballers. In 1982, Brian Woolnough, a highly respected football journalist, wrote *Black Magic: England's*

Black Footballers. In his study, he employed many of the stereotypical myths prevalent at the time. Media portrayals of black people outside the context of football were often hostile and derogatory and, within the game, their depiction of footballers could be distinctly unenlightened. Cyrille Regis remarked that a piece of great play or skill would be described as 'black magic', a talented black player would be described as a 'black pearl' or 'black gold', and black players would be described as having 'black power'. Even as Garth Crooks was saying to Woolnough, 'I believe the black pearl, black bombshell descriptions have served their purpose. I find it corny', Woolnough couldn't or wouldn't refrain.

In addition to negative or exotic portrayals of footballers, the media typically ignored racist attitudes or allowed them to go unchallenged. In a television interview during the 1983/84 season, Crystal Palace manager Alan Mullery, in responding to an assessment of Vince Hilaire that the attention he had received as a seventeen-year-old had contributed to his unfulfilled potential, defended him, describing Hilaire as being nice enough to want to take home, and then, casually and seemingly from left field, commented on Hilaire's 'great suntan'. The interviewer, perhaps embarrassed or surprised, went on to discuss other matters related to Palace's performance, leaving Mullery's remarks to go unchallenged. Even in 1990, England legend Geoff Hurst famously described the Cameroon side as 'niggers in the woodpile' while acting as a pundit during that year's World Cup. Again, Hurst's remarks were barely commented upon.

Racism manifests itself in a number of conflicting ways. Racist insults and banana throwing are the more extreme examples, but in the main it operates in far more nuanced and subtle ways. Media discussions about racism within the game often give the impression that verbal abuse and name calling are the limits of racism's reach, undertaken by extremists. However, as offensive and as much of an affront to one's dignity as racist insults undoubtedly are, they aren't the issues that affect black footballers most materially.

Racism's subtle and often intangible modus operandi impacts in a number of ways, most notably excluding black players from managerial and coaching appointments as well as from positions in clubs, FA committees and other forums where key decisions about the game are made. As Paul Davis articulated, football is an important part of the post-*Windrush* experience of black communities, and their contribution to how football is observed as both a domestic and global game is an important one. The game in England has traded significantly on its cosmopolitan and ethnically diverse nature in order to attract star players and sponsorship opportunities and, in this regard, the Premiership ranks ahead of other European leagues. The fact is that this situation has been attained in no small measure by the trials and tribulations suffered by those pioneers who experienced so much hostility without the safety net of anti-racist campaigns and official support. The novelty in the fact that today's generation of black footballers play without the sense of anxiety before going out in front of a baying, hostile crowd at Upton Park, The Den, Elland Road or Stamford Bridge is something many are unaware of. That those venues are largely free of the kind of poisonous atmosphere that was endemic up until the 1990s is testimony to those who went before them. In fact, many of those pioneers who faced such hostility express a degree of scorn at the inability of today's generation of footballers to deal with the relatively benign racism they suffer on occasions when it occurs.

That black footballers today express anger, surprise or hurt when they suffer racist insults is to be welcomed. Instances of racism within football and wider society should be viewed as a relic from a bygone age. But football reflects society and within society as a whole, racism persists, even as some outward forms decline. In football, the authorities still want to focus solely on name-calling. The game is quick to bring sanctions against racist insults and there are clear sanctions, bans and fines in place. Even high-profile black players like Rio Ferdinand and Paul Elliott have fallen foul of the guidelines and have faced fines and bans for the use of language that is inappropriate. But there are no guidelines to ensure that black players feel that they can still contribute to the game when they hang up their boots. Attempts to develop ways for this to happen in coaching and management have been met with resistance from football's movers and shakers and although the press and media in general often like to present themselves in opposition to the FA hierarchy, in practice they share a very similar outlook.

The ground for black footballers has shifted significantly and the current campaigns reflect the needs of footballers who have retired or are near retirement. The reason they keep going in the face of resistance, indifference and hostility is because of their love of the game and the frustration borne of having much to offer but no one willing to accept.

Today, football is fond of telling itself it's moved on. Moved on from banana throwing and moved on from monkey noises. When black players first became a feature of the game in Britain, there were no black people in the dugout or the press box, as commentators or administrators, in boardrooms or in the crowd. In over forty years, all that has been achieved is the freedom to play without being called a 'black bastard'. Taken in its entirety, it's difficult to assert that the game has made the kind of progress it very often claims for itself.

Football faces significant challenges in the next few years that will have a huge impact on how the game develops. Grassroots football, so important in nurturing the next generation of talented footballers, is in a state of crisis, with little more than an argument about paltry sums of money from a multi-billion-pound TV deal representing the action on the issue. The ageing profile of those who attend matches and do much to ensure that the professional game remains the glorious, colourful spectacle it is, is a demographic time bomb that the game's leaders seem unprepared to address. How can we get our national teams to regularly qualify and win big international tournaments? Above all, we desperately require some kind of vision or strategy in order to achieve this aim. While equality is about social justice, and that remains an important driver for change within the game, diversity is fundamentally about nurturing and developing the full range of resources and talent at your disposal in order address the key issues that affect the team, the club, the league or the game. Black people, who could bring their perspectives, remain largely absent from positions of influence and leadership within the game, allowed to contribute as players but no further.

John Barnes, frustrated by the way in which discussions about racism are framed, suggests that some kind of 'truth and reconciliation' process should be undertaken, enabling those guilty of acting in a racist manner to admit past misdemeanours in order to move the debate on from the current focus on who made a racist remark to whom. This may enable the game to think about how it might adequately harness the vital contribution that black people can make at all levels. The enduring legacy of the Three Degrees, Anderson, Podd, Bennett, Williams and so many others is difficult to accurately assess. They made giant strides and laid the foundations to allow future generations to play the game in a far healthier environment than they enjoyed – one in which black players now felt comfortable that their mothers, wives and children could watch without witnessing racist hostility. In some ways, they're football's Rosa Parks: they allowed others to pick up the baton and continue. When the boardroom, the dugout, the press box and the crowd start to look like more of what we see on the pitch, only then can we more accurately describe their legacy.

However, although that legacy is still to be determined, many of the key players who have contributed so much to the rich story of black British footballers have contributed massively to the game in the UK overall. These players hold records for appearances and goals for club and country, have played a key role in their team's greatest games or achievements, and are inducted into halls of fame. If football in the UK remains locked within the stark disparities of what is seen on the pitch and what is seen in other areas of the sport, nevertheless, the records and achievements, games, goals and performances of black players will continue to have an enduring impact on the beautiful game.

THE GREATEST BLACK BRITISH TEAM

TO FIND THE greatest black British team, each of the players who agreed to participate in *Pitch Black* was asked to select their best British XI. Although the survey was open to players from all the home nations, it transpired that only Englishmen received any nominations for the team, except one each for George Berry and, interestingly, Ryan Giggs, who, on account of having a black father, was a legitimate nomination. Amongst the selectors, there was a fair amount of unanimity about the back five, but the real debates took place around selection in midfield and in the forward line. The number of outstanding candidates for attacking midfielders and strikers caused some interesting tactical dilemmas as to how participants selected their formations. It's not a particularly scientific survey, but it's produced an attacking side with a solid back four, one holding midfielder, two attacking midfielders and three strikers offering creativity with plenty of goal threat. Overall, the selectors did a fine job.

GOALKEEPER: DAVID JAMES
James didn't have a great deal of competition for this spot, Alex Williams being an obvious alternative, but James was the stand-out contender for the keeper's berth and deservedly

so. In a league career spanning over twenty-five years, James made over 500 Premier League appearances, the third-highest number in history, and gained fifty-three caps for England. He occasionally suffered lapses in concentration, which meant that he could be an erratic performer, earning him the nickname 'Calamity James', but he was big, athletic, agile and an excellent shot stopper and in many ways he was the first modern keeper.

RIGHT-BACK: VIV ANDERSON

Closely challenged by the claims of Paul Parker and to a lesser degree by Danny Thomas, Viv Anderson makes the side in the right-back slot. A much better defender than he gives himself credit for, he was deceptively quick and also good in the air and a threat in set pieces. He was never afraid to put his foot in. As well as him being a fine defender, his status as the first black player to gain an England cap justifies his inclusion. He was also the first black manager of a league side since the 1960s and the first black player to win the European Cup. He was awarded an MBE in 2000 and inducted into the English Football Hall of Fame.

LEFT-BACK: ASHLEY COLE

Never seriously challenged for his position, Ashley Cole was selected by all but one *Pitch Black* participant for the left-back berth. Cole had a long career with Arsenal, Chelsea and Roma, and an examination of his medal haul makes impressive reading. He won three Premier Leagues, seven FA Cup winners' medals (the most of any player in history), one League Cup, three Community Shields, one Europa League and one Champions League. He was also twice the UEFA Player of the Year, once England Player of the Year and won

107 caps for England, making him the first black player to play for the country over 100 times.

The reason his selection was almost unanimous is because he was without peer. In an England side that consistently failed to live up to expectations, Cole was usually free of any blame. A quick, very consistent performer, he was an attacking left-back, but also excellent defensively, and had a couple of epic encounters at international level with Cristiano Ronaldo and managed to nullify him. Probably England's greatest ever left-back.

CENTRE-BACK: RIO FERDINAND

Unanimously selected for the team, Ferdinand won eighty-one caps, making him second only to Ashley Cole as the black player to win the most for England. He formed a centre-back partnership with Sol Campbell for England at the 2002 World Cup and was England's first permanent black captain, although injury prevented him from leading the team into the 2010 World Cup.

He captained Manchester United, with whom he won six Premier League titles, one FA cup, two League Cups, five Community Shields, one Champions League and one FIFA Club World Cup.

An excellent reader of the game, strong, quick, good in the air, excellent in bringing the ball out of defence and in his distribution, he was twice the most expensive defender in the world.

CENTRE-BACK: SOL CAMPBELL

Campbell comfortably made the team, although the claims of Des Walker made his selection far from a foregone conclusion. Quick, strong, dominant and good in the air, Campbell won fifty-three caps for England and was the first English player to represent the national team at six consecutive tournaments. He was also only the second black player to captain England. He was part of Arsenal's 'Invincibles' side that went unbeaten during the 2003/04 season, after his acrimonious move from Spurs. During his career he won two Premier League titles, three FA Cups, one League Cup and one Community Shield.

HOLDING MIDFIELDER: PAUL INCE

Ince appeared in just about every participant's team. He was a more creative influence during his West Ham days, before becoming a tough, combative, box-to-box midfielder. At Inter Milan, at Liverpool and for England he operated as a holding midfielder, winning fifty-three caps for his country. He won two league titles, two FA Cup winners' medals, one League Cup and one Cup Winners' Cup medal. He was the first black player to captain England and was the first black British manager to manage a Premier League side. He would be this team's captain.

ATTACKING MIDFIELDER: LAURIE CUNNINGHAM

It would be easy to dismiss Cunningham's inclusion as sentimental or iconic, but as a right-sided attacking midfielder, his inclusion makes sense. David Rocastle and Mark Chamberlain were both nominated, but Cunningham made the side ahead of them. Strong, skilful and lightning quick, he was the first black player of his generation to represent England and earned six caps for the full England side. He went on to become the first Englishman to play for Real Madrid.

ATTACKING MIDFIELDER: JOHN BARNES

A roll call of John Barnes's achievements is worth reflecting upon for a few moments. Seventy-nine England caps, PFA Footballer of the year, two Football Writers' Player of the Year awards, two league titles, two FA Cups, an MBE and a writing credit for the words for the rap in New Order's 'World in Motion'.

He started as a quick, skilful winger, and when his pace left him, he added maturity, experience and a few pounds to reinvent himself as a midfielder who kept things ticking along, always available for teammates and ready to deliver an incisive pass. Of all the ex-players who were surveyed for this team, only two didn't vote for him. One was Barnes himself, and the other was a player who admitted Barnes probably deserved the accolade but, for a variety of reasons, couldn't bring himself to include him. Winning the PFA and Football Writers' Award in the same season, and winning the Writers' Award two years later, bears testimony to the fact that for three or four seasons, he was the best player England had. He should probably have been the first black player to win 100 England caps but he was wasted by successive England managers who stifled his talent, then left him out of the side when inevitably he was ineffective.

After finishing his playing career he had extremely brief managerial spells at Celtic and Tranmere either side of a stint managing the Jamaican national side. His goal against Brazil is quite rightly lauded, but the final goal for Liverpool in a 4–0 win in October 1987 better showcased his wide range of talents. Pressing the ball and winning it on the halfway line, he carried it to the edge of the QPR penalty area, where he skipped past a challenge from Terry Fenwick and, showing superb balance and poise, beat another defender before calmly stroking the ball past David Seaman. Not only was he overwhelmingly selected for the greatest black British team, but he was also selected as the best black British player of all time.

STRIKER: ANDY COLE

There was a great deal of debate about Andy Cole's inclusion, not because he didn't deserve it, but for tactical reasons. The debates centred on whether Paul Davis should be included as an extra midfielder, but in the end Cole was selected as one of three strikers. Andy Cole is the second-highest goal scorer in Premier League history. During his career with Manchester United he won five Premier League titles, two FA Cups, two Charity Shields and one Champions League medal and later, with Blackburn Rovers, he won the League Cup, giving him a winner's medal for every domestic club honour. Cole won PFA Young Player of the Year and fifteen caps for England.

STRIKER: CYRILLE REGIS

Regis was almost unanimously selected for inclusion in the side. Given some of the strikers who failed to make the team, his selection demonstrates how good he was. Les Ferdinand might count himself unlucky to not be included in the team, but Regis's achievements make him more than worthy of inclusion. He graduated through non-league football to go on and win PFA Young Player of the Year as well as five England caps. Regis was nominated as an all-time great by both West Brom and Coventry City, where he won his only domestic honour, an FA Cup winners' medal. One of the legendary Three Degrees, he was awarded an MBE in 2008.

STRIKER: IAN WRIGHT

A unanimous inclusion, Ian Wright began his career in non-league football before going on to form a legendary strike partnership with Mark Bright at Crystal Palace. His goal-scoring exploits for Arsenal won him the First Division Golden Boot in 1991/92 and elevated him to iconic status. He became Arsenal's all-time post-war leading scorer until his record was broken by Thierry Henry. He won a Premier League, two FA Cups, one League Cup and one Cup Winners' Cup. He was awarded an MBE in 2000 and selected for the English Football Hall of Fame in 2005. He won thirty-three caps for England.

SUBSTITUTES

Les Ferdinand
Paul Davis
David Rocastle
Des Walker

BIBLIOGRAPHY

BOOKS

L. Back, T. Crabbe & J. Solomos, *The Changing Face of Football* (Berg, 2001)

P. Dimeo & G. P. T. Finn, 'Scottish Racism, Scottish Identities', in *Fanatics: Power, Identity and Fandom in Football*, ed. by Adam Brown (Routledge, 1998)

Peter Fryer, *Staying Power: The History of Black People in Britain* (Pluto Press, 1984)

J. Garland & M. Rowe, *Racism and Anti-Racism in Football* (Palgrave, 2001)

Rodney Hinds, *Black Lions: A History of Black Players in English Football* (SportsBooks Ltd, 2006)

Richie Moran, 'Racism in Football: A Victim's Perspective', in *The Future of Football: Challenges for the 21st Century*, ed. by J. Garland, D. Malcolm & M. Rowe (Frank Cass, 2000)

Ambalavaner Sivanandan, *A Different Hunger* (Pluto Press, 1991)

Rogan Taylor, *Football and its Fans* (Leicester University Press, 1992)

Phil Vasili, *Colouring Over the White Line: The History of Black Footballers in Britain* (Mainstream Publishing, 2000)

Brian Woolnough, *Black Magic: England's Black Footballers* (Pelham Books, 1983)

NEWSPAPERS AND JOURNALS

'Abused football trainee in new tribunal', Helen Carter, *The Guardian*, 26 July 2001

'Alexander Technique', Grahame Lloyd, *When Saturday Comes*, March 2004

'Are black footballers paid less than their white teammates?', Harry Harris, *Daily Mirror*, 27 November 2007

'A black day for Scots football', Andrew Smith, *The Scotsman*, 30 December 2010

'Blair slams racist abuse', Kick It Out News, 18 November 2004

'Blatter is not the only dinosaur football needs to slap down', Patrick Collins, *Mail on Sunday*, 20 November 2011

'Blind loyalty at Liverpool and Chelsea will not help racism', Ian Prior, *The Guardian*, 22 December 2011

'Di Matteo calls for calm as Ferdinand prepares to face "stick" from fans', Dominic Fifield, *The Guardian*, 28 April 2012

'England go through amid mass brawl and racist abuse of Onuoha', Jeremy Wilson, *The Guardian*, 18 June 2007

'Exclusive: Kick It Out slams top clubs for "year wasted in hypocrisy"', David Conn, *The Guardian*, 10 December 2012

'FA under pressure to act', Liz Fekete, IRR News, 29 July 2003

'Football clubs told to tackle racism or face the courts', Paul Kelso, *The Guardian*, 12 October 2004

'The Hard Left: White working class football supporters have always been targeted by racist right', David Eimer, *The Guardian*, 25 November 1994

'Improbable, implausible, contrived', Owen Gibson, *The Guardian*, 6 October 2012

'Leeds ban on racist fans', Martin Wainwright, *The Guardian*, 29 March 1988

'No black and white issue', Jonathan Wilson, *When Saturday Comes*, October 2007

'Paul Elliott fighting hard against football racism', Henry Winter, *Daily Telegraph*, 16 June 2008

'Paul Ince sets example for a generation', Jeremy Wilson, *Daily Telegraph*, 12 March 2008

'Professional Footballers Survey: Biggest concern is to walk straight into another job', Nick Harris, *The Independent*, 21 April 2000

'Race bias "still rife in football"', Vivek Chaudhary, *The Guardian*, 20 May 2004

'Racism in Spanish football exposed', Liz Fekete, IRR News, 11 December 2004

'Referee defeats Football League in race bias case', Anne Whitney, *The Independent*, 6 December 2001

'Ron and Ron again', David Stubbs, *When Saturday Comes*, February 2005

'Someone tell UEFA racism is not an English disease', Simon Jordan, *The Observer*, 19 February 2006

'Unequal use of stop and search against ethnic minorities', Alan Travis, *The Guardian*, 31 March 2006

PUBLICATIONS

2001 FA Premier League National Fan Survey

Ethnic minorities and coaching in elite level football in England: A call to action, Sports People's Think Tank, 2014

Football Task Force, Eliminating Racism from Football, 30 March 1998

Stephen Lawrence Inquiry: Report and an Inquiry, Sir William Macpherson, 1999

WEB

http://www.furd.org/default.asp?intPageID=63

http://www.theguardian.com/football/blog/2014/nov/21/fan-view-dave-whelan-wigan-antisemitic-remarks

http://www.mirror.co.uk/sport/football/news/sir-trevor-brooking-10-20-clubs-4363636

http://www.telegraph.co.uk/sport/football/11224598/Ipswich-Town-coaches-Kieron-Dyer-and-Titus-Bramble-slam-Rooney-Rule.html

http://www.dailymail.co.uk/sport/football/article-2036302/Martin-Samuel-Being-black-Cole-Co-held-back.html

http://metro.co.uk/2014/09/10/why-the-rooney-rule-isnt-the-answer-to-the-lack-of-black-football-managers-4863178/

http://www.wsws.org/en/articles/1999/10/ford-o07.html

ACKNOWLEDGEMENTS

THERE ARE SO many people without whom I'd never have been able to write this book and I apologise profoundly to those I've neglected to mention. To all the players who agreed to be interviewed, I cannot thank you enough for your time, insight and perspectives. A special thanks goes to Iffy Onuora, Bobby Barnes and Paul Davis at the PFA for helping me get such great contacts; Ged Grebby at Show Racism the Red Card for his encouragement and support; Andrew Sherlock for his constructive criticism; to the massive Onuora clan, especially Obi, Uzo, Chiz, Chika, Chiz Jnr, Anyika and Nkechi for their encouragement and expertise and to Auntie Rose and Auntie Chinwe. Thanks to Linda Atherton for the great title and Pete Atherton for all his support; Billy Dutton, Liza Durkin, Pauline Donald, Wendy Gutin, Cheryl Varley, Jakub Goscinny for support and inspiration; and Rod Alexander and Jimmy Jagne for being a sounding board and fountain of knowledge and ideas. Last and by no means least, to my agent Darryl Samaraweera for his belief and to Olivia Beattie, my editor, for her invaluable input and everyone else at Biteback Publishing for their support.

INDEX